HOW TO TEACH READING IN THE PUBLIC SCHOOLS

First published 1898
This edition published by Lector House in 2025

ISBN: 978-93-6138-022-8

Lector House LLP
Registered Office: H. No. 96, Block C, Tomar Colony,
Burari, Delhi – 110084, India
info@lectorhouse.com
www.lectorhouse.com

HOW TO TEACH READING IN THE PUBLIC SCHOOLS

SOLOMON HENRY CLARK

2025

LECTOR HOUSE LLP

HOW TO TEACH READING IN THE PUBLIC SCHOOLS

BY

S. H. CLARK, PH.B.

OF THE UNIVERSITY OF CHICAGO

Author of "How to Read Aloud"
and Associate Author of "Principles of Vocal Expression, Mental Technique and Literary Interpretation"

PREFACE

This book is intended as a manual for teachers of reading in the public schools. In its preparation the theory was, first, that the teacher should have a thorough knowledge of how thought and feeling are expressed—in other words he must have the criteria of expression; and, second, that he should have a definite graded method of instruction, in which the simple shall precede the complex, and in which one element, and one only, shall be presented at a time.

The book is, therefore, an endeavor to assist the teacher of reading, first, by explaining the psychology of the criteria of expression; second, by presenting a practical method of instruction; and, third, by discussing certain definite principles of literary interpretation.

Parts of this book have been given to the public by the author, in *Principles of Vocal Expression* and *How to Read Aloud,* the latter of which is now out of print. The interest in these two books is a cause for gratitude and it is hoped the present manual may serve its purpose equally well.

S. H. CLARK.

CONTENTS

PART THREE
LITERARY INTERPRETATION

INTRODUCTION

It is universally conceded that the public schools fail to give children much power as readers. One authority asserts that, after the child's twelfth year, his ability as a reader steadily declines. (Up to that time he is gradually acquiring greater mastery over words, and so, in a sense, may be said to be improving.) Testimony can be added that, by the time he reaches the university, the average student cannot read at all.

Many remedies have been suggested, from which two may be selected as typical. One is to call the attention of the child to the mechanics of vocal expression—to inflection, force, movement, and so forth. The other (that commonly employed), to tell the child to get the thought. It cannot be denied that both methods have, in isolated cases, been productive of some good, yet, on the whole, they have been well-nigh barren of results. Let us inquire briefly into the causes.

The mechanical method fails, especially with younger people, because it is dry, technical, unstimulating, and, in the main, uninteresting. It deals with rules for the use of the different elements of vocal expression, telling the child he must use a rising inflection here, a falling inflection there; that he must read parenthetical phrases and clauses in lower pitch and faster time; that this emotion should be manifested in normal quality, that emotion in orotund quality; and so on through weary, dreary rules and principles, the study of which has seldom done any good and oftentimes much harm. The "get-the-thought" method is a revolt against the other plan. Recognizing the fact that drills in the elements have done nothing toward elevating the standard of reading, the conscientious principal or superintendent tells his teachers that they must see to it that the scholars get the thought. This is a step in the right direction, but it must be acknowledged that it does not produce results. And the chief reasons for this are two. First, for one cause or another the finer shades of meaning escape too many teachers. Second, very few teachers have received the necessary training to enable them to discern quickly with what mental conditions various forms of vocal expression are associated. In other words, they have not the criteria of vocal expression; and, in consequence, helpful criticism is impossible.

Why have previous methods of teaching reading practically failed? There are three reasons: first, the lack of appreciation of the best literature on the part of the teacher; second, the complexity of vocal expression; and third, the intangibility of vocal expression.

Appreciation of the meaning and beauty of literature is the first requisite of a successful teacher of reading; and yet there is little opportunity afforded the teacher to get this appreciation. Is it not true that too many teachers have no love for real literature? The fault is not theirs, but that of the method of teaching literature that substitutes grammar, philology, history, and lectures about literature for the study of the meaning and beauty of the literature itself. One may safely assert that thousands of children would be better readers, even with the present faulty methods, if their teachers had a genuine interest in the best literature. Of what avail is it to put good literature into the schoolbooks if its merit does not appeal as well to the instructor as to the pupil? The stream can rise no higher than its source. There is, however, a rapidly growing sentiment against the substitution of parsing, history, philology, or ethics for genuine literary training. We are coming to recognize that literature is art, beauty, spirit; and, when this recognition becomes general, we shall have better teachers and better readers. For there is nothing that so stimulates our vocal expression as the desire to impress upon others the beauty and feeling of what has impressed ourselves.

Complexity may be defined by illustration. A phrase may be read fast or slowly; in high or low key; with one melody or another; with loud or subdued force; with this quality of voice or with that. Now all these elements are present at one time; so that, without proper training, the teacher is unable to discriminate between them and hence unable to give the needful correction, without which there can be no progress.

Intangibility may be explained by showing what is meant by a tangible subject. The spelling lesson is tangible; the arithmetic lesson is tangible. A mistake is easily recognized and corrected. Three months after a paper on these subjects has been handed in, the teacher can go back to it and examine it. But vocal expression is evanescent, and, by the untrained, can be recalled imperfectly, if at all, and then only a short time after it has been heard. In the presence of the combined difficulties due to complexity and intangibility, the teacher is appalled; and, conscientious though he be, he gives up in despair. The teaching becomes perfunctory; the children lose interest; and there is the end of reading. Reading, which should be the brightest and most inspiring of lessons, degenerates into a humdrum, dry-as-dust time-killer. Good reading is as rare as the classical bird. No idea of a pupil's reading ability can be gained from a knowledge of the class he is in. He is no better reader in the highest public-school grade than he is in the grade two or three below the highest. The teacher has come to recognize the futility of his efforts; and so, in many class rooms, the time set apart for reading is given up to language lessons, composition, and other studies, valuable in themselves, but only incidentally helpful in increasing the pupil's reading power.

It may be asked, what objects are to be attained as a result of reading lessons? There are two. First, to give us the power to extract thought from the printed page. After we leave school, our information is gained from books; and what we get from these is largely determined by our school training. Our system of education has a great deal to answer for when it fails to provide this training. The value of vocal expression is not to be depreciated, but of the utmost importance is the ability to get the author's meaning. Our teaching, from the primary grade to the university, is lamentably weak in this direction. A well-known college professor, in response to a school superintendent's question as to what would better the preparation of secondary-school students for college, replied: "For Heaven's sake, teach them how to read." Another college instructor—a learned authority on geology—states that he finds occasion to remark to his classes about once a month, "It's a great thing to be able to read a page of English." No one who examines the reading in our schools can fail to be struck, not so much with the absence of expressive power, as with the absence of mental grasp. We are so anxious to get on that we are content with skimming the surface, and do not take the time to get beneath it. The reading lesson should be, primarily, a thinking lesson, and every shade of thought should be carefully determined, no matter how long a time may be consumed. The habit of hurrying over the page, which is so prevalent, is clearly an outgrowth of schoolroom methods. Careless of all the future, we are too prone to push the pupil along, ignoring the simplest and most evident of psychological laws, that thought comes by thinking, and thinking takes time.

One tires of the universal excuse for the laxity of our methods: we have not the time. The reply to teacher, superintendent, and school board is, we have no time to teach a subject poorly. If thought-getting—genuine thought-getting—were insisted on from the outset, without doubt the work which now requires six or seven years to accomplish could be done in five. How much thought power has the public-school graduate? Very little. And yet, if all lessons—history, geography, arithmetic, and the rest—were made thought lessons, a child of fourteen would be on the road to educating himself when he left school. Is it not pitiful to see a bright boy or girl spending three or four hours a day in the preparation of his lessons, and then coming to class only to find that he has wasted and worse than wasted his time? In taking leave of this theme, the teacher is urged to ponder these noble words of a noble man, "When thou readest, look steadfastly with the mind at the things the words symbolize. If there be question of mountains, let them loom before thee; if of the ocean, let its billows roll before thy eyes. This habit will give to thy voice even pliancy and meaning. The more sources of interest we have, the richer is our life. To hold any portion of truth in a vital way is better than to have its whole baggage stored merely in one's memory." And, again, "He who thinks for himself is rarely persuaded by another. Information and inspiration he gladly receives, but he forms his own judgment. Arguments and reasons which, to the thoughtful, sound like mockery, satisfy the superficial and ignorant." And there is no better way to develop such a thinking person than by careful training in reading.

Most readers, like good-natured cows,
Keep browsing and forever browse;
If a fair flower come in their way
They take it too, nor ask, "What, pray!"
Like other fodder it is food,
And for the stomach quite as good.

Training in thought-getting is, then, the first result to be expected from the reading lesson. The second is the power of adequate vocal expression. The temptation to enlarge upon the many benefits to body, voice, mind, and soul, to say nothing of the practical worldly benefits of vocal expression, is resisted. It is taken for granted that they are recognized; so that we pass on to the discussion of a plan that may help us to get these benefits; prefacing the discussion with the statement that the evil results of our present laxity are not to be laid at the door of the individual teacher, but at that of the educational system in general.

This work makes no pretensions to treat in any detail reading as an art. Its sole object is to present the ideal of the reading lesson and suggest ways and means by which that ideal may be brought somewhat nearer to our grasp than it is at present. Nevertheless, to those who may desire to study reading as an art, it can be safely said, that we must first be good readers before we can be artists; and since this is so, there should be much gain to them from a careful, definite study of the fundamental principles herein set forth. For special teachers of elocution, also, it is hoped that the book may prove of some value, as dealing with those elements without the understanding of which successful teaching of advanced work is impossible.

Vocal culture, in the ordinary sense of the word, finds no place in this discussion. The reason for this omission will appear in the following pages. This much, however, may be stated here; except under particularly favorable circumstances, very little can be done in voice training in our public schools; but by the plan herein presented, the voices of our children may be made truly expressive, and that, after all, is of more value to them than mere technical facility.

While the subject of primary school reading is not discussed directly, the primary teacher should derive considerable assistance from the book, inasmuch as it aims to present the standard of criticism and the psychology of reading. With him rests to a great extent the success of any method of oral expression. That he should have a clear conception of the goal of the reading lessons and the manner of reaching it is therefore beyond dispute.

The book has a double purpose. First, to assist the teacher to teach reading; second, to help the teacher to improve his own reading. The latter purpose explains the amount of illustrative matter, and also the fact that some of this is beyond the grasp of young and immature minds.

PART ONE
THE CRITERIA OF VOCAL EXPRESSION

CHAPTER I

THE CRITERION OF TIME

It must be clear that no progress can be made in the teaching of any subject unless the teacher possess a definite standard of criticism; and, furthermore, it must be granted that the teacher of reading does not possess this standard. We have a standard in spelling, in arithmetic, in geography, but none in reading—at least none clearly apprehended and scientifically applied. It is, therefore, the purpose of the first part of this book to present those elements of vocal expression—the four criteria—a knowledge of which is indispensable to any progress in the teaching of reading. These are, Time, Pitch, Quality, and Force, the first of which we now proceed to study in detail.

In Professor Raymond's admirable work, *The Orator's Manual,* there appear these significant words: "The relative time apportioned to a word indicates the *mind's measurement* of it,—represents the speaker's judgment as to the amount of meaning or importance that it conveys." A moment's thought must convince us of the truth of this statement. Making due allowance for certain speakers, who, for one cause or another, have an unusually slow or fast utterance, the principle laid down by Professor Raymond is, without doubt, psychologically sound. In fact, it is a platitude; but like many another platitude, its truth is so close to us that we fail to perceive its meaning and application. An additional proof of the soundness of this principle is found in music. A solemn dirge, a funeral march, an anthem of praise is rendered in slow time; while moderate and fast time seem the fitting expression of the lighter moods.

Time, then, refers to the rate of vocal movement. It may be fast, or moderate, or slow, according to the amount of what may be called the collateral thinking accompanying the reading of any given passage. To put it another way: a phrase is read slowly because it means much; because the thought is large, sublime, deep. The collateral thinking may be revealed by an *expansive paraphrase*. For instance, in the lines

> Not a drum was heard, not a funeral note,
> As his corse to the ramparts we hurried,

why do we read slowly? The paraphrase answers the question. It was midnight. There lay our beloved leader, who should have been borne in triumphal procession to his last resting place. Bells should have tolled, cannon thundered, and thousands should have followed his bier. But now, alas! by night, by stealth, without even a single drum tap, in fear and dread, we crept breathless to the ramparts.

This, or any one of a hundred other paraphrases, will suffice to render the vocal movement slow. And so it is with all slow time. Let it be remembered that a profound or sublime thought *may* be uttered in fast time; but that when we dwell upon that thought, when we hold it before the mind, the time must necessarily be slow.

The succeeding passages will have a prevailingly slow movement. Measure the thought carefully, and think the expansive paraphrase. These drills are not to train us to read slowly (for any one can do that), but to think largely. The movement will take care of itself. It is further urged that the student give considerable attention to this part of the subject; for the time so spent will be valuable not only as it results in expressive movement, but because it is only through meditation that the fullest insight into the meaning of a passage can be acquired. Hence, dwelling for a long period upon a phrase or sentence gives opportunity for the enkindling of the imagination and emotion. It has been frequently found that where a student's movement was out of harmony with the sentiment of the passage, his emotional interpretation was equally poor. A farther careful study of the text to improve the movement has generally resulted in the improvement of the emotional expression.

> Mr. Speaker: The mingled tones of sorrow, like the voice of many waters, have come unto us from a sister State—Massachusetts—weeping for her honored son. The State I have the honor in part to represent once endured, with yours, a common suffering, battled for a common cause, and rejoiced in a common triumph. Surely, then, it is meet that in this the day of your affliction we should mingle our griefs.

> Search creation round, where can you find a country that presents so sublime a view, so interesting an anticipation? Who shall say for what purpose mysterious Providence may not have designed her! Who shall say that when in its follies or its crimes, the Old World may have buried all the pride of its power, and all the pomp of its civilization, human nature may not find its destined renovation in the New! When its temples and its trophies shall have mouldered into dust,—when the glories of its name shall be but the legend of tradition, and the light of its achievements live only in song, philosophy will revive again in the sky of her Franklin, and glory rekindle at the urn of her Washington.

> Often have I swept backward, in imagination, six thousand years, and stood beside our great ancestor, as he gazed for the first time upon the going down of the sun. What strange sensations must have swept through his bewildered mind, as he watched the last departing ray of the sinking orb, unconscious whether he should ever behold its return.

Wrapped in a maze of thought, strange and startling, he suffers his eye to linger long about the point at which the sun has slowly faded from view. A mysterious darkness creeps over the face of Nature; the beautiful scenes of earth are slowly fading, one by one, from his dimmed vision.

You think me a fanatic to-night, for you read history, not with your eyes, but with your prejudices. But fifty years hence, when Truth gets a hearing, the Muse of History will put Phocion for the Greek, and Brutus for the Roman, Hampden for England, La Fayette for France, choose Washington as the bright, consummate flower of our earlier civilization, and John Brown as the ripe fruit of our noonday, then, dipping her pen in the sunlight, will write in the clear blue, above them all, the name of the soldier, the statesman, the martyr, Toussaint L'Ouverture.

Figure to yourself a cataract like that of Niagara, poured in foaming grandeur, not merely over one great precipice of two hundred feet, but over the successive ridgy precipices of two or three thousand, in the face of a mountain eleven thousand feet high, and tumbling, crashing, thundering down with a continuous din of far greater sublimity than the sound of the grandest cataract. The roar of the falling mass begins to be heard the moment it is loosened from the mountain; it pours on with the sound of a vast body of rushing water; then comes the first great concussion, a booming crash of thunders, breaking on the still air in mid-heaven; your breath is suspended, and you listen and look; the mighty glittering mass shoots headlong over the main precipice, and the fall is so great that it produces to the eye that impression of dread majestic slowness of which I have spoken, though it is doubtless more rapid than Niagara. But if you should see the cataract of Niagara itself coming down five thousand feet above you in the air, there would be the same impression. The image remains in the mind, and can never fade from it; it is as if you had seen an alabaster cataract from heaven. The sound is far more sublime than that of Niagara, because of the preceding stillness in those Alpine solitudes. In the midst of such silence and solemnity, from out the bosom of those glorious, glittering forms of nature, comes that rushing, crashing thunder-burst of sound! If it were not that your soul, through the eye, is as filled and fixed with the sublimity of the vision as, through the sense of hearing, with that of the audible report, methinks you would wish to bury your face in your hands, and fall prostrate, as at the voice of the Eternal.

How lovely are thy dwellings fair!
O Lord of Hosts, how dear
The pleasant tabernacles are
Where thou dost dwell so near!

My soul doth long and almost die
Thy courts, O Lord, to see,
My heart and flesh aloud do cry,
O living God, for thee.

There even the sparrow, freed from wrong,
Hath found a house of rest;
The swallow there, to lay her young,
Hath built her brooding nest;

Even by thy altars, Lord of Hosts,
They find their safe abode;
And home they fly from round the coasts
Towards thee, my King, my God.

The following will illustrate fast movement. Let there be no attempt to accelerate the speed, but let the thought and emotion themselves govern that. No examples are given to illustrate moderate time, since the student gets sufficient practice of this kind in almost everything he reads.

> Gloriously, Max! gloriously! There were sixty horses in the field, all mettle to the bone; the start was a picture—away we went in a cloud—pell-mell—helter-skelter—the fools first, as usual, using themselves up. We soon pass them—first your Kitty, then my Blueskin, and Craven's colt last. Then came the tug—Kitty skimmed the walls—Blueskin flew over the fences—the colt neck-and-neck, and half a mile to run—at last the colt balked a leap and went wild. Kitty and I had it all to ourselves—she was three lengths ahead as we breasted the last wall, six feet, if an inch, and a ditch on the other side. Now, for the first time, I gave Blueskin his head—Ha, ha! Away he flew like a thunderbolt—over went the filly—I over the same spot, leaving Kitty in the ditch—walked the steeple, eight miles in thirty minutes, and scarcely turned a hair.

> Nice clothes I get, too, traipsing through weather like this! My gown and bonnet will be spoiled. Needn't I wear 'em, then? Indeed, Mr. Caudle, I *shall* wear 'em. No, sir! I'm not going out a dowdy to please you or anybody else. Gracious knows! it isn't often that I step over the threshold.

Before a quarter pole was pass'd,
Old Hiram said, "He's going fast."
Long ere the quarter was a half,

The chuckling crowd had ceased to laugh;
Tighter his frightened jockey clung
As in a mighty stride he swung,
The gravel flying in his track,
His neck stretched out, his ears laid back,
His tail extended all the while
Behind him like a rat-tail file!
Off went a shoe,—away it spun,
Shot like a bullet from a gun;
The quaking jockey shapes a prayer
From scraps of oaths he used to swear;
He drops his whip, he drops his rein,
He clutches fiercely for the mane;
He'll lose his hold,—he sways and reels,—
He'll slide beneath those trampling heels!
The knees of many a horseman quake,
The flowers on many a bonnet shake,
And shouts arise from left and right,
"Stick on! stick on!" "Hould tight! hould tight!
Cling round his neck; and don't let go,—
That pace can't hold,—there! steady! whoa!"

Then methought I heard a mellow sound,
Gathering up from all the lower ground;
Narrowing in to where they sat assembled,
Low voluptuous music winding trembled,
Wov'n in circles. They that heard it sigh'd,
Panted hand-in-hand with faces pale,
Swung themselves, and in low tones replied;
Till the fountain spouted, showering wide
Sleet of diamond-drift and pearly hail.
Then the music touch'd the gates and died;
Rose again from where it seem'd to fail,
Storm'd in orbs of song, a growing gale;
Till thronging in and in, to where they waited,
As 'twere a hundred-throated nightingale,
The strong tempestuous treble throbb'd and palpitated;
Ran into its giddiest whirl of sound,
Caught the sparkles, and in circles,
Purple gauzes, golden hazes, liquid mazes,
Flung the torrent rainbow round.
Then they started from their places,
Moved with violence, changed in hue,
Caught each other with wild grimaces,
Half-invisible to the view,
Wheeling with precipitate paces

To the melody, till they flew,
Hair, and eyes, and limbs, and faces,
Twisted hard in fierce embraces,
Like to Furies, like to Graces,
Dash'd together in blinding dew;
Till, kill'd with some luxurious agony,
The nerve-dissolving melody
Flutter'd headlong from the sky.

Let it not be supposed that any one of the foregoing extracts is to be read in uniformly slow or uniformly fast time; that will change with each variation in the importance of the thought. Without attempting to force any interpretation upon the student, an illustration is appended in which he may note how the relative importance of the ideas affects the rate of movement in the various phrases.

Med.	Wherefore rejoice? What conquest brings he home?
Med.	What tributaries follow him to Rome,
Fast.	To grace in captive bonds his chariot wheels?
Slow.	You blocks, you stones, you worse than senseless things!
Very slow.	O you hard hearts, you cruel men of Rome,
Med. and fast.	Knew you not Pompey? Many a time and oft
Fast.	Have you climb'd up to walls and battlements,
Fast.	To towers and windows, yea, to chimney-tops,
Med.	Your infants in your arms, and there have sat
Med.	The livelong day, with patient expectation,
Med.	To see great Pompey pass the streets of Rome:
Med.	And when you saw his chariot but appear,
Fast.	Have you not made an universal shout,
Fast.	That Tiber trembled underneath her banks,
Fast.	To hear the replication of your sounds
Fast.	Made in her concave shores?
Slow.	And do you now put on your best attire?
Med.	And do you now cull out a holiday?
Med.	And do you now strew flowers in his way,
Fast.	That comes in triumph over Pompey's blood?
	Begone!
Med.	Run to your houses, fall upon your knees,
Slow.	Pray to the gods to intermit the plague
Slow.	That needs must light on this ingratitude.

It must be evident that it is very difficult to suggest by a word the rate of speed at which one should render a given line. Fast and slow are relative terms. Certain speakers would consider slow reading what another would consider moderate. Yet there is on the whole a pretty general agreement as to the use of these terms. With this statement, we may proceed to an analysis of the selection to justify the marking.

The citizens of Rome have just declared to the tribunes, enemies of Caesar, why the people are making holiday: "We make holiday to see Caesar, and to rejoice in his triumph." Whereupon Marullus, one of the tribunes, begins his speech, endeavoring to convince the mob that there is absolutely nothing Caesar has done to merit this ovation. After the word "tributaries," the time is accelerated for the reason that all that follows, to the end of the query, is virtually repetitious, being included in the idea of tributaries. The indicated marking of lines four and five needs no justification. "Knew you not Pompey?" is a question containing reproach. The latter element will tend to retard the movement. "Many a time and oft" is repetitious; he is simply reminding them of well-known facts. When the speaker reaches "yea, to chimney-tops," the importance of the idea is at once manifest in the slower time, which continues to "arms," when it again changes to medium and fast. The student may find it a good drill to examine the remaining lines, to see whether he agrees with or differs from the time-markings.

Thus far we have been considering the element of time without regard to details. It is now necessary to note that time may be affected in two ways: by quantity and by pause. By dwelling upon the words the time may be retarded, and the same effect may be produced by frequent or long pauses. In the former instance, the mind is dwelling upon the thought while the voice is giving it expression; and in the latter, the mind is dwelling upon the idea or the collateral thought between the words or groups. The two methods may be illustrated in the following extract: "Our Father, which art in Heaven, hallowed be Thy name." One may read this with but one pause, after "Heaven"; or he may appropriately pause after "Father," "Heaven," and "hallowed."

GROUPING

Study carefully the following extract, and then read it aloud:

> But when the gray dawn stole into his tent,
> He rose, and clad himself, and girt his sword,
> And took his horseman's cloak, and left his tent,
> And went abroad into the cold wet fog,
> Through the dim camp to Peran-Wisa's tent.

We notice a tendency to break up the sentence into groups of varying length. This tendency is more or less instinctive; and while there may be some difference of opinion as to the number of groups, yet it must be conceded that there is a definite underlying principle, which admits of no exception. For instance, one might read the fourth line as if it were but one group; another, with virtually the same idea in mind, might divide it into two groups at the word "abroad." On the other hand, no one would read in this way: "And went abroad into the" — "cold wet fog through" — "the dim camp to Peran-Wisa's tent."

Read the following sentences aloud carefully, and it will be noticed that the same principle of grouping obtains:

> The star of Napoleon was just rising to its zenith as that of Washington was passing away.

> The name and memory of Washington will travel with the Silver Queen of Heaven through sixty degrees of longitude, nor part company with her till she walks in her brightness through the Golden Gate of California, and passes serenely on to hold midnight court with her Australian Stars.

The reading of these illustrations shows that grouping is entirely independent of punctuation. It is true that the spoken group may coincide with the grammatical group, but that is merely an accident. We group as we do, not because of punctuation marks, but for more fundamental and less conventional reasons. The function of the punctuation mark is to assist the reader in getting the author's thought. The following example will illustrate this:

> The slaves who were in the hold of the vessel had been captured in Africa.

It is plain that the clause introduced by "who" is a restrictive one, and implies that there were other slaves on the vessel besides those mentioned. If we now insert commas after "slaves" and "vessel," the sentence becomes equivalent to, The slaves, and they were all in the hold of the vessel, had been captured in Africa.

Note, again, how the sense would be obscured if the author had omitted the comma after "all" in this extract:

> For we are all, like swimmers in the sea,
> Poised on the top of a huge wave of fate.

We are not like swimmers in the sea, but poised on the top of a huge wave of fate, as swimmers in the sea are poised on waves of water.

To prove that grouping is independent of punctuation, let the student read aloud the following illustrations:

> But, look you, Cassius,
> The angry spot doth glow on Caesar's brow.

> I saw Mark Antony offer him a crown; and, as I told you, he put it by once; but, for all that, to my thinking he would have had it ... and, for mine own part, I dare not laugh.

In the two preceding extracts, the reader would hardly pause after "But," "you," and the "and's."

While we are on the subject of punctuation, it may be advisable to look at a few examples in which the understanding of the force of punctuation vitally affects the reading. In these lines from Tennyson's *Ode on the Death of the Duke of Wellington,* students carelessly connect the phrase "sad and slow" with "Lead out the pageant." As a matter of fact, a moment's thought must show us that the opening sentence is complete in itself, and that "sad and slow" modifies "go." A careful reading of the text would reveal this, but a mind that had been trained to observe these matters of punctuation would have observed at once that the colon separated the two ideas, and, further, that the word modified by "sad and slow" was to be sought further on. Here is the passage:

> Lead out the pageant: sad and slow,
> As fits a universal woe,
> Let the long long procession go,
> And let the sorrowing crowd about it grow,
> And let the mournful martial music flow,
> The last great Englishman is low.

Another passage, from *The Merchant of Venice,* is equally interesting and instructive. Shylock says:

> Yet his means are in supposition; he hath an argosy bound to Tripolis, another to the Indies; I understand moreover upon the Rialto, he hath a third to Mexico, a fourth for England; and other ventures he hath, squandered abroad.

Seven students out of ten read the last sentence as if "hath squandered" were the verb. The comma after "hath" shows this to be a mistake, and, moreover, denotes a shade of meaning that is very significant of Shylock's character.

The object in giving these illustrations has been to free the student from a very common misconception that the group is determined by the punctuation mark, and, further, to draw his attention to the necessity of scanning the punctuation with the utmost care. As a rule, the words are in themselves sufficient index of the author's meaning; but, as in the cases cited, there are times when carelessness regarding punctuation leads to serious and ridiculous misunderstanding. The punctuation will make the sense clear wherever such help is necessary; but after that, as far as grouping is concerned, the student need give it no further attention. In order to impress the fact that grouping and punctuation are independent of each other, the following examples should be thoughtfully considered and then read aloud:

> So every bondman in his own hand bears
> The power to cancel his captivity.

> And as the greatest only are,
> In his simplicity sublime.

Note that "only" modifies "greatest," and hence should be separated from "are." If the sentence were prose, it would read, "And as only the greatest are," in which case there would be no difficulty in the reading. As it is, we must bring out the relation by careful grouping.

> The first object of a free people is the preservation of their

liberty; and liberty is only to be preserved by maintaining constitutional restraints and just divisions of political power.

Soon after William H. Harrison's nomination, a writer in one of the leading administration papers spoke of his "log cabin" and his use of "hard cider," by way of sneer and reproach....

It did not happen to me to be born in a log cabin, but my elder brothers and sisters were born in a log cabin, raised amid the snowdrifts of New Hampshire, at a period so early that, when the smoke rose from its rude chimney and curled over the frozen hills, there was no similar evidence of a white man's habitation between it and the settlements on the rivers of Canada.

The following example is an excellent one to illustrate the necessity of paying careful attention to grouping:

Of Man's first disobedience, and the fruit
Of that forbidden tree, whose mortal taste
Brought death into the world, and all our woe,
With loss of Eden, till one greater Man
Restore us, and regain the blissful seat,
Sing, Heavenly Muse, that on the secret top
Of Oreb, or of Sinai, didst inspire
That shepherd, who first taught the chosen seed,
In the beginning how the Heav'ns and Earth
Rose out of Chaos.

It is to be remarked that the spirit did not teach the shepherd "in the beginning," but "how the Heav'ns and Earth rose" in the beginning, "out of Chaos." If we turn this last sentence into prose, it will assist us in getting the poet's meaning and consequently in giving the correct rendition.

THE PAUSE AS AN EXPRESSIVE ELEMENT

In the study of grouping, the student noticed that the groups were separated by pauses of varying duration. It may be said that the pauses were the results of the grouping rather than that the grouping was the result of the pauses. In other words, the pause could hardly be called expressive.

We are now to study the pause as an expressive element. No definite rule can be laid down for pausing; that is determined, to a large extent, by the temperament, the nature of the thought, and the occasion. It must be borne in mind, however, that the pause is not mere silence. A very little observation will show us that while the voice ceases, the thought continues to manifest itself in pantomimic expression. What is it, then, that determines the pause? The answer has a twofold aspect. First, pausing is an instinctive process, and comes as the result of certain psychological processes. We think in ideas, not in individual words, and these ideas are separated in our minds by pauses of varying length. We do not stop to consider whether or no we shall pause between the phrases of a sentence; the pause, as has been stated, comes instinctively, and is a manifestation of psycho-psychological action. In the second place, the pause is made as the result, to a greater or less degree, of collateral thinking. In other words, any given idea may call up another train of thought, with which the mind may engage itself, and such engagement would find actual expression in the pause. It must be remembered that the collateral thinking may take the mind backward or forward. According to the amount of this collateral thinking will be the duration of the pause.

An extract from the play of *Julius Caesar* will illustrate this point. In the fifth act, Brutus and Cassius have taken their "everlasting farewell," and Brutus ends the interview with these words:

> Why then, lead on.—O, that a man might know
> The end of this day's business, ere it come!
> But it sufficeth, that the day will end,
> And then the end is known.

The first four words of this speech are addressed to the onlookers. The word "on" takes the mind of the thoughtful and considerate leader to the battlefield where the fate of Rome is to be decided. He perceives that the future of his beloved city hangs trembling in the balance. The appearance on the preceding night of the ghost of Caesar, warning him that it will see him at Philippi, fills Brutus with apprehension. And then, how many of his followers, now so ready to do battle under his standard, will, ere night, lie cold in death upon the bloody field! All this and more passes through his mind, and his solicitude and apprehension manifest themselves in his features and in his body. Then even the stoical Brutus cannot repress his anxiety, which we note in the words, "O, that a man might know." This extract, therefore, well illustrates what was said above,—that the pause, as we here consider it, is not mere silence, but cessation of voice while the expression continues in the body. In the second place, it is plain that the collateral thinking determines the length of the pause.

Another element that determines the duration of the pause is the distance apart of the thoughts separated by the pause. Let us illustrate this:

> If this law were put upon our statute books there would not be, five years from to-day, a dissenting voice raised against it from the Atlantic to the Pacific.

Let it not be understood that there are no occasions when the phrase "from the Atlantic to the Pacific" would not be uttered with scarcely any pause after Atlantic. This phrase, and others like it, may have become a mere commonplace to describe extent; but in such a passage as the above, where the speaker is hyperbolically expressive, he no doubt intends to convey the idea that not one objection would be heard even in all the three thousand miles between the oceans. If the student will stop for a moment to analyze his own consciousness while uttering this sentence, he will scarcely fail to see the vast extent of territory separating the two oceans.

Many writers on the subject have given emotion as a reason for the pause. Strictly speaking, however, emotion, as distinct from thinking, seldom or never is the cause of the pause, unless it completely choke the utterance. In the example quoted above from *Julius Caesar* there is no doubt considerable emotion during the pause; but it is the thought, and not the emotion arising out of it, that leads to the silence.

The following excerpt is from the speech of Satan in *Paradise Lost*. Satan has been cursing his lot and the author of his punishment. Finally, his judgment tells him that he himself, and not God, is responsible for the downfall. The pauses, indicated by the vertical lines, are suggestive of the proper rendition. Of course, the pauses vary in duration from the briefest cessation of voice to pauses of considerable length:

Nay, | curs'd be thou; | since against his | thy will
Chose freely | what it now | so justly rues.
Me | miserable! which way shall I fly
Infinite wrath, | and infinite despair? |
Which way I fly | is Hell; | myself | am Hell;
And in the lowest deep | a lower deep |
Still threat'ning to devour me | opens wide |
To which the Hell I suffer | seems a Heav'n.
But say I could repent | and could obtain |
By act of grace | my former state, | how soon
Would height | recall high thoughts, | how soon unsay |
What feign'd submission | swore.
This | knows my punisher; therefore | as far
From granting | he, as I | from begging | peace.

The student should practice the following examples until he perceives clearly the force of the preceding principles. The group is the thought unit, and the proper rendition of the sentence depends upon our grasp of the units that compose it. Hence, a conscientious study of the phrasing will lead not only to careful grouping, but to a grasp of the thought in its entirety that cannot fail to affect for good the reading of the whole selection:

... and there were drawn
Upon a heap a hundred ghastly women
Transformed with their fear, who swore they saw
Men all in fire walk up and down the streets.

He were no lion, were not Romans hinds.

Those that with haste will make a mighty fire
Begin it with weak straws.

A piece of work that will make sick men whole.

Danger knows full well
That Caesar is more dangerous than he.
We are two lions litter'd in one day,

And I the elder and more terrible.

No more in soldier fashion will he greet
With lifted hand the gazer in the street.

Before the starry threshold of Jove's court
My mansion is, where those immortal shapes
Of bright aerial spirits lived inspher'd
In regions mild of calm and serene air.

Whether 'tis nobler in the mind to suffer
The slings and arrows of outrageous fortune,
Or to take arms against a sea of troubles,
And by opposing end them?

And the sunset paled and warmed once more
With a softer, tenderer afterglow;
In the east was moonrise with boats off-shore;
And sails in the distance drifting slow.

O may I join the choir invisible
Of those immortal dead who live again
In the minds made better by their presence:

Moses, who spake with God as with his friend,
And ruled his people with the twofold power
Of wisdom that can dare and still be meek,
Was writing his last word, the sacred name
Unutterable of that Eternal Will
Which was and is and evermore shall be.

We stood far off and saw the angels lift
His corpse aloft until they seemed a star
That burnt itself away within the sky.

Messer Bernado del Nero was as inexorable as Romola had expected in his advice that the marriage should be deferred till Easter, and in this matter Bardo was entirely under the ascendency of his sagacious and practical friend. Nevertheless, Bernado himself, though he was as far as ever from any susceptibility to the personal fascination in Tito which was felt by others, could not altogether resist that argument of success which is always powerful with men of the world.

Some of the softening effects of advancing age have struck me very much in what I have heard or seen here and elsewhere. I just now spoke of the sweetening process that authors undergo.

Do you know that in the gradual passage from maturity to helplessness the harshest characters sometimes have a period in which they are gentle and placid as young children? I have heard it said, but I cannot be sponsor for its truth, that the famous chieftain, Lochiel, was rocked in a cradle like a baby, in his old age. An old man, whose studies had been of the severest scholastic kind, used to love to hear little nursery stories read over and over to him. One who saw the Duke of Wellington in his last years describes him as very gentle in his aspect and demeanor. I remember a person of singularly stern and lofty bearing who became remarkably gracious and easy in all his ways in the later period of his life.

Whatever Lionel had said to his wife that evening she had found something to say to him: that Laura could see though not so much from any change in the simple expression of his little red face and in the vain bustle of his existence as from the grand manner in which Selina now carried herself. She was "smarter" than ever and her waist was smaller and her back straighter and the fall of her shoulders finer; her long eyes were more oddly charming and the extreme detachment of her elbows from her sides conduced still more to the exhibition of her beautiful arms.

At the moment when death so suddenly stayed his course the greatness of Henry the Fifth had reached its highest point. He had won the Church by his orthodoxy, the nobles by his warlike prowess, the whole people by his revival of the glories of Crecy and Poitiers. In France his cool policy had transformed him from a foreign conqueror into a legal heir to the crown; his title of Regent and of successor to the throne rested on the formal recognition of the estates of the realm; and his progress to the very moment of his death promised a speedy mastery of the whole country. But the glory of Agincourt and the genius of Henry the Fifth hardly veiled at the close of his reign the weakness and humiliation of the Crown when the succession passed to his infant son.

PEDAGOGICAL ASPECTS

From what has been stated, it must be clear that drills in fast time or slow time are useless and fraught with much danger of affectation. Any of us can read slowly or rapidly; that is merely a matter of mechanics. The object to be attained is the development of such power of discrimination in the child that the value of each phrase and sentence shall be carefully determined; and then the degree of extent, depth, sublimity or grandeur of the thought will determine the rate of movement. Training in Time for its own sake is valueless. From the very beginning, the teacher must use Time as a test, as a standard of criticism; and all corrections must be made with a clear perception on the part of the teacher of the psychology of Time.

If a child read too rapidly, it is because his mind is not sufficiently occupied with the thought; if he read too slowly, it is because he does not get the words; or because he is temperamentally slow; or because, and this is the most likely explanation, he is making too much of a small idea.

The only excuse for drills in Time is when a pupil reads everything at about the same rate. In such a case, in the upper grades, the teacher may choose certain selections for the proper expression of which approximately fast or slow movement, as the case may be, would be required. Then let the teacher, through careful analysis and question, lead the child to understand the passages as the teacher understands them, and the proper rate of utterance will follow. This process may seem slow; but let us bear in mind that we are dealing with fundamental principles of thinking, and too much time cannot be spent in building our foundations strong and solid. Furthermore, if the rate of utterance is not the instinctive manifestation of the child's thought measurement, it is nothing at all. To tell him to read fast or slowly is but to make him affected, and incidentally, even if unconsciously, to impress upon him that reading is a matter of mechanics and not of thought-getting and thought-giving.

In order to teach grouping, various rules have been laid down. Pupils have committed a long list of these without much practical benefit. A few of these rules are given to show the mechanical nature of such a method of teaching. "In every direct period, the principal pause comes at that part where the sense begins to form, or the expectation excited by the first member begins to be answered." Or, "A loose sentence requires a longer pause between its first member (usually a period direct or inverted), and the additional member which does not modify it." And, again, "Where the adjective follows the substantive or noun it modifies, and has modifiers of its own, constituting a descriptive phrase, it should be separated from its noun by a short pause." Now, it may be quite true that these rules are valid, but is it not clear that the pedagogy which makes use of them in the earlier stages approaches the subject from the wrong side? It lays stress upon the objective rather than upon the subjective aspect.

The pause should never be taught merely as pause. If the principles herein discussed have any meaning, they must surely teach us that the pause must come spontaneously. The pedagogic point to be remembered is that the pupil must be trained to extract the thought piece by piece, and to express it. The pause will then appear without consciousness. The attempt to teach pauses as such must result in mechanical silences, during which the face of the pupil is a perfect blank, the indubitable sign of mental blankness.

It should certainly now be clear that it is wrong to draw the attention of the pupil to the pause as such, and that it is useless and often misleading to give him at the beginning rules of pausing. We must approach the printed page in the spirit with which we approach one who is speaking to us, and, having grasped the meaning, repeat the ideas. Then the pauses will come as the unconscious expression of certain definite mental action.

Perhaps there is no better way of bringing home to the reader the psychological action lying behind grouping and pausing than by calling his attention to a chapter from a brief but most attractive work by Ernest Legouvé, of the *Conservatoire Française*:

> To conclude what we have to say on the first portion of our subject, the material part of reading, we must now occupy ourselves a little with what may be called punctuation.
>
> The tongue punctuates as well as the pen.
>
> One day, Samson, sitting at his desk, sees himself approached by a young man apparently pretty well satisfied with himself.
>
> "You wish to take reading lessons, sir?"
>
> "Yes, Monsieur Samson."
>
> "Have you had some practice in reading aloud?"
>
> "O yes, Monsieur Samson, I have often recited whole passages from Corneille and Molière."
>
> "In public?"
>
> "Yes, Monsieur Samson."
>
> "With success?"
>
> "Well, yes, Monsieur, I think I may flatter myself that far."
>
> "Take up that book, please. It is Fontaine's Fables. Open it at the *Oak and the Reed*. Let me hear you read a line or two."
>
> The pupil begins:
>
> "The Oak one day, said to the Reed— —"
>
> "That's enough, sir! You don't know anything about reading!"
>
> "It is because I don't know much, Monsieur Samson," replies the pupil, a little nettled, "it is precisely because I don't know much that I've come to you for lessons. But I don't exactly comprehend how from my manner of reading a single verse— —"
>
> "Read the line again, sir."
>
> He reads it again:
>
> "The Oak one day, said to the Reed— —"
>
> "There! You can't read! I told you so!"
>
> "But— —"
>
> "But," interrupts Samson, cold and dry, "but why do you join the adverb to the noun rather than to the verb? What kind of an Oak is an Oak one day? No kind at all! There is no such tree! Why, then, do you say: *the Oak one day, said to the Reed*? This is the way it should go: *the Oak (comma) one day said to the Reed*. You understand, of course?"

"Certainly I do," replies the other, a new light breaking on him. "It seems as if there should be an invisible comma after Oak!"

"You are right, sir," continues the master. "Every passage has a double set of punctuation marks, one visible, the other invisible; one is the printer's work, the other the reader's."

"The reader's? Does the reader also punctuate?"

"Certainly he does, quite independently too of the printer's points, though it must be acknowledged that sometimes both coincide. By a certain cadenced silence the reader marks his period; by a half silence, his comma; by a certain accent, an interrogation; by a certain tone, an exclamation. And I must assure you that it is exclusively on the skillful distribution of these insensible points that not only the interest of the story, but actually its clearness, its comprehensibility, altogether depends."

CHAPTER II

THE CRITERION OF PITCH

The second criterion is that of Pitch. By Pitch is meant everything that has to do with the acuteness or gravity of the tone,—in other words, with keys, melodies, inflections and modulations. Again we are indebted to Professor Raymond for a clear statement regarding this most subtle of all the elements of expression. His words are as follows: "The melody of the movement taken by the voice represents, therefore, like the melody in music, the *mind's motive,*—indicates its purpose in using the particular phraseology to which the melody is applied; and because pitch, through the kinds of inflections and melody chosen, reveals the motives, we shall find that the use of this element in ordinary conversation is constantly causing precisely the same phraseology to express entirely opposite meanings." Before proceeding further, it may be well to illustrate this principle, in order that the reader may follow more clearly the subsequent discussion.

Let us suppose some one to ask the question, "Do you think Mr. Jones is a good teacher?" and that the reply is given, "Oh, yes," with a melody that virtually says, "Oh, I suppose so; he is not a very great teacher; in fact, there are many things about his teaching that might be a great deal better, but he manages to get along." Now, all of this paraphrase, which reveals the motive, is manifested in the significant melody upon the two words, "Oh, yes." Let us suppose further that a few days later Mr. Jones comes to us and calls us to account for speaking disparagingly of his teaching. "What," we reply, "we say anything against your teaching! Why, when Smith asked us whether we considered you a good teacher, we said in the most unequivocal manner, 'Oh, yes'!" And this time we utter the words with strong, positive assertiveness. The words in both cases are the same, but the different melodies indicate entirely opposite motives behind the words.

Read aloud such a sentence as, "John rode to the park last Christmas," changing the meaning by transferring the significant inflection successively to all the important words, thus:

John rode to the park last Christmas.

John *rode* to the park last Christmas.

John rode to the *park* last Christmas, etc.

Does it not appear that, with each change in the motive, the melody changes?

We often hear it said that in such cases as the last we have been changing the emphasis. This is true. But emphasis is a broad term, and one often confused with force. As a matter of fact, the changes in the successive readings were changes of melody due in every case to changes of motive.

Again, "When we are in our graves our children will honor it. They will celebrate it with thanksgiving, with festivities, with bonfires, with joy." The inflections on the last four nouns would probably be falling. Why? Because each would be held to be of sufficient importance to be emphasized by itself, and cut off from the others. To read them with rising inflections would be to manifest the fact that the mind was thinking of them in the aggregate. Once again, the melody shows the motive.

The melody is an indubitable sign of the discriminative ability of the reader. It is the severest test of his power to perceive sense, or logical, relations. So important a feature of the work is this that it appears necessary to emphasize it and to illustrate it in many ways.

Bassanio desires to show his love for Antonio. He says:

Antonio, I am married to a wife,
Which is as dear to me as life itself;
But life itself, my wife, and all the world,
Are not with me esteem'd above thy life:
I would lose all, ay, sacrifice them all
Here to this devil, to deliver you.

It is evident that he does not wish to assert that he is married, nor that he is married to a wife; but that he is married to a wife as dear as life itself. And yet many a pupil reads the passage as if Bassanio were desirous of insisting upon the fact that he is married to a wife. Not a very remarkable condition of affairs, truly. It is no argument to say that the comma after "wife" indicates the necessity of a rising inflection on that word. As has been already intimated, and as will be later developed, the punctuation has nothing to do with the inflection.

Meanwhile King Robert yielded to his fate,
Sullen and silent and disconsolate.
Dressed in the motley garb that Jesters wear,
With look bewildered, and a vacant stare,
Close shaven above the ears, as monks are shorn,
By courtiers mocked, by pages laughed to scorn,
His only friend the ape, his only food
What others left,—he still was unsubdued.

In the preceding passage, note that from the third line to the clause at the end of the sentence the mind is glancing forward, and this fact will be evident in the rising inflection at the end of every important statement. Notice, further, that all of these statements will be uttered in what is virtually the same melody. The reason for this is that they are co-ordinate, and having the same motive behind them will be read with the same melody.

Observe the different melodies in the following sentences, and how the difference manifests the varying motive:

I said *one*, two, three, four, five.

I said one, *two*, three, four, five.

I said one, two, *three*, four, five.

I said one, two, three, *four*, five.

I said one, two, three, four, *five*.

When Mark Antony uses the phrase, "honorable men," in the beginning of his oration, there can be no doubt that he avoids even the slightest indication of sarcasm in his voice. Whatever his ultimate purpose may be, his immediate intention is to conciliate the mob. This purpose, his motive, is shown by the unequivocal melody with which he says:

Here, under leave of Brutus and the rest,—
For Brutus is an honorable man,
So are they all, all honorable men,—
Come I to speak on Caesar's funeral.

It is hardly necessary to consider this aspect farther. Let us, however, examine the subject in detail. The first consideration is that of Key. Key has been defined as "the fundamental tone of a movement to which its modulations are referred, and with which it generally begins and ends; keynote." (Webster.) Perhaps the meaning of the current phrases "high key" and "low key" will make the definition clear. When we say of one that he speaks in a high key, we should be understood as meaning that his pitch is prevailingly high; and that the reverse is true when we say of one that he speaks in a low key. While it is true that the key differs in individuals, yet experience shows that within a note or two we all use the same keys in expressing the same states of minds. The question for us is, What determines the key? It can be set down as a fixed principle that controlled mental states are expressed in the low keys, while the high keys are the manifestation of the less controlled mental conditions.[1] This principle will be more readily understood

[1] In describing what is small, delicate, nice, we often note the tendency to use a rather high key. This is no doubt due to the tension that results from unconscious imitation. The

when we consider the states finding expression in low or high key in music. We should hardly awaken much enthusiasm by playing *Yankee Doodle* in a key an octave below that in which it is written; nor should we catch the subtle meaning of Chopin's *Funeral March* if it were played in a key an octave higher than the original key. Let the reader study the spirit of the following extracts, and read them aloud. He will find in such practice the best proof of the truth of the principle we are here discussing:

Over his keys the musing organist,
Beginning doubtfully and far away,
First lets his fingers wander as they list,
And builds a bridge from Dreamland for his lay:
Then, as the touch of his loved instrument
Gives hope and fervor, nearer draws his theme,
First guessed by faint auroral flushes sent
Along the wavering vista of his dream.—*The Vision of Sir Launfal.* LOWELL.

It is but a legend, I know,—
A fable, a phantom, a show,
Of the ancient Rabbinical lore;
Yet the old mediæval tradition,
The beautiful, strange superstition,
But haunts me and holds me the more.

When I look from my window at night,
And the welkin above is all white,
All throbbing and panting with stars,
Among them majestic is standing
Sandalphon the angel, expanding
His pinions in nebulous bars.

And the legend, I feel, is a part
Of the hunger and thirst of the heart,
The frenzy and fire of the brain,
That grasps at the fruitage forbidden,
The golden pomegranates of Eden,
To quiet its fever and pain.—*Sandalphon.* LONGFELLOW.

I had a dream, which was not all a dream.
The bright sun was extinguished; and the stars
Did wander darkling in the eternal space,
Rayless, and pathless; and the icy earth
Swung blind and blackening in the moonless air;
Morn came, and went,—and came, and brought no day.

The world was void;

voice is to a certain extent squeezed in endeavoring to express the smallness of the idea, with the result that the key is raised. Note how the child's key rises when he asks for a "leetle, teeny bit."

The populous and the powerful was a lump,—
Seasonless, herbless, treeless, manless, lifeless,—
A lump of death—a chaos of hard clay.
The rivers, lakes, and ocean, all stood still;
And nothing stirred within their silent depths:
Ships, sailorless, lay rotting on the sea;
And their masts fell down piecemeal: as they dropped,
They slept on the abyss without a surge;—
The waves were dead; the tides were in their grave;
The moon, their mistress, had expired before;
The winds were withered in the stagnant air;
And the clouds perished: Darkness had no need
Of aid from them, She—was the universe. —*Darkness.* BYRON.

A fool, a fool!—I met a fool i' th' forest,
A motley fool;—a miserable world!—
As I do live by food, I met a fool;
Who laid him down, and bask'd him in the sun,
And rail'd on lady Fortune in good terms,
In good set terms,—and yet a motley fool.
"Good morrow, fool," quoth I; "No, sir," quoth he,
"Call me not fool, till heav'n hath sent me fortune;"
And then he drew a dial from his poke:
And looking on it with lack-lustre eye,
Says, very wisely, "It is ten o'clock;
Thus may we see," quoth he, "how the world wags;
'Tis but an hour ago, since it was nine;
And after one hour more 'twill be eleven;
And so, from hour to hour, we ripe and ripe,
And then, from hour to hour, we rot and rot,
And thereby hangs a tale." When I did hear
The motley fool thus moral on the time,
My lungs began to crow like chanticleer,
That fools should be so deep contemplative.
And I did laugh, sans intermission
An hour by his dial. O noble fool!
A worthy fool! Motley's the only wear. —*As You Like It,* Act ii., Sc. 7.

Haste thee, nymph, and bring with thee
Jest, and youthful jollity,
Quips, and cranks, and wanton wiles,
Nods, and becks, and wreathed smiles,
Such as hang on Hebe's cheek,
And love to dwell in dimple sleek;
Come, and trip it as ye go,
On the light fantastic toe. —*L'Allegro.* MILTON.

Where sweeps round the mountains
The cloud on the gale,
And streams from their fountains
Leap into the vale,—
Like frighted deer leap when
The storm with his pack
Rides over the steep in
The wild torrent's track,—
Even there my free home is;
There watch I the flocks
Wander white as the foam is
In stairways of rocks.
Secure in the gorge there
In freedom we sing,
And laugh at King George, where
The eagle is king. —*Song*. T. B. Read.

The reason for low pitch or high pitch is psycho-physiological. Nerve tension means muscular tension, and, since the muscles controlling the vocal chords are subject to the same laws as the other muscles, the greater the tension the higher the pitch. Hence, since what we have called the controlled states are accompanied by relatively low muscular tension, it necessarily follows that they will be expressed in relatively low keys.

The desire to communicate thought to another has a tendency to raise the key. To illustrate: if we are addressing an audience in a small room, we shall speak in a moderately low key. If the auditorium is large, the key will be higher. If we are speaking in the open air, the chances are that we shall use a key considerably above that of ordinary conversation. On the other hand, when one is communing with himself, the absence of desire to reach others removes the tension, and in consequence the pitch is low. It is well to bear in mind that all soliloquies are not read in low key. Soliloquies are often full of uncontrolled passion, in which case the principle first laid down would apply, and the pitch would be high, according to the degree of tension. What has been said in this paragraph we may sum up in a few words: those states in which there is strong desire to communicate (objective states) are manifested in high key; while the introspective (subjective) states find expression in the lower keys. Henry V., inciting his soldiers to attack the enemy's fortifications, says:

Once more unto the breach, dear friends, once more;
Or close the wall up with our English dead!
In peace, there's nothing so becomes a man,
As modest stillness, and humility:
But when the blast of war blows in our ears,
Then imitate the action of the tiger;
Stiffen the sinews, summon up the blood,
Disguise fair nature with hard-favor'd rage:
Then lend the eye a terrible aspect;

Let it pry through the portage of the head,
Like the brass cannon; let the brow o'erwhelm it,
As fearfully as doth a gallèd rock
O'erhang and jutty his confounded base,
Swill'd with the wild and wasteful ocean.
Now set the teeth, and stretch the nostril wide;
Hold hard the breath, and bend up every spirit
To his full height!—On, on, you noblest English,
Whose blood is fet from fathers of war-proof!—

* * * * *

The game's afoot;
Follow your spirit: and, upon this charge,
Cry—God for Harry! England! and Saint George!

—*Henry V.*, Act iii., Sc. 1.

The tension of the speaker is evidently high, owing to the exhilaration of the moment, and to the desire to project his voice (of which he may be unconscious), and consequently the key will be high. It is the joy of the English people that Tennyson voices in his Welcome to Alexandra. Again the key is relatively high.

Sea-kings' daughter from over the sea, Alexandra!
Saxon and Norman and Dane are we,
But all of us Danes in our welcome of thee, Alexandra!
Welcome her, thunders of fort and of fleet!
Welcome her, thundering cheer of the street!
Welcome her, all things youthful and sweet,
Scatter the blossoms under her feet!
Break, happy land, into earlier flowers!
Make music, O bird, in the new-budded bowers!
Blazon your mottoes of blessing and prayer!
Welcome her, welcome her, all that is ours!
Warble, O bugle, and trumpet, blare!
Flags, flutter out upon turrets and towers!
Flames, on the windy headland flare!
Utter your jubilee, steeple and spire!
Clash, ye bells, in the merry March air!
Flash, ye cities, in rivers of fire!
Rush to the roof, sudden rocket, and higher
Melt into stars for the land's desire!
Roll and rejoice, jubilant voice,
Roll as a ground-swell dashed on the strand,
Roar as the sea when it welcomes the land,
And welcome her, welcome the land's desire,
The sea-kings' daughter as happy as fair,
Blissful bride of a blissful heir,
Bride of the heir of the kings of the sea.

O joy to the people and joy to the throne,
Come to us, love us, and make us your own;
For Saxon or Dane or Norman we,
Teuton or Celt, or whatever we be,
We are each all Dane in our welcome of thee, Alexandra!

—*Welcome to Alexandra.* TENNYSON.

Hamlet's soliloquy will find expression in moderately low key when one grasps the idea that Hamlet is meditating upon:

To be, or not to be,—that is the question;
Whether 'tis nobler in the mind to suffer
The slings and arrows of outrageous fortune,
Or to take arms against a sea of troubles,
And by opposing end them? To die,—to sleep,—
No more; and by a sleep to say we end
The heart-ache, and the thousand natural shocks
That flesh is heir to,—'tis a consummation
Devoutly to be wish'd. To die,—to sleep;—
To sleep! perchance to dream!—ay, there's the rub;
For in that sleep of death what dreams may come
When we have shuffled off this mortal coil,
Must give us pause: there's the respect
That makes calamity of so long life;
For who would bear the whips and scorns of time,
Th' oppressor's wrong, the proud man's contumely,
The pangs of disprized love, the law's delay,
The insolence of office, and the spurns
That patient merit of th' unworthy takes,
When he himself might his quietus made
With a bare bodkin? who would fardels bear,
To grunt and sweat under a weary life,
But that the dread of something after death,—
The undiscover'd country from whose bourn
No traveler returns,—puzzles the will,
And makes us rather bear those ills we have
Than fly to others that we know not of?
Thus conscience does make cowards of us all;
And thus the native hue of resolution
Is sicklied o'er with the pale cast of thought;
And enterprises of great pith and moment
With this regard their currents turn awry,
And lose the name of action. —*Hamlet,* Act iii., Sc. 1.

The following lines are delivered by Hamlet when he appreciates the fact that while his father's blood cries out for vengeance he stands idle, beset by doubts and fears. The speech is a soliloquy, but it would be rendered in a moderately high pitch owing to the mental tension of the speaker:

O, what a rogue and peasant slave am I!
Is it not monstrous, that this player here,
But in a fiction, in a dream of passion,
Could force his soul so to his own conceit,
That from her working all his visage wann'd;
Tears in his eyes, distraction in 's aspect,
A broken voice, and his whole function suiting
With forms to his conceit? and all for nothing!
For Hecuba!
What's Hecuba to him, or he to Hecuba,
That he should weep for her? What would he do,
Had he the motive and the cue for passion
That I have? He would drown the stage with tears,
And cleave the general ear with horrid speech;
Make mad the guilty, and appal the free,
Confound the ignorant, and amaze indeed
The very faculties of eyes and ears. Yet I,
A dull and muddy-mettled rascal, peak,
Like John-a-dreams, unpregnant of my cause,
And can say nothing; no, not for a king
Upon whose property and most dear life
A damn'd defeat was made. Am I a coward?
Who calls me villain? breaks my pate across?
Plucks off my beard, and blows it in my face?
Tweaks me by th' nose? gives me the lie i' the throat,
As deep as to the lungs? who does me this?
Ha!
'Swounds, I should take it; for it cannot be
But I am pigeon-liver'd, and lack gall
To make oppression bitter; or, ere this,
I should have fatted all the region kites
With this slave's offal. Bloody, bawdy villain!
Remorseless, treacherous, lecherous, kindless villain!
O vengeance! —*Hamlet*, Act ii., Sc. 2.

The principle just discussed,—that key depends on the degree of tension, first mental, then physical,—is of very wide application. As a matter of fact, it explains the whole subject of melody. In passing from a controlled to a less controlled state, the voice rises, and vice versa. To illustrate: Brutus says to Cassius, "You yourself are much condemned to have an itching palm"; and Cassius replies, "I an itching palm!" On the word "I" the voice of Cassius strikes upward through, perhaps, an octave of the scale, and this inflection manifests the increasing tension of Cassius' mind as he utters the exclamation. It is almost impossible to restrain the tension of throat and hand while reading the passage. Note how the muscular tension increases while one is speaking the words of Cassius. Bearing in mind what has been said of the relation of bodily tension to pitch, the explanation of Cassius' inflection will not be far to seek. Again, Brutus says, "The name of Cassius honors this corruption, and chastisement doth therefore hide his head." Cassius replies in one word, "Chastisement." There are two interpretations of this word: one, that Cassius replies, as if questioning, "Do you dare say this to me?" and the other, that, astounded at the bluntness of Brutus's speech, Cassius replies, speaking to himself, "He dared speak of chastisement to me!" In the first case the inflection would be rising, denoting the increase of tension; in the second case, the inflection would be falling, marking a gradual decrease of tension. Let the reader experiment on this example, and observe how the mental tension corresponds with the physical tension.

The melody in which any phrase or sentence is given consists of a series of waves, the crests of which mark the maximum of tension. It is a difficult matter to indicate speech melody, but it is hoped the following illustrations will be at least sufficiently suggestive to make clear the psychology of melody. In the following sentence there is a gradual ascent of the voice, since the intensity increases from the first word to the end.

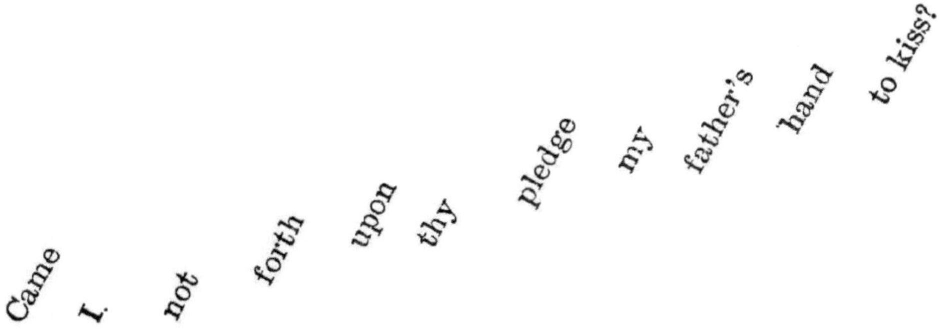

Again, we have a very similar melody in this:

Would you wrest the wreath of fame
From the hand of fate?

The descending melody, denoting that the maximum of tension is at the beginning of the sentence, is found in the following:

"Dead" marks the crest of the wave of tension in the following. Observe how the melody rises to that word and descends after it:

dead, So
pleasure sadness
strike breathes
from
cold
out
dungeons
the
from mould
breathed where
Burns
vapors
is
As laid.

For those who have no musical ear, it may be somewhat difficult to catch these speech melodies. But, fortunately, in most cases, an acute musical ear is not necessary. Melody takes care of itself. When we have determined the principal word in each phrase, the melody will rise or fall from that without any effort on our part. And furthermore, even those without an ear for tune recognize instinctively the appropriateness of a given melody which they may be unable to analyze in detail. Nevertheless, the ability to analyze speech tunes is a great aid to the teacher; and it is to be hoped that the foregoing explanation will materially assist him in his work of developing the logical acumen of his class.

Melody is made up of skips and inflections. The inflection needs no definition; the skip is simply a discreet passage from one note to another. As the violinist draws his bow over the string and simultaneously runs his finger up or down the string, we have the analogy of the inflection. The pianist cannot do more than skip from one note to another, although there is an approximation to the glide, or inflection, in *legato* playing. The skip is found in such a sentence as this:

tus ue tors?
Give a with
Bru his ces
stat an

The psychology of the skip is precisely that of the inflection, i. e., transition from less to more tension, or the reverse. In such an exclamation as, "Thou tattered upstart!" it is next to impossible to use the wide rising inflection that would be natural on the first syllable of "upstart," owing to the nature of the syllable. Hence, there would be a skip between "up" and "start." But let it be carefully observed that, including the skip, the voice traverses exactly the interval it would have passed through had it been possible to use one inflection, as, for instance, on "boy" in "Thou tattered boy!" Our attention may now be turned to inflections.

Inflections are not a matter of accident, nor are they a conventional device. Their meaning is definite and fixed, and their force instinctively recognized by all. Although we do not stop to analyze them, they convey to all alike a distinct shade of thought. And further, the same shade of thought will always find expression through the same inflections. We must bear in mind that it is not claimed that all will be moved in the same way by the same stimulus, nor that all will take the same meaning from a given passage. What is claimed is, that the same purpose will find expression, with all, in fundamentally the same melody (of which inflections form the larger part). If this were not so, how should we understand one another? We discern a speaker's purpose quite as much in his melody as in his words. For example, if one were to ask, "Are you going out?" with the object of acquiring information, he would use instinctively a rising inflection on "out." If he were surprised at our intention to go out, he would use a wider rising inflection. And if he had asked the question several times without receiving a reply, and were now insisting on an answer (his motive now being to assert his right to an answer) he would use a wide downward inflection on "out." And so should we all under like conditions, and the meaning of all would be alike understood by all. We need enlarge no further on this. Let it suffice that if given inflections had not always the same meaning and were not always instinctively used to express the same purpose, conversation would be impossible.

The rising inflection is the sign of incomplete sense. Whenever the mind points forward the significant inflection is upward. Test this in the following illustrations. The rising inflection will be particularly noticed on the italicized words, which are not necessarily to be strongly emphasized:

> In *1815* M. Charles *Myriel* was the bishop of D— —. He was a man of about seventy-five years of *age*, and had held the see of D— — since 1806. Although the following details in no way affect our *narrative*, it may not be useless to quote the rumors that were current about *him* at the moment when he came to the diocese; for what is said of *men*, whether it be true or *false*, often occupies as much space in their *life*, and especially in their *destiny*,[2] as what they do.
>
> The beams of the rising *sun* had gilded the lofty domes of *Carthage*, and *given*, with its rich and mellow *light*, a tinge of *beauty* even to the frowning ramparts of the outer harbor.

When, for any reason, we do not desire to assert strongly; when what we have to say is trite, trivial, repetitious; when we are uncertain or doubtful; when we entreat; when we ask a question to which the answer yes or no is expected, we also use the rising inflection.

> I do not claim this is the only method.
>
> I cannot promise definitely, but I think you may rely upon getting it.
>
> I shall wait for you in the lobby, if you don't tarry too long.

[2] The rising inflection will be heard only on the last syllable of this word. Note the discreet skip of the voice between the first and second syllables.

It doesn't look like rain, does it?

There are some arguments in its favor, but they are not weighty.

No, nobody claims that.

I grant I may have taken the honorable gentleman by surprise.

I cannot tell what you and other men
Think of this life, but, for my single self,
I had as lief not be as live to be
In awe of such a thing as I myself.

I do not charge the gentleman with wilful *misstatement*, but I would rather say he is a great economizer of the truth.

I do not like to think that the opposition is purposely delaying the vote on this question.

Never fear *that*: if he be so resolved,
I can o'ersway him.

You won't leave me, father.

Good friends, sweet friends, let me not stir you up to such a sudden flood of mutiny!

O, Hamlet, speak no more.

Pity the sorrows of a poor old man.

It would be idle to base an opinion on any argument of Mr. Webster.

O, that is of no consequence; you don't believe that.

It is hardly necessary for me to go over the charges of the attorney for the *plaintiff*; they are trivial and unimportant.

It goes without saying that you know the early history of these people.

There are very few who haven't a bowing acquaintance with this subject.

You know me well, and herein spend but time

> To wind about my love with circumstance.

> Not that I loved Caesar *less*, but that I loved Rome more.

> It is not that I doubt the gentleman's *honesty*, but that I question his authority.

> It was at the end of the war that this incident occurred; not at the *beginning*.

Uncertainty, confusion, hesitation, and other forms of doubt, are really questions,—the mind seeking solution of difficult and perplexing problems.

> I wish I could find some way out of this, but—

> There ought to be some other method of solving this *difficulty*: let me see, let me see.

> I would I had been there.

> Are you the owner of this house?

> Can you tell me what time it is?

Care must be taken not to confuse this form of interrogation with Figurative Interrogation. The latter is often strongly assertive. For instance:

> God of battles, was ever a battle like this in the world before?

This is equivalent to asking a question and answering it at the same time. It asks in words, "was ever?" It answers in inflection, "there never was." Grammatically, then, it is a question; rhetorically, it is an exclamation. Here is another form of Figurative Interrogation:

> Are you going out? (No answer.) Are you going out? (I demand an answer.)

In this case, the second question becomes a demand. The speaker cares for an answer not so much because of any interest in it as such, but because he desires his authority respected.

The following examples of Figurative Interrogation should be carefully studied:

> Is there a single atrocity of the French more unprincipled and inhuman than that of Russia, Austria, and Prussia, in Poland?

> Did he not know that he was making history that hour? Did he not know this, I say?

> If I were to propose three cheers for Washington, is there a single man, woman, or child in this vast audience who would refuse to lift his voice?

> Have you, gentlemen of the jury, considered the price the state asks the prisoner to pay for what is only an indiscretion at most? I repeat, have you considered the price?
>
> Has the gentleman *done*? Has he *completely* done?

A very interesting psychological question arises in connection with Figurative Interrogation. It has been shown how the grammatical question becomes an oratorical assertion; but there is a point in assertion beyond which it may pass and become an intense emotional question. In this sentence, "Shall not the Judge of all the earth do right?" we have an illustration. There are three possibilities here. First: a simple question looking for information. Second: an exclamation equivalent to, Who does not know that the Judge of all the earth shall do right? Third: a skeptical question (with considerable emotion) is it possible that any one would deny that the Judge of all the earth shall do right?

It would be easy to multiply examples and make many refinements of this principle underlying the use of the rising inflection. A careful study, however, of those given should suffice to impress upon the reader that the rising inflection will be given whenever for any reason whatsoever there is no desire to assert.

Incompleteness (implied or otherwise) is marked by the rising inflection; completeness by the falling. We are all aware that the falling inflection marks completed sense, so that this principle will require neither elaboration nor illustration. Attention must be called, however, to the fact that we often assert strongly in the middle of a sentence. This phase of the subject has been so well described by another[3] that we quote as follows:

> "Momentary Completeness.—This applies to any clause, phrase, or even word, which has, for any reason, enough separate force to constitute, at the moment, an entire thought, and to call for a separate affirmation of the mind. This momentary completeness may arise:
>
> "1. From the logical importance of the clause, phrase, or word requiring a strong affirmative emphasis.
>
> "2. From an elliptical construction—one in which each part could be reasonably expanded into a complete proposition.

"*Example* of 1 would be this sentence from Webster:

> It comes, if it come at all, like the outbreaking of a fountain from the earth, or the bursting forth of volcanic fires, with spontaneous, original, native force.

"Here the ideas of spontaneity, originality, nativeness, are each so important to the thought that the mind is called upon to make a separate affirmation upon each one.

[3] Prof. W. B. Chamberlain in his "Rhetoric of Vocal Expression." This work is now out of print, but a revision and enlargement of it is published by Scott, Foresman & Co., of Chicago, under the title "Principles of Vocal Expression and Literary Interpretation."

"*Examples* of 2 are found in some of the connected clauses in this passage from Byron's *Dream of Darkness*:

I had a dream, which was not all a dream.
The bright sun was extinguished, and the stars
Did wander, darkling, in the eternal space,
Rayless and pathless, and the icy earth
Swung blind and blackening in the moonless air.
Morn came and went—and came, and brought no day,
And men forgot their passions in the dread
Of this their desolation; and all hearts
Were chilled into a selfish prayer for light.

"The 'loose' sentence presents a typical case of momentary completeness, each added clause or element giving a separate, subjoined thought.

"In the following cases the period mark inclosed in brackets, [.], indicates the place at which the sentence might close; and the words in parentheses are those which might be supplied in constructing separate complete propositions. The reconstruction suggests the probable process of thought.

> The next day he voted for that repeal [.], and he would have spoken for it too [.], if an illness had not prevented it.

> The Englishman in America will feel that this is slavery—that it is *legal* slavery, will be no compensation, either to his feelings or his understanding.

"The Englishman in America will feel that this is slavery [.]. (The mere fact) that it is *legal* slavery will (in his estimation) be no compensation (at all). (It will not be (in any degree) satisfactory) either to his feelings or his understanding.

"Completeness is marked in the voice by a falling slide; that indicating finality usually descends at least a fifth (from *sol* down to *do*), and is preceded by a more or less distinct rising melody. This cadential melody may carry the voice so high in pitch that the falling slide will be as great as an octave. The indication of momentary completeness is also a falling slide, varying in extent from a third to a fifth, but not so marked as that of finality, and usually not preceded by any special rising melody.

"In the following example note momentary completeness on 'man,' 'woman,' 'child,' and finality on the climacteric word 'beast.' Thus:

They saw not one màn, not one wòman, not one chìld,

b
footed e
four a
one s
not t.

"It is especially important to study the relation of momentary completeness in connection with dependent clauses. As a rule, a definitive clause does not stand in the relation of momentary completeness, but in that of subordination or anticipation. A supplemental clause, on the other hand, is distinctively complete. This relation is not always shown, either by the punctuation, or by exact use of relative pronouns. In strictness, 'who' and 'which', as already said, should always mark supplemental relations; 'that,' definitive. Considerations of euphony, however, often overrule grammatical and rhetorical principles. The problem in regard to dependent clauses is; to decide whether the subordinate clause contains additional thought, or only modifying thought. The best practical test will be found in paraphrasing. If a dependent clause is truly definitive, it may be reduced to a brief element,—often to a single word, which may be incorporated in the first clause.

> *Example.*—Lafayette was intrusted by Washington with all kinds of services ... the laborious and complicated, which required skill and patience; the perilous, that demanded nerve.—EVERETT.

"In this example, it is obvious that the clause introduced by 'which' and the one beginning with 'that' stand in precisely the same relation, the change being made for euphony. It is obvious also that both dependent clauses are supplemental rather than definitive. In both of these clauses, therefore, there is an added thought, and this gives the relation of momentary completeness at the words 'complicated' and 'perilous.'

"The ear, under the guidance of the logical and rhetorical insight, gives a much more sensitive and more accurate punctuation than can be indicated by printer's marks or grammarian's rules. Not the words, nor the grammatical elements, nor the customary and traditional rendering, determine grouping or inflection, but rather the speaker's immediate purpose at the moment of the utterance.

"The principle of momentary completeness is strikingly exemplified in the case of a 'division of the question' in parliamentary proceedings. Division is called for because each item is considered as separately important enough to demand the entire attention. The same is often true in the announcement of a proposition containing several different elements, or of a text of Scripture suggesting many separate thoughts."

It need hardly be said that the rule so often given, that "the voice should rise at a comma," is ridiculous. It often does, it is true,—not because of the comma, but because of the motive.

The purpose of the following drills is not to train the student in the manner of making inflections, but rather to impress upon his mind the fact that rhetorically a sentence may be complete even though the point of completion be not marked by a full stop. In other words, the drill is one in mental, rather than vocal, technique.

The student must determine the purpose in every case, and then trust his voice to manifest that purpose.

> Hence! *home,*[4] you idle *creatures,* get you home.

---

[4] The falling inflection may properly be given on the italicised words; but the latter

Speak, what trade art thou?

Where is thy leather *apron,* and thy rule?

You *blocks,* you *stones,* you *worse* than senseless things.

Many a time and oft
Have you climb'd up to walls and battlements,
To towers and windows, yea, to *chimney-tops.*
Your infants in your *arms,* and there have sat
* * * * *
To see great *Pompey* pass the streets of Rome.

Be gone!
Run to your *houses,* fall upon your *knees,*
Pray to the gods to intermit the *plague*
That needs must light on this ingratitude.

Then, Brutus, I have much mistook your passion;
By means whereof this breast of mine hath buried
Thoughts of great *value,* worthy cogitations.

I was born free as *Caesar,* so were you;
We both have *fed* as well, and we can both
Endure the winter's *cold* as well as he.

His coward lips did from their color *fly,*
And that same eye whose bend doth awe the world
Did lose his lustre.

Ye *gods,* it doth *amaze* me,
A man of such a feeble temper should
* * * * *
... bear the palm alone.

Why, man, he doth bestride the narrow world
Like a *Colossus,* and we petty men
Walk under his huge legs and peep about
To find ourselves dishonorable graves.

Let me have men about me that are *fat,*
Sleek-headed men, and such as sleep o' nights.

Seldom he *smiles,* and smiles in such a sort,
As if he mocked himself.

---

are not therefore necessarily to be emphasized.

Such men as he be never at heart's ease
Whiles they behold a greater than *themselves,*
And therefore are they very dangerous.

Come on my *right* hand, for this ear is *deaf,*
And tell me *truly* what thou think'st of him.

Why, there was a *crown* offered him; and, being offered him, he put it by with the back of his *hand,* thus.

I can as well be *hanged* as tell the manner of it; it was mere *foolery,* I did not mark it.

You look *pale,* and *gaze,*
And put on *fear,* and case yourself in wonder,
To see the strange impatience of the heavens.

Stand *close* awhile, for here comes one in haste.

How that might change his *nature, there's* the question.

But when he once attains the upmost round
He then unto the ladder turns his *back,*
Looks in the *clouds,* scorning the base degrees
By which he did ascend.

... let us not break with *him,*
For he will never follow *anything*
That other men begin.

It is often a matter of judgment whether we shall interpret a phrase as momentarily complete or as pointing forward, incomplete. Sometimes either interpretation would be acceptable, but, as a rule, one conveys the author's intention better than the other. For instance, in the following extract from *The American Indian,* the author says:

> As a race they have withered from the land. Their arrows are broken, their springs have dried up, their cabins are in the dust. Their council-fire has long since gone out on the shore, and their war-cry is fast fading to the untrodden West.

It seems clear that in the second sentence the author is not enumerating minor details which form one larger whole, but that each statement is a sentence complete in itself, and so important that spontaneously we separate it from the others not merely by a pause but by a downward inflection.

If we were saying to another, "I bought my children firecrackers, torpedoes, skyrockets, and pinwheels," we should use rising inflections until we closed our sentence on "pinwheels." But it would be quite natural for the child, greatly excited by his presents, to use the downward inflection on those words, and these inflections would mark the importance, to him, of each separate gift. He would say, "I have firecrackers,—torpedoes,—skyrockets,—and pinwheels."

Circumflex inflections are the expression of complex mental states. Note this in the following examples:

> Not inferior to this was the wisdom of him who resolved to shear the wolf. What, shear a *wolf*! Have you considered the *danger* of the attempt? No, says the madman, I have considered nothing but the *right*.
>
> *Oh, no!* He wouldn't accept a *bribe*; of course not.
>
> You meant no *harm*; oh, no: your thoughts are innocent.
>
> It isn't the *secret* I care about; it's the slight, Mr. Caudle.

Difficult as is the subject of circumflex inflections, the difficulty is very much reduced when we bear in mind that the elements which compose them are the same as those with which we have been dealing. In Longfellow's *King Robert of Sicily*, the Angel asks the king, "Who art thou?" To which Robert answers, sneeringly, "I am the King." Now, on the word "I" we may expect to hear the rising circumflex (composed of a falling followed by a rising inflection) which the following paraphrase will justify: He dares ask me who I am! What audacity! Do you dare ask such a question of me? Would you know who I am? Perhaps a diagram will make this clearer:

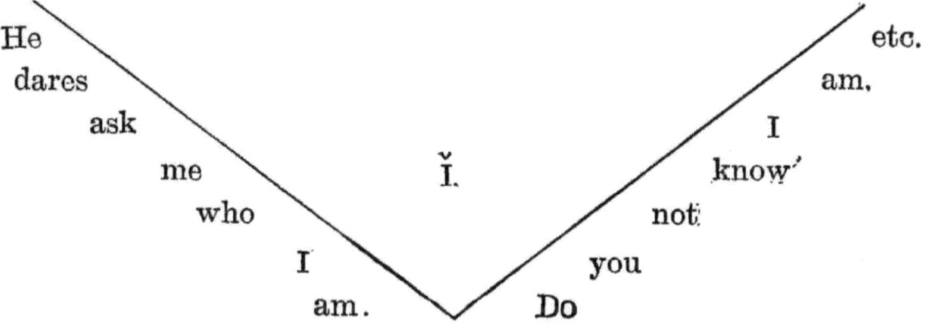

Professor Chamberlain has made this question so clear that we quote from him again:

"Paraphrase for Complex Relations: These, as already seen, are cases of combined ideas, expressed by composite motions of the voice, called circumflexes. In order to justify such double motion of the voice, the mind of the reader needs to recognize the combination implied in the words. He will make himself surer of this by analyzing, or separating into its component parts, each composite idea.

> Be not too tâme neither.

"Here is a plain implication of one member of the antithesis; and it might be expanded thus, As you are not to be too extrávagant in your expression, so you are not to be too quìet.

"This combination of separable elements might be illustrated by diagram, thus:

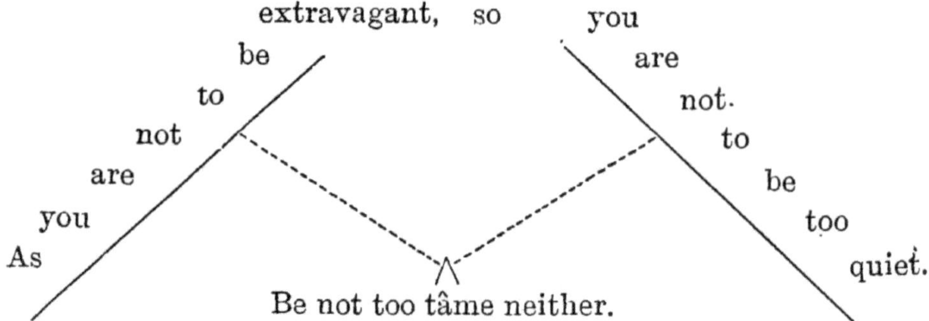

"Here the negative, or anticipatory, clause is, in the condensed form, suggested by the negative, or rising, part of the circumflex; the positive clause, by the falling part of the tone.

"In a similar way two separate elements, both of which are verbally expressed, may be combined in one elliptical or complex clause; e. g.:

I come to bûry Caesar, not to práise him.

"Inverting clauses:

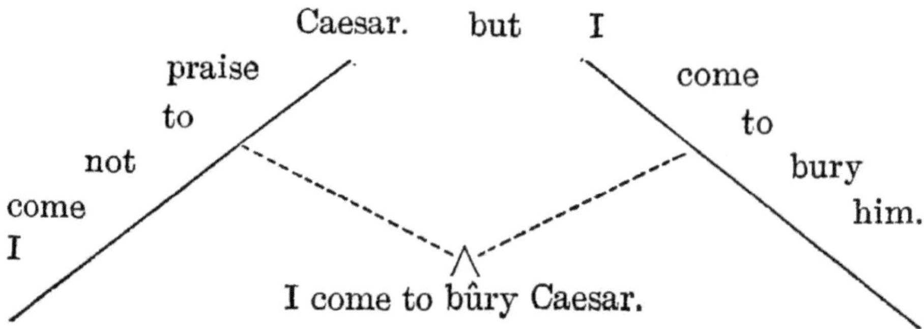

"The same method of illustration may be extended *ad libitum*."

There is one feature of circumflex inflection somewhat common but seldom treated, the understanding of which is very helpful to the teacher. This feature is observed when there are assertion and incompleteness in the same word. For instance, "John Brown," being the important idea in the following sentence, would be uttered with a falling inflection; but since the mind is glancing forward from "Brown" the rising inflection would mark that fact. Hence, the two states of mind would be manifested in a combined inflection the psychology of which should now be clear.

John Brown was one of the most striking figures of the anti-slavery agitation.

We have the same phenomenon on the word "Sicily" in the following extract, except that the falling inflection is on the first two syllables and the rising on the third:

Robert of Sicily, brother of Pope Urbane
And Valmond, Emperor of Allemaine
* * * * *
... heard the priests chant the Magnificat.

The extent, or width, of the inflection depends upon the amount of collateral thinking. Thus a simple question as, "Is your name Brown?" will take an inflection of about a third of the musical scale, while the inflection of Cassius on "Chastisement," in the example previously given, will be probably a full octave. The length of the inflection is explained by the philosophy of "Time": it is a matter of the importance or non-importance of the idea. The direction of the inflection is explained by the philosophy of "Pitch": it is determined by the purpose, or motive.

Varied melody is found in the speech of every-day life. Note how the voice continually runs up and down in a conversation on commonplace topics. The moment the subject grows serious and dignified, the discriminative elements largely disappear and with them the varied melody; until in solemn prayer, invocation, and certain forms of meditation in the absence of desire to insist on the importance of any one word, or the absence of the purpose to discriminate between one phase and another, we approach very close to the monotone. Let us remember, however, that it is not the emotion as such that affects the melody, but the mental content of the emotion.

In order that the reader may see the application of the foregoing principles, an analysis of a complete poem is appended. There may be a difference of opinion concerning details, but it must be remembered that the value of this analysis for the student lies in the fact that it should teach him that some interpretation is to be definitely decided on. The average reading is haphazard; so that one must gain a great deal through the mental drill necessary to decide the various questions that come up in the course of such an analysis as that here undertaken. It is a common experience to hear a pupil read a passage one way at one time and a different way at another. It would therefore seem to be better to read a passage incorrectly with some reason behind the error, than to read it correctly as a matter of accident, with the chance that the next time it is read the expression will be quite different. The greatest value of such analyses is found in the improvement in the student's power of discrimination. *The melody, which manifests the purpose, the motive, is the very life of good reading.*

Up from the meadows rich with corn,
Clear in the cool September morn,

The clustered spires of Frederick stand
Green-walled by the hills of Maryland.

Round about them orchards sweep,
Apple and peach tree fruited deep,

Fair as the garden of the Lord
To the eyes of the famished rebel horde,

On that pleasant morn of the early fall
When Lee marched over the mountain wall;

Over the mountains winding down,
Horse and foot, into Frederick town.

Forty flags with their silver stars,
Forty flags with their crimson bars,

Flapped in the morning wind: the sun
Of noon looked down, and saw not one.

Up rose old Barbara Frietchie then,
Bowed with her fourscore years and ten;

Bravest of all in Frederick town,
She took up the flag the men hauled down;

In her attic window the staff she set,
To show that one heart was loyal yet.

Up the street came the rebel tread,
Stonewall Jackson riding ahead.

Under his slouched hat left and right
He glanced; the old flag met his sight.

"Halt!"—the dust-brown ranks stood fast.
"Fire!"—out blazed the rifle-blast.

It shivered the window, pane and sash;
It rent the banner with seam and gash.

Quick, as it fell, from the broken staff
Dame Barbara snatched the silken scarf;

She leaned far out on the window-sill,
And shook it forth with a royal will.

"Shoot, if you must, this old gray head,
But spare your country's flag," she said.

A shade of sadness, a blush of shame,
Over the face of the leader came;

The nobler nature within him stirred
To life at that woman's deed and word;

"Who touches a hair of yon gray head
Dies like a dog! March on!" he said.

All day long through Frederick street

Sounded the tread of marching feet:

All day long that free flag tost
Over the heads of the rebel host.

Ever its torn folds rose and fell
On the loyal winds that loved it well;

And through the hill-gaps sunset light
Shone over it with a warm good-night.

Barbara Frietchie's work is o'er,
And the Rebel rides on his raids no more.

Honor to her! and let a tear
Fall, for her sake, on Stonewall's bier.

Over Barbara Frietchie's grave,
Flag of Freedom and Union, wave!

Peace and order and beauty draw
Round thy symbol of light and law;

And ever the stars above look down
On thy stars below in Frederick town!

—*Barbara Frietchie.* WHITTIER.

l. 3.—Note momentary completeness on "Frederick."

l. 1-3.—These lines are anticipative.

l. 5, 6.—Each line a complete affirmative statement, although separated from the rest of the poem only by commas.

l. 7.—"Lord," momentary completeness.

l. 8.—Rising inflection on "horde," since the sense is incomplete until we come to "wall." A good example, since lines 9 and 10 would make very good sense without the succeeding two.

l. 12.—Momentary completeness on "foot."

l. 13-14.—The motive being the same in both lines, note that the melody is the same.

l. 16.—"Noon" is contrasted with "morning"; hence the rising circumflex on the former word.

l. 17.—Transition here. Observe the higher key commencing on "up."

l. 19.—This line is anticipative. Supply "being" before "bravest," and note how the temptation to use the falling inflection on "town" disappears.

l. 21.—Optional rising or falling inflection on "set."

l. 23.—Transition in key. Why?

l. 24.—What difference in motive would be conveyed by rising and falling inflections on "Jackson"?

l. 25-28.—Transitions on "under," "halt," "the," "fire," "out." Explain.

l. 29.—Note the comma after "window." What is its function?

l. 31.—Observe that "as it fell" is subordinate. Many read this couplet incorrectly. The idea is not "as it fell from the broken staff," but that she snatched it "from the broken staff."

l. 33.—Anticipative.

l. 35.—Transition.

l. 37.—(1) Observe how the key lowers. Why? (2) What shades of meaning are conveyed by the following readings: *a,* momentary completeness on "sadness," and "shame"; *b,* anticipation on "sadness," momentary completeness on "shame." Which do you prefer? Why?

l. 41.—Transition. Is the key higher or lower?

l. 43-44, 45-46, 47-48.—Why is the melody about the same in these couplets?

l. 49-50.—Many opportunities for choice of inflection on "hill-gaps," "light," "over."

l. 51.—Rising or falling inflection on "o'er"? Why?

l. 56.—No momentary completeness on "Union." Why?

l. 59, 60.—Contrast between "above" and "below."

No attempt has been made in this analysis to do more than direct attention to the portions of the poem in which inflection and melody are affected by the interpretation.

PEDAGOGICAL ASPECTS.

Much of what has been said concerning the pedagogical aspects of the discussion of "Time" may be repeated here. Drills in inflections as such are of very little value and potentially very harmful. Occasionally we hear the argument that a pupil has no ear for inflections, and that the drill is to train his ear. Most pupils have no difficulty in making proper inflections, so that for them class drills are time wasted; for those whose reading is monotonous, because of lack of melodic variety, the best drills are those which teach them to make a careful analysis of the sentences, and those which awaken them to the necessity of impressing the thought upon others. We deceive ourselves when we proceed to correct the error of monotony in any mechanical, artificial way.

We have learned that, when a pupil has the proper motive in mind and is desirous of conveying his intention to another, a certain melody will always manifest that intention. The melody, then, is the criterion of the pupil's purpose. We expect a certain melody with certain phrases. When that melody is heard, we are scarcely conscious of its presence; when another is heard, we are struck as by a discord of music when we expect concord. The moment a pupil loses sight of the exact meaning of a phrase and its relation to the other phrases, that moment his melody betrays him. Now the teacher must be able to translate the false melody. He must determine the pupil's purpose (or absence of any purpose) behind the incorrect melody, remove the wrong purpose, put in its stead the true purpose, and rely upon natural instincts to do the rest. Herein lies the great value to the teacher of a knowledge of the psychology of the criterion of pitch.

Suppose a pupil reads, "Up from the meadows green with corn," using a rising circumflex on "meadows." This would show at once that "meadows" was contrasted in his mind with something else. Remove the contrast, direct his mind forward from that word to the next phrase, and the proper melody will come. Some teachers, especially those engaged in the teaching of young children, have a somewhat patronizing melody in all they say and read. This melody is overflowing with circumflexes, which are soon copied by the class. Let the teacher free himself from this patronizing mental condition and talk to the children as if they were men and women, and the peculiar melody will disappear from the voices of both teacher and pupil. It is rather difficult to present this melody in graphic form, but the following diagram may prove suggestive:

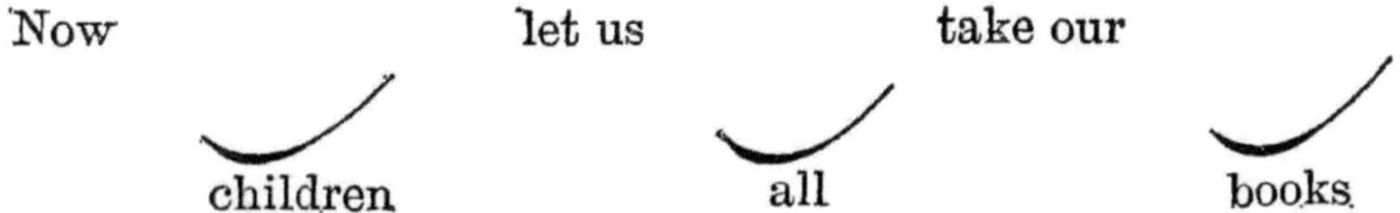

It is hardly to be believed that there is so much ignorance as to the meaning of inflection. During the past two years, in schools of our largest cities, the author has heard teachers reprimand their pupils for allowing their voices "to fall at a comma." As if commas were intended to indicate vocal expression! Once when a bright lad used a falling inflection on "want," in such a sentence as "What do you want?" a class nearly shook their hands off in their endeavors to attract the teacher's attention, in order that, when he said, "What's wrong?" they might shout at the top of their voices, "He let his voice down at a question mark."

One of the commonest of misunderstandings that prevail among us, is that the rising inflection is always to be given upon words preceding commas, and also that it must never be given at the end of a sentence. It is hoped that these fallacies have been entirely exploded, and that the teacher has learned that motive, and motive only, governs the inflection. We used to be told to count one at a comma, two at a semi-colon, and four at a period. Such admonitions are exactly on a par with those just referred to.

Teachers should bear in mind that pupils do not need to have a musical ear in order to read with correct melody. As we have stated again and again, melody is the result of varying tension, and that has nothing to do with the ability to recognize tones. With singing this is different. There we must strike certain notes, and ear training is necessary; but speech melody is instinctive, and all that is necessary for its development is mental training and practice in reading—not voice drills as such.

The melody of long sentences presents a case of peculiar difficulty. Where the sentence is long, especially where it is long and involved, the pupil's melody is often faulty because he cannot hold the thought in mind from beginning to end. Pupils should be trained on sentences specially chosen to develop their powers of continuous thinking. These sentences should be carefully analyzed and thoroughly discussed before reading. The following examples, while too difficult for younger pupils, will afford good practice for the teacher:

> While the Union lasts, we have high, exciting, gratifying prospects spread out before us, for us and our children. Beyond that I seek not to penetrate the veil. God grant that in my day, at least, that curtain may not rise. God grant that on my vision never may be opened what lies behind. When my eyes shall be turned to behold for the last time the sun in heaven, may I not see him shining on the broken and dishonored fragments of a once glorious Union; on States dissevered, discordant, belligerent; on a land rent with civil feuds, or drenched, it may be, in fraternal blood! Let their last feeble and lingering glance, rather, behold the gorgeous ensign of the republic, now known and honored throughout the earth, still full high advanced, its arms and trophies streaming in their original luster, not a stripe erased or polluted, not a single star obscured—bearing for its motto no such miserable interrogatory as, "What is all this worth?" nor those other words of delusion and folly, "Liberty first, and Union afterward;" but everywhere, spread all over in characters of living light, blazing on all its ample folds as they float over the sea and over the land, and in every wind under the whole heavens, that other sentiment, dear to every true American heart—"Liberty *and* Union, now and forever, one and inseparable."—*Reply to Hayne*. WEBSTER.

Note that the force of "may I not see him" continues to "fraternal blood," and consequently that there should be rising inflections on "Union," "dissevered," "discordant," "belligerent," "feuds," and "blood." And note further that "What is all this worth?" and "Liberty first, and Union afterward," are anticipative and hence will take a rising inflection on "worth" and "afterward."

> At Atri in Abruzzo, a small town
> Of ancient Roman date but scant renown,
> One of those little places that have run
> Half up the hill, beneath a blazing sun,
> And then sat down to rest, as if to say,
> "I climb no further upward, come what may,"
> The Re Giovanni, now unknown to fame,
> So many monarchs since have borne the name,
> Had a great bell hung in the market place.
>
> —*The Bell of Atri.* LONGFELLOW.

The town would have used a falling inflection on "may" because for it the sense would have been completed with that word; but with us this phrase is subordinate, and hence the inflection on "may" will be rising.

And as a hungry lion who has made
A prey of some large beast—a hornèd stag
Or mountain goat—rejoices, and with speed
Devours it, though swift hounds and sturdy youths
Press on his flank, so Menelaus felt
Great joy when Paris, of the godlike form,
Appeared in sight, for now he thought to wreak
His vengeance on the guilty one, and straight
Sprang from his car to earth with all his arms.

—*The Iliad,* Book II. HOMER (BRYANT).

But when public taste seems plunging deeper and deeper into degradation day by day, and when the press universally exerts such power as it possesses to direct the feeling of the nation more completely to all that is theatrical, affected, and false in art; while it vents its ribald buffooneries on the most exalted truth, and the highest ideal of landscape, that this or any other age has ever witnessed, it becomes the imperative duty of all who have any perception or knowledge of what is really great in art, and any desire for its advancement in England, to come fearlessly forward, regardless of such individual interests as are likely to be injured by the knowledge of what is good and right, to declare and demonstrate, wherever they exist, the essence and the authority of the beautiful and the true.—*Modern Painters.* RUSKIN.

CHAPTER III

THE CRITERION OF QUALITY

Thus far we have been considering the criteria of states essentially intellectual. "Time" has to do with the extent of the thought; "Pitch" with the purpose. Quality manifests emotional states. By Quality we mean that subtle element in the voice by which is expressed at one time tenderness, at another harshness, at another awe, and so on through the whole gamut of feeling.

In order to prove that the quality (*timbre,* the French call it) of the voice is the result of emotional conditions, we must first understand what we may term the physics of quality. The number of air waves striking the ear in a given time determines the pitch; the width of the waves determines the volume of sound; the shape of the waves determines the quality. But how is the shape of air waves affected? It would take us too far from our subject to discuss this question in detail.[5] Let it suffice that the shape of the air wave, and hence the quality, is dependent upon the texture of the vibrating body. We recognize at once the different qualities respectively of the flute, piano, violin, harp or cornet; it is the difference in the texture of the vibrating substances that enables us to do this. Why will the artist pay thousands of dollars for a Stradivarius or Cremona violin? Not because of its age, but because of the quality of the tone he can bring out on that instrument, which is impossible on other makes of violins. The fashioners of these old instruments possessed a secret of treating or seasoning the wood that gave to their products a tone quality the violin-makers of to-day endeavor in vain to reproduce. This treatment affected the texture of the wood, and hence the quality.

To him who plays upon the human instrument of the voice, is given a great advantage over other artists. He can change the quality of his tone almost at will, while they can only approximate these changes. The tone as it comes from the vocal bands is comparatively colorless, but the size and shape of the reinforcing cavities (the larynx, pharynx, mouth, and nares), and the texture of their membranes, determine the quality of the tone that reaches the ear. Now, the size and shape of some of these can be changed at will, and are often modified unconsciously by emotion. The same may be said of the texture of the surface against which the tone impinges as it comes from the larynx. The shape of the nares and the texture of its membrane are virtually fixed, as is the texture of the roof of the mouth and the pharynx. Herein is the explanation of the individuality of voices. But the shape of the mouth and of the pharynx may be considerably modified by the action of the tongue, the raising, lowering, or contracting of the larynx, and the movements of

[5] See Tyndall on "Sound;" or Prof. Halm on the same subject.

the soft palate. It is, therefore, clear that the quality of the voice is partly fixed and partly changeable.

Before we proceed to discuss the effect of emotion upon the quality, we must first recognize that voice defects are of three kinds: (1) Those arising from disease or accident, such as catarrh, obstructions in the nose, enlarged tonsils, broken nose, and many others. These require medical or surgical treatment. (2) Those arising from congenital defects, which can be only partially removed, such as cleft palate, abnormally narrow nares, and the like. (3) Those arising out of the temperament of the man and the improper use of his voice.

It should now be plain that when we say that emotion affects the quality of the tone, we mean the peculiar quality of a particular man. If a speaker's voice is nasal, we do not claim that that quality is expressive of any emotion. On the contrary, nasal quality is the distinguishing characteristic of his voice, but that quality can be modified by emotion. In other words, there can be a nasal-tender quality, or a nasal-harsh quality, the tender or harsh feeling accounting for the difference.

Paul Heyse has said, "The voice is the man." What did he mean by that? He did not mean that a throaty voice indicated one temperament, and a nasal voice another, but that the emotional man, the spiritual man, has a certain texture of muscle. This texture affects the quality of his natural voice, whatever that voice may be, and consequently the quality of the voice manifests the man. If we will interpret this dictum broadly, no fault will be found with it. Who does not recognize the blustering man by his bellowing tone? the fawning hypocrite by his oily quality? the aggressive, assertive individual by his harsh guttural? In all probability, Heyse meant more than quality, in the sense in which we use it here; but granting this, his saying is of very wide application even in this restricted realm.

How does emotion affect the quality of the voice? Emotion is essentially a muscular condition. This condition is determined by the amount of nervous energy sent to the muscles, and this energy determines the muscular texture. Tender emotions mean tender texture, a relaxed condition of the muscles; while harsh quality is the result not only of throat contraction (change in the shape of the reinforcing cavity) but of constricted muscle, harsh texture. This is all there is to the philosophy of "Quality."

Dr. Rush, in his *Philosophy of the Human Voice,* has named many of these qualities. He calls them Normal, Orotund, Guttural, Pectoral, Falsetto, and so on; and mentions the emotional conditions that manifest themselves through these various forms. On the whole, his classification is sound; but there is one gross error, due either to himself or his followers, that must be considered here. The Orotund (the enlarged natural) quality is more than a loud voice. It is a full voice with a quality that cannot better be described than by the term richness. Many students have endeavored to obtain this quality by shouting, or by holding the mouth as if gaping, and have developed only loudness without a trace of soulfulness, or merely a round, hollow hot-potato-in-the-throat kind of voice. There is no objection to the use of the term Orotund to characterize that rich, full tone suggestive of deep, full, enlarged feeling; but we must bear in mind that loudness is not only not necessary for the Orotund, but is often no part of it at all. The Orotund, as we have said, is that quality of which the main characteristics are roundness and richness. One who is restricted is not likely to use this quality. It can come only when there is the utmost freedom of the entire vocal region. When we have removed the tension which may be "the man," or the result of bad vocal training, we shall get that enlarged quality, which should not, as is so often the case, manifest merely the larger emotional states, but should be the natural voice of the speaker. The Orotund manifests dignity above all else; it manifests the large, grand spirit. Of course, we do not mean an affected Orotund, but an easy, large, unrestricted quality showing the largeness of the soul behind it. To develop this quality, let the student use his imagination. Let him dwell for a long time upon the sublimity and grandeur of such passages as follow. Then let him abandon himself to the emotion aroused through his contemplation, and in time the genuine Orotund will come. And so only can it come. So important is this phase of the subject that we repeat: The tone expressive of elevated feeling "cannot be mechanically produced, or manufactured independently of the general mental and physical conditions." The imagination must lead, otherwise we shall have big voices without big quality. That peculiar quality expressive of enlarged feeling is not necessarily loud. In fact, the voice may not be strong, but, at the same time, it may *suggest* grandeur and sublimity far better than a voice that has sheer loudness. But, if the student will practice faithfully, he may be assured that his voice will receive more genuine training through these exercises than through a whole volume of *merely* technical drills. Develop the imagination, the soul, and the voice will grow through the effort of the soul to go out in expression. But let him avoid mere shouting and vociferating, even if he never gets a voice.

If the student has not the imagination, he must develop it. There are many loud voices, but few with soulful quality. But what avails this loudness? Certainly it enables one to be heard above the din of voices and the roar of the waves, but it never stirs the nobler emotions of an audience; and unless one can do that he is anything but an orator. Mere loudness is rant—nothing less.

Many students, for one reason or another, either have no ability to express elevated feeling in public, or repress it through diffidence or shyness. Let such remember that we are constantly experiencing and expressing this feeling in our everyday life; that it is simply an enlargement of a more or less commonplace feeling; and let him begin with the simple examples that are set down first. Any one can say, What a lovely day this is! Well, that is a mild form of elevated feeling. Let him imagine it is graduation day, and that rain had been threatening to fall all the previous night. It is daylight now; and as he opens his eyes and looks up at the cloudless sky, will he not exclaim with elevated feeling, What a glorious day we're going to have!

By "elevated feelings" one must not understand those only that are serious and solemn. Whenever the imagination is enkindled by the contemplation of what is large, dignified, grand, sublime, the emotions are stirred, and find expression in enlarged, soulful quality.

Ay, every inch a king.

Think of it! a building that could hold a hundred thousand people!

Here will be their greatest triumph.

Who shall put asunder the best affections of the heart?

We loved the land of our adoption!

A good name is better than precious ointment.

Gird up thy loins now, like a man.

Comfort ye my people.

O Zion, that bringest good tidings, get thee up into the high mountain!

He is as honest a man as ever breathed.

Search creation round, where will you find a country that presents so sublime a spectacle, so interesting an anticipation?

Most of all, fellow-citizens, if your sons ask whose example they shall imitate, what will you say? For you know well it is not music, nor the gymnasiums, nor the schools, that mold young men; it is much more the public proclamations, the public example. If you take one whose life has no high purpose, one who mocks at morals, and crown him in the theater, every boy who sees it is corrupted. When a bad man suffers his deserts, the people learn; on the contrary, when a man VOTES AGAINST WHAT IS NOBLE AND JUST, and then comes home to teach his son, the boy will very promptly say, "Your lesson is impertinent and a bore." Beware, therefore, Athenians, remembering posterity will rejudge your judgment, and that the character of a city is determined by the character of the men it crowns.

Right forever on the scaffold, Wrong forever on the throne;
But that scaffold sways the future, and behind the dim unknown
Standeth God within the shadow, keeping watch above his own.

Thou, too, sail on, O Ship of State!
Sail on, O UNION, strong and great!
Humanity, with all its fears,
With all the hopes of future years
Is hanging breathless on thy fate!
We know what Master laid thy keel,

What workmen wrought thy ribs of steel,
Who made each mast, and sail, and rope,
What anvils rang, what hammers beat,
In what a forge, and what a heat,
Were shaped the anchors of thy hope!

Fear not each sudden sound and shock;
'Tis of the wave, and not the rock;
'Tis but the flapping of the sail,
And not a rent made by the gale!
In spite of rock and tempest's roar,
In spite of false lights on the shore,
Sail on, nor fear to breast the sea!
Our hearts, our hopes, are all with thee:
Our hearts, our hopes, our prayers, our tears,
Our faith triumphant o'er our fears,
Are all with thee,—are all with thee! —*The Ship of State.* LONGFELLOW.

See what a grace was seated on this brow;
Hyperion's curls; the front of Jove himself;
An eye like Mars, to threaten and command;
A station like the herald Mercury
New-lighted on a heaven-kissing hill;
A combination and a form indeed,
Where every god did seem to set his seal,
To give the world assurance of a man. —*Hamlet*, Act iii., Sc. 4.

Awake, my soul! Not only passive praise
Thou owest; not alone these swelling tears,
Mute thanks, and secret ecstasy. Awake,
Voice of sweet song! Awake my heart, Awake!
Green vales and icy cliffs, all join my hymn! —COLERIDGE.

And the evening star was shining
On Schehallion's distant head,
When we wiped our bloody broadswords,
And returned to count the dead.
There we found him, gashed and gory,
Stretched upon the cumbered plain,
As he told us where to seek him,
In the thickest of the slain.
And a smile was on his visage,
For within his dying ear
Pealed the joyful note of triumph,
And the clansman's clamorous cheer:
So, amidst the battle's thunder,
Shot, and steel, and scorching flame,

In the glory of his manhood
Passed the spirit of the Græme!

Open wide the vaults of Atholl,
Where the bones of heroes rest,—
Open wide the hallowed portals
To receive another guest!
Last of Scots and last of freemen,—
Last of all that dauntless race,
Who would rather die unsullied
Than outlive the land's disgrace!

—Aytoun.

Bury the great Duke
With an empire's lamentation,
Let us bury the Great Duke
To the noise of the mourning of a mighty nation,
Mourning when their leaders fall,
Warriors carry the warrior's pall,
And sorrow darkens hamlet and hall.

Where shall we lay the man whom we deplore?
Here, in streaming London's central roar,
Let the sound of those he wrought for,
And the feet of those he fought for,
Echo round his bones forevermore.

Lead out the pageant: sad and slow,
As fits a universal woe,
Let the long, long procession go,
And let the sorrowing crowd about it grow,
And let the mournful martial music blow;
The last great Englishman is low.

All is over and done:
Render thanks to the Giver,
England, for thy son.
Let the bell be toll'd.
Render thanks to the Giver,
And render him to the mold.
Under the cross of gold
That shines over city and river,
There he shall rest forever
Among the wise and the bold.
Let the bell be toll'd:
And a reverent people behold
The towering car, the sable steeds:
Bright let it be with his blazon'd deeds
Dark in its funeral fold,
Let the bell be toll'd:

And a deeper knell in the heart be knoll'd;
And the sound of the sorrowing anthem roll'd
Thro' the dome of the golden cross;
And the volleying cannon thunder his loss;
He knew their voices of old.
For many a time in many a clime
His captain's ear has heard them boom,
Bellowing victory, bellowing doom:
When he with those deep voices wrought,
Guarding realms and kings from shame;
With those deep voices our dead captain taught
The tyrant, and asserts his claim
In that dread sound to the great name
Which he has worn so pure of blame,
In praise and in dispraise the same,
A man of well-attemper'd frame.
O civic Muse, to such a name,
To such a name for ages long,
To such a name,
Preserve a broad approach of fame,
And ever-echoing avenues of song.

—*Ode on the Death of the Duke of Wellington.* TENNYSON.

Venerable men! you have come down to us from a former generation. Heaven has bounteously lengthened out your lives, that you might behold this joyous day. You are now where you stood fifty years ago, this very hour, with your brothers and your neighbors, shoulder to shoulder, in the strife for your country. Behold, how altered! The same heavens are indeed above your heads; the same ocean rolls at your feet; but all else how changed!

You hear now no roar of hostile cannon, you see no mixed volume of smoke and flame rising from burning Charlestown. The ground strewed with the dead and dying; the impetuous charge; the steady and successful repulse; the loud call to repeated assault; the summoning of all that is manly to repeated resistance; a thousand bosoms freely and fearlessly bared in an instant to whatever of terror there may be in war and death; all these you have witnessed, but you witness them no more.

All is peace. The heights of yonder metropolis, its towers and roofs, which you then saw filled with wives and children and countrymen in distress and terror, and looking with unutterable emotions for the issue of the combat, have presented you to-day with the sight of its whole happy population come out to welcome and greet you with a universal jubilee. Yonder proud ships, by a felicity of position appropriately lying at the foot of this mount,

> and seeming fondly to cling around it, are not means of annoyance to you, but your country's own means of destruction and defense.—WEBSTER.

> What lesson shall those lips teach us? Before that still, calm brow let us take a new baptism. How can we stand here without a fresh and utter consecration? These tears! how shall we dare even to offer consolation? Only lips fresh from such a vow have the right to mingle their words with your tears. We envy you your nearer place to these martyred children of God. I do not believe slavery will go down in blood. Ours is an age of thought. Hearts are stronger than swords. That last fortnight! How sublime its lesson! the Christian one of conscience,—of truth. Virginia is weak, because each man's heart said amen to John Brown. His words,—they are stronger even than his rifles. These crushed a State. Those have changed the thoughts of millions, and will yet crush slavery. Men said, "Would he had died in arms!" God ordered better, and granted to him and the slave those noble prison hours,—that single hour of death; granted him a higher than the soldier's place,—that of teacher; the echoes of his rifles have died away in the hills,—a million hearts guard his words. God bless this roof,—make it bless us. We dare not say bless you, children of this home! you stand nearer to one whose lips God touched, and we rather bend for your blessings. God make us all worthier of him whose dust we lay among these hills he loved. Here he girded himself and went forth to battle. Fuller success than his heart ever dreamed God granted him. He sleeps in the blessings of the crushed and the poor, and men believe more firmly in virtue, now that such a man has lived. Standing here, let us thank God for a firmer faith and fuller hope.—WENDELL PHILLIPS.

A great deal of space has been given to the preceding illustrations because the quality necessary to express the emotions in those selections is very rare. Rare for two reasons: first, because we dwell so much of the time in the realm of the so-called practical that we lose interest in the sublimer aspects presented in poetry; and, secondly, we do not express these larger emotions freely and often. Expression, like all other powers, comes through practice.

The second distinct quality is what has been called the Normal. This is the voice of everyday life, the voice in which we carry on the conversation of the home, the schoolroom, and the business of life generally. We need no special practice in this quality, but it is well to recognize it in order that we may compare with it the other qualities. The following extract would be expressed in Normal quality.

> Speak the speech, I pray you, as I pronounced it to you, trippingly on the tongue; but if you mouth it, as many of your players do, I had as lief the town crier spoke my lines. And do not saw the air too much with your hand, thus; but use all gently: for in

the very torrent, tempest, and (as I may say) whirlwind of your passion, you must acquire and beget a temperance that may give it smoothness. Oh, it offends me to the soul to hear a robustious, periwig-pated fellow tear a passion to tatters, to very rags, to split the ears of the groundlings, who, for the most part, are capable of nothing but inexplicable dumb-shows and noise. I would have such a fellow whipped for o'erdoing Termagant; it out-herods Herod: pray you avoid it.

Be not too tame either, but let your own discretion be your tutor: suit the action to the word, the word to the action, with this special observance, that you o'erstep not the modesty of Nature; for anything so overdone is from the purpose of playing, whose end, both at the first, and now, was, and is, to hold, as 'twere, the mirror up to Nature, to show Virtue her own feature, Scorn her own image, and the very age and body of the time his form and pressure. Now, this overdone, or come tardy off, though it make the unskillful laugh, cannot but make the judicious grieve; the censure of the which one must, in your allowance, o'erweigh a whole theater of others. Oh, there be players that I have seen play—and heard others praise, and that highly—not to speak it profanely, that, neither having the accent of Christians, nor the gait of Christian, pagan, or man, have so strutted and bellowed that I have thought some of Nature's journeymen had made men, and not made them well, they imitated humanity so abominably.—*Hamlet*, Act iii., Sc. 2.

In a work which makes no pretension to cover the whole realm of elocution, it would be out of place to discuss the more extravagant forms of emotion, such as terror, rage, hate, and the like. In order, however, to give this phase of the subject a certain approximation to complete treatment, it may be well to touch upon these abnormal emotional states and the respective qualities in which they find expression.

There is a wide range of feeling that so affects the action of the vocal apparatus as to produce a breathy tone. It would be idle and misleading to enumerate all the occasions upon which we might expect to hear this aspirated voice. Suffice it that a sense of oppression resulting from any one of many causes: the desire not to be overheard; the weakness of old age and disease—any of these conditions may produce the aspirated tone. Aspiration does not manifest any one emotion, but may accompany many. There may be considerable aspiration mixed with the expression of joy, as well as with the expression of hate or despair. It is well to bear this in mind, for many text books give the "Aspirated Quality" as a specific kind of voice manifesting specific emotions and those only. When we observe that this quality is found in awe, terror, hate, and like emotions; in debility; and when we wish to whisper; the unscientific nature of such a classification becomes sufficiently clear. A few examples are appended:

St! Don't make any noise: he's asleep.

Walk softly: I think they're listening.

Go away! I hate you.

Oh! I'm so tired; help me along.

How can I tell him the truth!
There is no hope.

"Charge, Chester, charge! On, Stanley, on!"
Were the last words of Marmion.

O horror! horror! horror!
Tongue, nor heart, cannot conceive, nor name thee!

Measureless liar!

Spare me, great God! Lift up my drooping brow;
I am content to die; but, oh, not now.

I pray you, give me leave to go hence;
I am not well.

Dear master, I can go no further: O, I die for food! Here lie I down, and measure out my grave. Farewell, kind master.

How ill this taper burns! Ha! who comes here?
I think it is the weakness of my eyes
That shapes this monstrous apparition.
It comes upon me. Art thou any thing?
Art thou some god, some angel, or some devil,
That mak'st my blood cold, and my hair to stare?—
Speak to me what thou art.—*Julius Caesar*, Act iv., Sc. 3.

LADY MACBETH. Alack! I am afraid they have awak'd,
And 'tis not done. The attempt, and not the deed,
Confounds us. Hark!—I laid their daggers ready,
He could not miss them.—Had he not resembled
My father as he slept, I had done 't. My husband!

MACBETH. I have done the deed. Didst thou not hear a noise?

LADY MACBETH. I heard the owl scream, and the crickets cry.
Did you not speak?

MACBETH. When?

LADY MACBETH. Now.

MACBETH. As I descended?

LADY MACBETH. Ay.

MACBETH. Hark!
Who lies i' th' second chamber?

LADY MACBETH. Donalbain.

MACBETH. This is a sorry sight. [*Looking at his hands.*

LADY MACBETH. A foolish thought, to say a sorry sight.

MACBETH. There's one did laugh in 's sleep,
And one cried, "Murder!" that they did wake each other;
I stood and heard them: but they did say their prayers,
And address'd them again to sleep. —*Macbeth,* Act ii., Sc. 2.

Stern, severe, harsh feelings have a tendency to contract the throat; hence, we get a quality that is called the Guttural. It is heard only where the passion grips the throat.

Mend, and change home,
Or by the fires of heaven, I'll leave the foe,
And make me wars on you: look to 't: Come on!

"Curse on him!" quoth false Sextus:
"Will not the villain drown?
But for this stay, ere close of day
We should have sacked the town!"

Never, Iago. Like to the Pontic Sea,
Whose icy current and compulsive course
Ne'er feels retiring ebb, but keeps due on
To the Propontic and the Hellespont,
Even so my bloody thoughts, with violent pace,
Shall ne'er look back, ne'er ebb to humble love,
Till that a capable and wide revenge
Swallow them up. Now, by yond' marble heaven,
In the due reverence of a sacred vow
I here engage my words. —*Othello,* Act iii., Sc. 3.

Blow winds, and crack your cheeks! rage! blow!
You cataracts and hurricanes, spout
Till you have drench'd our steeples, drown'd the cocks!
You sulphurous and thought-executing fires,
Vaunt couriers to oak-cleaving thunderbolts,
Singe my white head! And thou, all-shaking thunder,
Strike flat the thick rotundity o' the world!
Crack Nature's molds, all germens spill at once,
That make ungrateful man! —*King Lear,* Act iii., Sc. 2.

There are two opposite qualities of voice well known to singers: the bright, ringing tone, and the dark, sombre, covered tone. This distinction is, for the purposes of the public-school teacher, far more valuable than most others. Joy, happiness, buoyancy, exuberance, are likely, when there are no marked physical defects, to find expression in the bright tone; while sorrow and the moods of introspection may often modify the texture of the vibrating substances so as to produce the darker quality.

EXTRACTS TO ILLUSTRATE "DARK" QUALITY.

King. O, my offense is rank, it smells to Heaven;
It hath the primal eldest curse upon't,
A brother's murder! Pray can I not:
Though inclination be as sharp as will,
My stronger guilt defeats my strong intent;
And, like a man to double business bound,
I stand in pause where I shall first begin,
And both neglect. What if this cursèd hand
Were thicker than itself with brother's blood,
Is there not rain enough in the sweet Heavens
To wash it white as snow? Whereto serves mercy
But to confront the visage of offense?
And what's in prayer but this twofold force,—
To be forestallèd ere we come to fall,
Or pardon'd being down? Then I'll look up;
My fault is past. But, O, what form of prayer
Can serve my turn? *Forgive me my foul murder?*
That cannot be; since I am still possess'd
Of these effects for which I did the murder,
My crown, mine own ambition, and my Queen.
May one be pardoned and retain th' offense?... —*Hamlet,* Act iii., Sc. 3.

Alas! my noble boy! that thou shouldst die!
Thou who wert made so beautifully fair!
That death should settle in thy glorious eye,
And leave his stillness in this clustering hair!
How could he mark thee for the silent tomb,
My proud boy, Absalom!

Cold is thy brow, my son! and I am chill
As to my bosom I have tried to press thee!
How was I wont to feel my pulses thrill
Like a rich harp-string yearning to caress thee,
And hear thy sweet "*my father!*" from those dumb
And cold lips, Absalom!

But death is on thee! I shall hear the gush
Of music, and the voices of the young;
And life will pass me in the mantling blush,

And the dark tresses to the soft winds flung;—
But thou no more, with thy sweet voice, shalt come
To meet me, Absalom!

And oh! when I am stricken, and my heart,
Like a bruised reed, is waiting to be broken,
How will its love for thee, as I depart,
Yearn for thine ear to drink its last deep token!
It were so sweet, amid death's gathering gloom,
To see thee, Absalom! —*David's Lament over Absalom.* N. P. Willis.

Lear. You Heavens, give me patience,—patience I need!
You see me here, you gods, a poor old man,
As full of grief as age; wretched in both!
If it be you that stir these daughters' hearts
Against their father, fool me not so much
To bear it tamely; touch me with noble anger;
And let not women's weapons, water-drops,
Stain my man's cheeks!—No, you unnatural hags,
I will have such revenges on you both,
That all the world shall—I will do such things,—
What they are, yet I know not; but they shall be
The terrors of the earth. You think I'll weep;
No, I'll not weep:
I have full cause of weeping; but this heart
Shall break into a hundred thousand flaws,
Or e'er I'll weep.—O Fool, I shall go mad! —*King Lear*, Act ii., Sc. 4.

EXAMPLES TO ILLUSTRATE "BRIGHT" QUALITY.

Gratiano. Let me play the fool:
With mirth and laughter let old wrinkles come,
And let my liver rather heat with wine
Than my heart cool with mortifying groans.
Why should a man, whose blood is warm within,
Sit like his grandsire cut in alabaster?
Sleep when he wakes and creep into the jaundice
By being peevish? I tell thee what, Antonio—
I love thee, and it is my love that speaks—
There are a sort of men whose visages
Do cream and mantle like a standing pond,
And do a willful stillness entertain,
With purpose to be dress'd in an opinion
Of wisdom, gravity, profound conceit,
As who should say, "I am Sir Oracle,
And when I ope my lips let no dog bark!"

O my Antonio, I do know of these
That therefore only are reputed wise
For saying nothing, who, I am very sure,
If they should speak, would almost damn those ears
Which, hearing them, would call their brothers, fools.
I'll tell thee more of this another time:
But fish not, with this melancholy bait,
For this fool gudgeon, this opinion.
Come, good Lorenzo. Fare ye well awhile:
I'll end my exhortation after dinner. —*The Merchant of Venice,* Act i., Sc. 1.

She mounts her chariot with a trice,
Nor would she stay for no advice,
Until her maids, that were so nice,
To wait on her were fitted.
But ran herself away alone;
Which when they heard, there was not one
But hasted after to be gone,
As she had been diswitted.

Hop, and Mop, and Drap so clear,
Pip, and Trip, and Ship, that were
To Mab their sovereign dear,
Her special maids of honor;
Fib, and Tib, and Pinck, and Pin,
Tick, and Quick, and Jill, and Jin,
Tit, and Nit, and Wap, and Win,
The train that wait upon her.

Upon a grasshopper they got,
And what with amble and with trot,
For hedge nor ditch they spared not,
But after her they hie them.
A cobweb over them they throw,
To shield the wind if it should blow,
Themselves they wisely could bestow,
Lest any should espy them. —*Queen Mab.* DRAYTON.

Cheer answer cheer, and bear the cheer about.
Hurrah, hurrah, for the fiery fort is ours!
"Victory, victory, victory!"

Hear the sledges with the bells,—silver bells;
What a world of merriment their melody foretells!
How they tinkle, tinkle, tinkle,
In the icy air of night!
While the stars that oversprinkle
All the heavens, seem to twinkle

With a crystalline delight;
Keeping time, time, time,
In a sort of Runic rhyme,
To the tintinnabulation that so musically wells
From the bells, bells, bells, bells, bells,—
From the jingling and the tinkling of the bells.

—*The Bells.* POE.

PEDAGOGICAL ASPECTS.

For the third time, it is well to be reminded that drills in the elements of expression as such have no place in public-school training. Perhaps in no part of the work is more care necessary than in the development of the pupil's power to express feeling. If we were discussing methods of teaching elocution outside of the public school, the author would be compelled to protest strongly against a prevalent practice of endeavoring to develop the different vocal qualities apart from the emotion that produces these qualities. But the difficulty in public-school methods is that they pay comparatively little attention to emotional expression. As a general thing, so educators say, there is either no feeling ("no expression," some put it), or, what is worse, there is a palpable affectation of feeling. Somehow, it has come to be considered "girlish" for a boy to put feeling into his reading, especially tender feeling; and for the girl to do so is considered a sure indication of weakness. The atmosphere of the school-room is not conducive to the development of emotional power, and if, by any chance, a shoot should peep out of the soil, it dies for want of light and warmth. Emotion in itself is a good thing, when properly guided; but we need emotion in reading because it is a sign that the pupil can be moved by the contemplation of the noble, the tender, the true. It is a sign that the children have that precious gift of imagination. Where there is no opportunity for the expression of feeling, there must result a great loss in expressive power and eventually in power of imagination. Such a loss is irremediable, for there follows in its wake inability to appreciate the finer breath and spirit of literature.

Our public schools, except in particularly favored districts, can do very little towards training the voices of the pupils. Even when there are special teachers the best results are found not so much in the voices as in the ability to read music. To train the human voice requires genius and much particular training, and we cannot expect that school communities will appoint such teachers for many, many generations. But development of the child's powers of expression through the stimulation of his imagination and emotions will do wonders for his voice. So that here we have a third reason for pleading so earnestly for more careful attention to this aspect of vocal expression. One hears so often the excuse, "Oh, he hasn't any voice; that's why he can't read." The author believes with that great specialist in the child voice, William L. Tomlins, that, except when there are serious structural defects, the imagination and soul will make a voice. Let it be remarked, that the claim is not made that vocal training is unnecessary. But when we look at the conditions that make impossible the appointment of skilled specialists in voice, we give up in despair of effecting for some time to come any radical change. Further, a good voice does not imply a good reader. Since, then, we can not get the voice teacher; and since, when we can, we are not assured he will develop good expressionists, it should be a great stimulus to the conscientious teacher to learn that the very highest quality of the voice, soulfulness, may be developed through stimulation of the imagination. And, further, let us note that expression that comes in this way can never be affected.

The teacher now knows that emotion affects the quality of tone. Let him then use this knowledge as he has learned to use his knowledge of the other criteria. We recognize instinctively the quality that expresses sorrow, tenderness, joy and the other states of feeling. When the proper quality does not appear it is because the child has no feeling or the wrong feeling—generally the former. There is but one way to correct the expression, i. e., by stimulating the imagination.

This is a most difficult task, but that fact does not excuse us from attempting it. In Part II this feature will be treated at length.

CHAPTER IV

THE CRITERION OF FORCE

Force manifests the degree of mental energy. When we speak in a loud voice there is much energy; when softly, there is little. This criterion is the easiest of the four to understand, because, perhaps, it is the most tangible. We need not stay, therefore, to illustrate, but may pass on to consider a subdivision of Force, the understanding of which is very necessary to good teaching.

In reading the following lines note how explosive is the utterance on the emphatic words:

> Down! down! your lances, down!
> Bear back both friend and foe!

Now observe how differently we apply the force on the emphatic words of this extract:

> Ye gods! ye gods! Must I endure all this?

In the first example, upon the emphatic words, there was heard a loud explosion of the voice, followed by a gradual diminution in force; in the second, the voice perceptibly swelled on the significant words. This swell or diminish has been called "Stress." Perhaps it is not the best word, but since its meaning in the sense in which we are using it here is generally understood, it may be well to retain it. "Stress" refers to the manner of applying the force to the emphatic syllable. In the first of the preceding illustrations, the greatest force was at the beginning of the emphatic syllable. This form is called "Radical" stress. In the second, the force was applied in the opposite manner. This form is denominated "Final" stress.

Radical stress marks all forms of animated utterance. It is the result of the normal action of the vocal chords, which, coming together before syllabic impulses, suddenly part, causing a slight degree of explosion. Absence of this form of stress gives the delivery a kind of drawling effect. It is further to be noted that even in those utterances characterized by other forms of stress this form yet manifests itself on most of the syllables. After the student has practiced the other forms of stress, he will better understand this remark. He will have noticed that the other forms are significant just in so far as they differ from this one, which is the normal; and, further, that because the radical stress *is* normal, the use of other forms of stress on a comparatively few (emphatic) syllables will give a very significant coloring to a whole paragraph.

We must guard against over-developing this abruptness. If we do not, our delivery will be very likely to become explosive, and then we shall create the impression of being too dogmatic. On the other hand, slovenliness and drawling may be overcome by drilling on this element of expression, and much vitality will thereby be imparted to the speaking.

All speech, then, has this abrupt character. It has become so familiar to us that we do not notice it except, as it were, in its absence, when the delivery becomes drawling or slovenly. Hence, we can say that radical stress in its milder forms is not essentially expressive; it is an inherent part of our vocal production. It becomes expressive only in its stronger forms. The student whose delivery is sufficiently vital need not practice on the milder form. It need hardly be said that the form and the thought should not be separated in this practice.

It should also be borne in mind that there are different degrees of stress as well as kinds. Professor Raymond truly says, "Never confuse the kind of stress with the degree." To illustrate: the decided stroke of the voice is heard in,

> Come, and trip it as ye go
> On the light fantastic toe;

but a strong attack would spoil the daintiness. Let us remember that a grain of gunpowder explodes as well as a ton. This admonition applies as well to other forms of stress.

It has been urged, that if the claim is true that the complete assimilation of the thought and feeling will, through practice, lead to adequate expression, why bother the student with such drills as these? The answer is plain. One's temperament may be of such a nature that he cannot express a single sentence without, say, the greatest insistency. The insistency is temperamental, and it shows in everything the speaker does. By a careful study of "Stress," he is introduced to his own consciousness, soon recognizes his weakness, and his delivery is improved through improving his mental action. If this is true for the creative speaker, the orator, how much more is it true of him who reads or recites the words of another.

A few years ago, a well-known minister spoke these words: "You may read the tragedies of Sophocles, and the philosophy of Plato and Aristotle; you may be familiar with the lore of the Hindus and the Brahmins; you may know your Shakespeare, your Milton, and your Dante, your Wordsworth, your Browning, and your Tennyson, but [raising aloft a limp-covered Bible] it's *all here*!" And he brought the book down on the palm of his hand with a thwack that was heard throughout the building. He fairly exploded on "all here," and the congregation laughed. Paraphrased, his stress said, I—I, who know what I am talking about, tell you people—deny it if you can—it's all here. There was no appeal, no tenderness, no gentle persuasiveness. His purpose ought to have been (to avoid argument, let it be said that the context justifies this remark—he was appealing for a more careful and reverential study of the Bible) to express, Oh, my friends, this holy work, this revelation of God's goodness, contains all you need. Why not take it up, and study it? You read all literatures; will you not read this too? The trouble was that the preacher, being naturally of an aggressive nature, lost sight of his final purpose, and spoiled what might have been a very effective appeal, by obtruding himself between his illustration and his audience. It may be of interest to state that the speaker's attention was called to this; and he admitted the justice of the criticism, while disclaiming all knowledge of what he had done, and how he had done it.

This illustrates the contention. He had had no idea that he had become so assertive that he virtually said, *I* tell you so, on every emphatic word. A study of "Stress" and its psychology would certainly have helped him.

In *The Orator's Manual* the author sums up this matter of radical stress thus: "The radical stress is exerted on account of a subjective ... motive; in other words, because a man desires chiefly to express an idea on his own account.... In [this] case the sound bursts forth abruptly, as if the man were conscious of nothing but his own organs to prevent the accomplishment of his object.... It is used whenever one's main wish is to express himself so as to be distinctly understood. In its mildest form, it serves to render articulation clear and utterance precise; when stronger, it indicates bold and earnest assurance, positiveness, and dictation.... Without [this] stress, gentleness becomes an inarticulate and timid drawl, and vehemence mere brawling bombast. With too frequent use of it, one's delivery becomes characterized by an appearance of self-assertion, assurance, or preciseness." In other words, it is the "I" stress.

Of final stress, Professor Raymond says: "It is exerted on account of an objective idea. The sound is pushed forth gradually, as if the man were conscious of outside opposition, and of the necessity of pressing his point. It is used whenever one's main wish is to impress his thoughts on others. It gives utterance, in its weakest form, to the whine or complaint of mere peevishness demanding consideration; when stronger to a pushing earnestness or determination; in its strongest form, to a desire to cause others to feel one's own astonishment, scorn, or horror.... Without final stress there can be no representation of childish weakness or obstinacy, or of ... resolution; used too exclusively, or excessively, it causes delivery to be characterized by an appearance of wilfulness, depriving it of the qualities of persuasion that appeal to the sympathies."

A very little of final stress will give a decided coloring to the delivery. The student should be careful, therefore, not to overdo it. To illustrate: a speaker is urging the colonists to abandon the idea of war, claiming that they are weak, and so on. Patrick Henry rises and says, "Sir, we are *not* weak if we make a proper use of those means which the God of nature hath placed in our power. Three millions of people armed in the holy cause of *liberty*, and in such a country as that which *we* possess, are *invincible* by *any* force which our enemy can send against us." On the word "not," the speaker is plainly pushing aside the argument of his opponent. When he utters "liberty," we note again the insistent idea. He tells us by his stress, Other revolutions may have failed through lack of numbers, but the gentleman forgets that ours will be a struggle for liberty. Again, in "we," "invincible," and "any," we plainly discern the idea of overcoming opposition. Now, it must be clear that while it is only on the five words italicized we note the insistence, yet the whole statement is strongly tinged by it.

There is a third form of stress commonly called "Median." This is a combination of the final and radical, and manifests a combination of the objective and subjective states. There are other combinations and forms of stress, but they are rarely heard and need not be dwelt upon here.

Attention needs to be directed to the fact that stress sometimes extends through several words and gives a characteristic color to an entire phrase or sentence. For instance, we note that the swell continues from the opening word to "despised," in the following speech of Cassio, who is opposing Iago's plan. Note further the same effect on phrases italicized:

> I will rather sue to be despised, than to deceive so good a commander, with *so slight, so drunken,* and *so indiscreet* an officer. Drunk! and speak parrot? and squabble? swagger? swear? and discourse fustian with one's own shadow? O thou invisible spirit of wine, if thou hast no name to be known by, let us call thee—devil!—*Othello,* Act ii., Sc. 3.

Observe how the force increases up to "Lord" and dies away to the end in the following:

> O, sing unto the Lord a new song.

It may be well to remark here that there are certain writers who hold that the study of stress is misleading, or at best useless. To these answer is made that music uses these stresses very much in the sense in which they are used here. The attack necessary for pure singing or instrumental tone is our radical (normal) stress. The "staccato" and "sforzando" are more intense forms of this stress. The "crescendo," "diminuendo," and "swell" are respectively equivalent to "final," prolonged "radical," and "median" stresses.

It may be well to call attention to a very general confusion of ideas in the use of the word "low." It is applied to force and pitch indiscriminately, to the loss of an important distinction. Low pitch is the result of low tension, while soft force is diminished mental energy. High pitch may accompany soft force, and loud force may be simultaneous with low pitch. It is because low pitch has generally accompanied soft force that the confusion has arisen.

EXAMPLES ILLUSTRATING THE USE OF RADICAL STRESS.

Are you ready? Go!

Carry—Arms.
Present—Arms.
Right about—face.
Halt.

Stop, don't take another step.

Give me that pencil; it's mine.

Leave the room, sir.

One, two, three, fire.

Back! beardless boy!
Back! minion! Holdst thou thus at naught
The lesson I so lately taught?

Man, who art thou who dost deny my words?

But in the gloom they fought, with bloodshot eyes
And laboring breath; first Rustum struck the shield
Which Sohrab held stiff out; the steel-spiked spear
Rent the tough plates, but fail'd to reach the skin,
And Rustum pluck'd it back with angry groan.
Then Sohrab with his sword smote Rustum's helm,
Nor clove its steel quite through; but all the crest
He shore away, and that proud horsehair plume,
Never till now defiled, sank to the dust. —*Sohrab and Rustum.* M. Arnold.

He spoke, and Rustum answer'd not, but hurl'd
His spear; down from the shoulder, down it came,
As on some partridge in the corn a hawk,
That long has tower'd in the airy clouds,
Drops like a plummet; Sohrab saw it come,
And sprang aside, quick as a flash; the spear
Hiss'd, and went quivering down into the sand,
Which it sent flying wide;—then Sohrab threw
In turn, and full struck Rustum's shield; sharp rang,
The iron plates rang sharp, but turn'd the spear.
And Rustum seized his club, which none but he
Could wield. —*Sohrab and Rustum.* M. Arnold.

Girl! nimble with thy feet, not with thy hands!
Curl'd minion, dancer, coiner of sweet words!
Fight, let me hear thy hateful voice no more. —*Ibid.*

Thou art not in Afrasiab's garden now
With Tartar girls, with whom thou art wont to dance;
But on the Oxus sands, and in the dance
Of battle, and with me, who make no play
Of war; I fight it out, and hand to hand.
Speak not to me of truce, and pledge, and wine!
Remember all thy valor; try thy feints

And cunning! all the pity I had is gone;
Because thou hast shamed me before both the hosts
With thy light skipping tricks, and thy girl's wiles. —*Ibid.*

The armaments which thunderstrike the walls of rock-built cities,
Bidding nations quake, and monarchs tremble in their capitals;
The oak leviathans, whose huge ribs make their clay creator
The vain title take of lord of thee, and arbiter of war,—

These are thy toys; and as the snowy flake they
melt into thy yeast of waves,
Which mar alike the Armada's pride, or spoils of Trafalgar. —BYRON.

EXAMPLES ILLUSTRATING THE USE OF FINAL STRESS.[6]

I *won't*!

No, sir; I am not guilty.

Away, slight man!

Must *I* budge? Must *I* observe you?

I am *astonished, shocked,* to hear *such* principles avowed in *this* house.

CASSIUS. *Ye gods! ye gods!* Must I endure *all this*?

BRUTUS. All this? Ay, more.

SHYLOCK. May I speak with Antonio?

BASSANIO. If it please you to dine with us.

SHYLOCK. Yes, to smell *pork;* to eat of the habitation which your prophet the Nazarite conjured the *Devil* into. I will *buy* with you, *sell* with you, *talk* with you, *walk* with you, and so following; but I will not *eat* with you, *drink* with you, nor *pray* with you.—*The Merchant of Venice,* Act i., Sc. 3.

SALARINO. Why, I am sure, if he forfeit, thou wilt not take his flesh: What's that good for?

SHYLOCK. To bait fish withal: if it will feed nothing else, it will

[6] A few words are italicized in order to draw attention to the places where we should be likely to use this stress. Observe, too, how the stress impresses us with the desire of the speaker to push away opposition.

feed my revenge. He hath disgraced me, and hinder'd me half a million: laugh'd at my losses, mock'd at my gains, scorned my nation, thwarted my bargains, cooled my friends, heated mine enemies; and what's his reason? I am a Jew. Hath not a Jew eyes? hath not a Jew hands, organs, dimensions, senses, affections, passions? fed with the same food, hurt with the same weapons, subject to the same diseases, healed by the same means, warmed and cooled by the same winter and summer, as a Christian is? If you prick us, do we not bleed? if you tickle us, do we not laugh? if you poison us, do we not die? and if you wrong us, shall we not revenge?—*The Merchant of Venice*, Act iii., Sc. 1.

WORCESTER. Those same noble Scots,
That are your prisoners,—

HOTSPUR. I'll keep them all;
By heaven, he shall not have a Scot of them.
No, if a Scot would save his soul, he shall not.
I'll keep them, by this hand.

WORCESTER. You start away,
And lend no ear unto my purposes.—
Those prisoners you shall keep.

HOTSPUR. Nay, I will; that's flat.—
He said, he would not ransom Mortimer;
Forbade my tongue to speak of Mortimer;
But I will find him when he lies asleep,
And in his ear I'll holla—Mortimer!
Nay,
I'll have a starling shall be taught to speak
Nothing but Mortimer, and give it him,
To keep his anger still in motion.

—*King Henry IV.*, Part I., Act i., Sc. 3.

And now, go bring your sharpest torments. The woes I see impending over this guilty realm shall be enough to sweeten death, though every nerve and artery were a shooting pang. I die! but my death shall prove a proud triumph; and, for every drop of blood ye from my veins do draw, your own shall flow in rivers. Woe to thee, Carthage! Woe to the proud city of the waters! I see thy nobles wailing at the feet of Roman senators! thy citizens in terror! thy ships in flames! I hear the victorious shouts of Rome! I see her eagles glittering on thy ramparts. Proud city, thou art doomed! The curse of God is on thee—a clinging, wasting curse. It shall not leave thy gates till hungry flames shall lick the fretted gold from off thy proud palaces, and every brook runs crimson to the sea.—*Regulus to the Carthaginians.* KELLOGG.

EXAMPLES ILLUSTRATING THE USE OF MEDIAN STRESS.

Arise, shine; for thy light is come, and the glory of the Lord is risen upon thee.

For, behold, darkness shall cover the earth, and gross darkness the people: but the Lord shall arise upon thee, and his glory shall be seen upon thee.

And nations shall come to thy light, and kings to the brightness of thy rising.

Lift up thine eyes round about, and see: they all gather themselves together, they come to thee; thy sons shall come from far, and thy daughters shall be nursed at thy side.

Then thou shalt see, and be lightened, and thine heart shall tremble and be enlarged; because the abundance of the sea shall be unto thee, the wealth of the nations shall come unto thee.—*Isa.* lx. 1-5.

Thou kingly Spirit throned among the hills,
Thou dread ambassador from earth to heaven,
Great hierarch! tell thou the silent sky,
And tell the stars, and tell yon rising sun,
Earth, with her thousand voices, praises God.—COLERIDGE.

The Lord reigneth; he is appareled with majesty;
The Lord is appareled, he hath girded himself with strength:
The world also is stablished that it cannot be moved.
Thy throne is established of old:
Thou art from everlasting.
The floods have lifted up, O Lord.
The floods have lifted up their voice;
The floods lift up their waves.
Above the voices of many waters,
The mighty breakers of the sea,
The Lord on high is mighty.
Thy testimonies are very sure:
Holiness becometh thine house,
O Lord, for evermore.—*Ps.* xciii. 1-5.

He was a man, take him for all in all,
I shall not look upon his like again.—*Hamlet*, Act i., Sc. 2.

This was the noblest Roman of them all.
*   *   *   *   *
His life was gentle; and the elements

So mix'd in him, that Nature might stand up
And say to all the world, *This was a man!*—*Julius Caesar*, Act v., Sc. 5.

For even then, Sir, even before this splendid orb was entirely set, and while the western horizon was in a blaze with his descending glory, on the opposite quarter of the heavens arose another luminary, and, for his hour, became lord of the ascendant.... And I did see in that noble person such sound principles, such an enlargement of mind, such clear and sagacious sense, and such unshaken fortitude, as have bound me, as well as others much better than me, by an inviolable attachment to him from that time forward.... I stood near him; and his face, to use the expression of the Scripture of the first martyr—his face was as if it had been the face of an angel. I do not know how others feel; but if I had stood in that situation, I never would have exchanged it for all that kings in their profusion could bestow. I did hope that that day's danger and honor would have been a bond to hold us all together forever.—BURKE.

O, sing unto the Lord a new song:
Sing unto the Lord, all the earth.
Sing unto the Lord, bless his name;
Show forth his salvation from day to day.
Declare his glory among the nations,
His marvelous works among all peoples.
For great is the Lord, and highly to be praised:
He is to be feared above all gods.
For all the gods of the people are idols:
But the Lord made the heavens.
Honor and majesty are before him:
Strength and beauty are in his sanctuary.—*Ps.* xcvi., 1-6.

Ho! gallant nobles of the League, look that your arms be bright!
Ho! burghers of St. Genevieve, keep watch and ward to-night!
For our God hath crushed the tyrant, our God hath raised the slave,
And mocked the counsel of the wise, and the valor of the brave.
Then glory to his holy name, from whom all glories are;
And glory to our sovereign lord, King Henry of Navarre.

—*The Battle of Ivry.* MACAULAY.

PEDAGOGICAL ASPECTS.

These aspects, having been dwelt upon at some length in the preceding discussion, may be dismissed with a few words. The knowledge of the psychology of Force and Stress is to serve as a standard of criticism, not as a foundation for mechanical drills. There is a school of reading pedagogy, with lamentably extended sway, that argues, since there are found various kinds of stress in our speech, therefore we must drill our pupils on these. Nothing could be farther from the truth. Stress denotes a state of mind. If our philosophy of stress is sound, it should teach us that the mental state finds instinctive expression in one form of stress or another, and consequently we must get the state before we can get the stress. We might add that this is true of Time, Pitch, and Quality, as well as of Stress.

Do not tell a child to read louder. If you do, you will get loudness—that awful, grating schoolboy loudness—without a particle of expression in it. Many a child reads well, but is bashful. When we tell him to read louder, he braces himself for the effort and kills the quality, which is the finer breath and spirit of oral expression, and gives us a purely physical thing—force. Put your weak-voiced readers on the platform; let them face the class and talk to you, seated in the middle of the room, and you will get all the force you need. On the whole, we have too much force rather than too little. Let the teacher learn that we want quality, not quantity, and our statement of the mental action behind force will be of much benefit in creating the proper conditions.

PART TWO
METHOD OF INSTRUCTION

CHAPTER V

THE MENTAL ATTITUDE OF THE READER

In our knowledge of the psychology of the elements of expression, we have the solution of the difficulties resulting from the complexity and intangibility of vocal expression. The teacher now knows what to look for, and hence is enabled to diagnose the case. There is now the second step to be taken in the development of the teacher: he must have method. It can hardly be claimed that there is any definite progression in our instruction. In the primary grades, the pupils learn the letters, their sounds, and a meagre amount of expression. After that the teaching is haphazard. This is not the case with arithmetic or history, or geography; why should it be so in reading? The answer is clear. For many reasons, not difficult to ascertain, the child has a vague idea that reading is simply vocal utterance; that his work as a reader is done when he has pronounced the words. This state of mind may be attributed, first, to his primary training, and, second, to the perfunctoriness of the reading lesson in the grammar grades. We seem to be satisfied, in the beginning, if a pupil learns to recognize and pronounce words. This is a serious error. We should never for a moment forget that our purpose in giving pupils the ability to recognize words is to enable them to extract the thought from the printed page. Hence, from the outset, as was enjoined in the Introduction, we should lay the least possible stress upon word-getting, and, contrariwise, all possible stress on thought-getting. If the primary teachers should succeed in developing the state of mind that would cause the pupils to go to the printed page as they go to the feet of one who has a story to tell, we should be willing to ask for nothing else of them as a result of all their teaching.

But let us accept reading as we find it to-day, and let us suppose the pupil is about ten or eleven years of age. What is the first step? To impress upon him that the printed page is a picture; that it contains ideas, sights, sounds; that it takes the place of the author, and that he must listen to it as to the voice of the author. This is the all-important factor. Many of us think we are following this plan, when, in reality, we defeat our ends by the way we use the means. We allow slovenly reading and pass over the grossest carelessness; so that, unconsciously, the pupil forms the loosest habits of expression. Then the pupil must be stimulated to hold the thought; to let it hold him, if you will. This, too, is a very necessary part of the training. The defective reading of preachers and authors is not due to the fact that they cannot get the thought, but that they are not dwelling upon it in detail while reading. The third stage in the first step is to train the pupil so that he will never get up to read without the consciousness that he has something to give. Let the pupils, and, first of all, the teacher, close their books, and so give the poor reader some encouragement. Do not have him read to the backs of the class. How should we like to address an audience of inexpressive backs? The following of this last suggestion will produce wonderful results, and quickly too. But it has another value: it compels the class to think, to follow the reader, to get thought through the ear (a talent becoming rarer every day), and, above all, it stimulates the imagination. Summarized, the first step means, *Get the thought, hold the thought, give the thought*. Keep at this for a month, if necessary.

The one object of this lesson is to impress upon the mind of the pupil that words have no meaning unless they stimulate thought. It is, perhaps, needless to add that the teacher should be on his guard against teaching inflections and pauses and the like, as such. No other aim should be held in mind than that of getting the pupil to see clearly and to express forcibly.

The teacher should use constantly such criticism as, "Is that the thought?" or, "Won't you tell that to me?" This method will soon set the pupil to thinking. It will gradually impress upon him the true function of the reading lesson. There will soon disappear that dreadful perfunctoriness so characteristic of class-room reading. How much preparation does the pupil now give to his reading? Practically none. He prepares those lessons in which he gradually learns he can be definitely tested: his arithmetic, spelling, composition, geography. Then, if he has any time, he may look over his reading lesson to discover if there are any "hard" words, and when he has mastered these he thinks his work is done. But let us remember that such preparation is by no means adequate. There are passages in every lesson which require patient study, even though each word may be simple. Words in themselves mean little; it is words in relation that we must study.

This first step includes all the others. It may be asked then, "Why are there others?" The subsequent chapters will deal with this question, but it may be explained here that the purpose of this first step is to create and make permanent the proper atmosphere of the reading hour. The criticisms should be general, not particular, and the teacher should be careful to offer no discouraging criticism. Every effort should be made to stimulate the pupil. He should be urged to get the thought, and especially impressed with the idea that the class depends upon him for their understanding of the text.

Choose selections from all sources—from the history lesson, and from the geography lesson. Let these selections be fairly simple, and above all, vital and interesting. *Barbara Frietchie*, Longfellow's *Peace-Pipe* from *Hiawatha*, and Browning's *Ride from Ghent to Aix*, or *The Pied Piper*, and even shorter extracts of prose or poetry, are excellent material. Give out a dozen of these, let each pupil learn one by heart, and tell it,—not declaim it,—to his classmates.

Let the teacher not worry because this process is slow and threatens to leave the work outlined for a given term incomplete. It is not the quantity but the quality we are after. But by this method we shall in time cover more ground than we now do in a given period. If we continually offer such criticism as will impress the pupil that thought-getting is everything, that reading is but the expression of that thought, he will go to his history, and geography, and arithmetic lesson for thought; so that the time spent in the reading hour is virtually just the training for every other lesson. Finally, this is the true preparation for the making of sight-readers. It is true, one should be able to read better after some preparation than he does at sight; but everyone should be able, by the time he leaves the public school, to read any ordinary passage at sight without blundering. The mental attitude formed by the method urged will cause the student to approach the printed page warily, prepared to deal with its difficulties, and will thus produce better reading.

A word to those who ride the sight-reading hobby too hard. It is only the experienced reader who can read well at sight. To ask an immature pupil to read at sight is to do one of two things: if he is timid, it frightens him; if he is a poor reader it simply fastens the careless habits upon him, by leading him to believe, by implication, that reading is merely pronunciation. In the upper grades, there should be sight-reading, but only where the previous training has been methodical. It is well to give the class a chance to read over the selection for a few minutes before the test is made.

Each teacher must decide for himself how he will develop the foregoing principles. The following plan, however, representing the actual work of a teacher before his class, will be suggestive:

> We are going to study how to read; and the first thing we must know is, What is reading?
>
> Now, before we answer this question, let us try to get an answer to another: What is speaking? Speaking is telling someone what I am thinking or feeling. So, if you were in the author's school, he could tell you the thoughts he has. But you are not, and so he must write them. Now we are ready to answer the question, What is reading? Reading is getting thought from the printed or written page.
>
> Let us go a little further. Suppose a writer wants to say something to you through the printed page, what does he do? He first thinks over very carefully what he has to say, and then chooses and writes the words that will give you his meaning. But remember, you must study his words and think about them as carefully as he did when he wrote them.
>
> Have you been attentive so far? Let us see. Can you tell me what speaking is? what reading is? If you can not, do you not see you have not been paying attention?
>
> Getting thought from the printed page should be just like listening carefully to speaking. Yes, you must be more careful in reading, because the author is not here to explain things to you, or to repeat his words. You have only the printed words, and if you do not listen very carefully to what they say, you will not understand him. Now let us see whether this is clear. Here is a sentence;

can you see what I see? "The next day, which was Saturday, the king called his generals and some of his friends to the royal tent, and told them, in a quiet voice, that at daybreak on Tuesday he was going to return to London and give up the war."

Now take your eyes off the blackboard and tell us all you saw, and tell it in just the order the pictures occur on the board. If you miss any steps, you must read again and again until you see the whole thought so clearly that it seems real; then I am sure you will be able to tell it correctly. You need not use my words; just use your own language.

Now you are ready to take the next step. Read the sentence to the class so that you make them see just what you see. Be sure you never forget this.

You must remember that unless you *try* to make them see the pictures you have in mind, they will be very likely not to understand you.

Now, what have we been doing? First, we studied the meaning of the words; second, we got several pictures; and third, we tried to give those pictures to others. So we see there are two kinds of reading: the first for ourselves, the second for others. The first kind must always go before the second: for if we have nothing in our mind to tell, how can we give it to others?

Let us remember then, that reading for others is just like talking to them, and unless we get from the page just the thought the writer had in mind we cannot give that thought to another. Sometimes it is not easy to get this thought; but if you will study carefully, it will become clearer and clearer, until at last it is just as easy to understand as if it had been your own. I want to give you a short drill, and then our first lesson will be over. "In the summer the grass is green, but it turns brown in the fall." Can you imagine how green grass looks? how brown grass looks? Do you notice that fall is the time when grass is brown? Again, "He was a very tall man, with light, curly hair, tanned skin and blue eyes. His shoulders were stooped like those of a farmer or of one who has been digging in the mines." Close your eyes and then call up the picture of this man. Do you see him as a real man? Now read this sentence aloud so that your classmates may get the same picture that you have.

These are the three things we have learned in our first lesson, and they are very, very important: We must *get* the thought; we must *hold* the thought; and we must *give* the thought. This is reading aloud.

Remember, I want you to be getting these pictures from everything you read; from your geography lesson, your history lesson, and even your arithmetic lesson. I am sure you will get these lessons better than you ever did before.

Here are some interesting stories and parts of stories which you must tell to the class. Be sure you understand them, and then tell them so that your classmates will understand them too.

[7]Keep busy! 'tis better than standing aside
And dreaming, and sighing, and waiting the tide.
In life's earnest battle, they only prevail
Who daily march onward, and never say fail.

There's a rogue at play in my sunlit room,
And scarcely he rests from fun;
Floor, window, shelf, or closet's gloom
All are to him as one.

He opens the books and peeps within,
The paper turns inside out,
Snatches my thread, and thinks no sin
To throw my work about.

He clutches the curtains and whisks them down,
Then pulls at the picture cords,
Tosses my hair in the way of his own,
Nor heeds my coaxing words.

I wonder if one so glad and young
Will ever be prim and old?
He answers not, for he has no tongue—
Yet tells sweet tales as are told.

He climbs the walls, yet has no feet;
No wings, but flies the same;
No hands, no head, but breath so sweet—
For West Wind is his name.

In closing this chapter, it should be remarked that the time to be spent on this and subsequent steps depends upon the circumstances. In the lower grades more time will be necessary than in the upper. If the teacher of the eighth grade (the highest) wishes to devote some time to teaching reading, he should make a careful study of the needs of the class, and then use such of the steps, and in such order, as are most likely to meet those needs. In the lower classes it is suggested that the teacher follow in a general way the plan set forth in this book. About one step a month is all that a pupil can grasp. After he has the principle, let the teacher take up the regular reading lesson, laying special stress upon the principles already covered.

[8]It is believed that the reading lessons contained in this series

[7] Other examples should be found by the teacher. With a little care much valuable material may be selected.

[8] From the introduction to the author's "How to Read Aloud," which is out of print.

are the first attempt to present in an orderly and philosophic manner the difficulties the pupils have in learning to read.

There is very little doubt that the reading lesson hardly pays for the time spent upon it. All authorities are agreed that, except in rare cases, pupils do not read any better at the end of the school year than they do at the beginning, except that they may pronounce with a little more facility or are possessed of a somewhat wider vocabulary. In many class rooms, reading becomes a lesson in composition, spelling, definition, and the like.

The method in vogue in certain districts of telling pupils about Inflections, and Time, and Kinds of Emphasis, is certainly faulty. On the other hand, very little more progress has been made by those who, in a very general and vague manner, tell the pupil to get the thought. As a result of the methods heretofore in use, it has been found impossible for the teacher in any given grade to determine how much real knowledge of reading a pupil has who has just been promoted from a lower grade.

In the lessons here presented, it is impressed upon the pupil not only that he must get the thought, but he is shown how to get it. The various difficulties of reading are presented one at a time, and further, are so graded that the least difficult shall precede the more complex. It is well known that the reading lesson, as a reading lesson, gets little or no preparation by the pupils. By the method here laid down careful preparation is a necessity; and the lesson which, as a rule, is very ill prepared, may now be studied at home with a very definite object in view, and more important still, the pupil can be held responsible for definite results.

It must be remembered that the young pupil knows nothing of inflections, emphasis, etc., and cares still less about them. While the teacher may be thoroughly conversant with the whole range of vocal technique in reading, he should try to avoid the use of technical terms with the pupils, especially with the younger ones. This is the very essence of the present method, which is based upon a well-established psychological law: If the thought is right, the expression will be right. Talking to pupils about technique, only confuses them and in many cases results in gross affectations. The mind is taken from the thought to the form of its expression. We must remember that shyness, and other forms of self-consciousness (which so often mar the reading) are really but signs that the pupil's mental action is awry. The reading may be more quickly and more permanently improved by eradicating the self-consciousness than by resorting to technical drills. Make the pupil *want to read*, and the chances are strongly in favor of his losing self-consciousness.

All the essential features, however, are included in the present work.

While it is not possible in the space allotted the author of these articles to give the fullest possible instruction, yet these lessons will serve a definite purpose by presenting to the pupils, in a rational order, the various difficulties everyone has to overcome in learning to read. There may be certain phases of technique that a teacher may miss in this series of lessons, but it is certain, that if they are carefully taught, the pupils will improve not only along the particular line laid down in each lesson, but along the whole line of reading in general.

This method is introduced in the hope that the measure of a pupil's progress will not be gauged by the number of selections he reads in a given period. It is better to prepare carefully and philosophically six or eight lessons in one-half of the school year, than to endeavor to cover three times as many in the usual hurried fashion. The teacher may be sure that when the first six or eight lessons are thus carefully prepared, the progress thereafter will be more rapid. There is no doubt that the pupil who will spend two years in this graded work will be able to read any ordinary selection with ease, and with pleasure to the listener.

It is urged (1) that the teacher use additional examples under each new principle, in order that the pupil may have the principle impressed upon him by selecting new examples for himself and by reading them aloud in class; (2) that the same lesson be repeated as many times, with the same or new illustrations, as may be necessary to assure the teacher that the class has thoroughly grasped the spirit of the lesson; and (3) that the teacher insist upon most careful and adequate preparation. So, and so only, can we hope to teach reading.

The main objects of the first lessons are two. First; to develop what may be termed the logical side of reading; in other words, the intellectual side. The greatest stress should be laid on getting the sense, which is, of course, the basis of all reading. The emotional side need not be altogether neglected, but should be always subsidiary to the intellectual. If the teacher succeed in getting the expression *vital,* nothing more should be expected. To get the sense and to express it with earnestness is the first step. Second; the teacher is urged not to follow mechanically the order of the general reading lessons. If Lesson XX offer a better opportunity than, let us say, Lesson X for illustrating the principle laid down in any of the special lessons, the former should be used, no matter what the preceding general lesson may have been. The teacher should be acquainted with the pedagogical possibilities of all the general lessons, and should use such, irrespective of their place in the book, as are best adapted at the moment to assist the pupils in mastering the principle in any given special reading lesson. I have found much good in keeping a little note book on the following plan: I give a page to each of the steps, and every example I come across, no matter in what book—history, geography, reader—is noted. Thus:

EXAMPLES OF CONTRAST.

Book.	Page.	Paragraph.
——'s History,	250	3
——'s History,	109	1
Reader (3)	87	8

In this way, the teacher has always plenty of illustrative matter on hand.

While not in entire sympathy with the method that compels teachers to cover a certain number of reading lessons in a given time, yet I am sensible that it would be useless to attempt to change all this at once. Recognizing the futility of such an effort, I advise the teacher to conform to this arbitrary and unscientific method until the community is educated to the newer method. The best results may be obtained, under the circumstances, by following some such plan as this: Begin with the first special lesson as soon as possible. Then, having dwelt on that as long as necessary, pass to the regular reading lessons, bearing in mind that until the second special lesson, the principle of the first should be constantly reiterated. For the entire time (say a month) between the first and second special lessons let the teacher revert to the former again and again. Let the corrections be made over and over by asking such questions as, "Is that the way you would say it if you were talking?" or, "You are not trying to make us see the picture," and so on. After the second special lesson has been taken up in class, and before the third, the endeavor of a teacher should be to enforce the principles of the first two lessons. This plan should be kept up until the last lesson has been taught.

CHAPTER VI

GROUPING

If the work of the first step has been carefully done, the transition to the second step will present few difficulties. As a matter of fact, the pupil has been grouping unconsciously, but in a way more or less uncertain. The purpose of the next step is to fix firmly the habit of grouping. As a general rule, the pupil pronounces as many words in one group as his eye can take in and his voice utter; consequently, his reading is choppy and often meaningless.

At the outset care should be exercised in the choice of extracts. Any extract will not do. Simple passages, with simple ideas, are needed. Avoid complex, involved, inverted rhetoric. Later on, when proper habits have been formed, the difficulties may be increased; but we shall meet only with discouragement if we introduce them too soon. The following is just difficult enough to bring out the efforts of an ordinary child of ten or eleven:

> Once upon a time there lived a very rich man, and a king besides, whose name was Midas; and he had a little daughter, whom nobody but myself ever heard of, and whose name I either never knew, or have entirely forgotten. So, because I love odd names for little girls, I choose to call her Marygold.—*The Golden Touch.* HAWTHORNE.

The teacher should use a great many isolated extracts. These may not be so interesting as entire selections, but if chosen carefully and read with a definite object, it is surprising how they hold the attention of the class. It may also be possible to find short stories to supplement the extracts. Many good extracts may be found in the reader or even in some of the other books the children are using.

The reason for urging this plan is that few reading books present the difficulties of reading, in a rational, graded manner. Any selection may contain the simplest problem and the most difficult in one paragraph. The pupil must be trained to get his ideas from the printed page in groups, and such training can surely be gained better by using carefully selected passages than by the present aimless wandering among a labyrinth of words. It is admitted that a good teacher of reading may be able to get along without calling the attention of the class to grouping as a definite step; but he must certainly have that step in mind as part of the development of a reader.

In this lesson we begin exercises in what might be called "mental technique." It must be borne in mind that these lessons are planned with the object of presenting one element at a time, and the pupil must not be expected to read well where he has had no previous drill. In this lesson, therefore, the pupil should be held responsible for what he has learned in the first and second lessons only. It must further be remembered that all corrections should be made by putting such questions as, "Is that the whole picture?" or, "Have you not given us more than one picture?" Never tell a pupil to make a pause here or a pause there, or to read faster or more slowly. Such corrections are useless. We must learn to rely upon the thinking to govern the rate of speed, or the length and frequency of the pauses.

It might be well to bear in mind that in colloquial speech pauses are less frequent. In other words, the groups are longer.

As a result of such training as the pupil gets in this lesson we shall note that he will learn to look ahead, and so rid himself of the too general tendency to utter words as soon as he sees them, regardless of the sense. The process of recognizing words and pronouncing them simultaneously is attended with no small amount of danger. It begets a fatal facility in reading that is a positive detriment to the pupil. There are thousands who read glibly and yet are utterly ignorant of the meaning of what they read. To prevent the formation of such a habit or to break it up where it already exists, there is no better plan than that herein advocated for the study of grouping. It need hardly be said that the method of telling a pupil "to pause before a relative pronoun, inverted adjectives, prepositional phrases," and the like, is virtually useless. The thought, and not the grammatical construction, determines the pause.

Another suggestive lesson for the teaching of grouping is offered:

> You remember that in our last lesson we learned that we must first get the thought before we could read. Now we are to study how to get the thought.
>
> Did you ever notice how you think? If you hear the word "Car," what do you think of? Some, of a horse car, some, of an electric car, and some, of a steam car. So you see the word "Car" by itself does not give us a very clear picture. The words, "I saw," do not mean very much either. For unless we know what you saw we get nothing to think about. The two words "in a" do not mean much, and by this time you know why.
>
> Let us put all these words together and add a word or two: "I saw a man in a steam car." Now we have a clear picture. What do we learn from this? We learn that a single word does not give us a clear picture, and that it takes three, and four, and sometimes many words, to give us a picture. We can think "I saw a man" or "in a steam car," but we get a complete thought only when we put these two groups of words together. We notice also that while it takes just a moment to see a picture, it often takes many words to describe it.
>
> What we have done is called grouping; that is, reading several words together just as we read the syllables of a word. Let us try

some examples. "Charles gave a sled to his brother." Here there are two groups: One ending at "sled," the other, at "brother." "I went to King Street with my sister to buy a new hat." Here we have three groups. Can you pick them out?

The last thing we are to learn in this lesson is that every group of words has a picture in it, and that we must not read aloud any word until we have got the thought or the picture in the group.

Pick out the groups in the following sentence, and then read aloud, but be sure you pay attention to the picture in each group: "When-our-school-closes for-the-summer-vacation, some-of-us-go-to-the-country, others-go-to-the-lakes, some-go-to-the-mountains, and-many stay-in-the-city."

For to-morrow's lesson[9] I want you to bring in the groups in the following examples, putting hyphens between the words of each group, just as we did in the sentence about the summer vacation.

[9] The teacher should select the examples, not too many, and write them on the board; or they may be selected from the reader. Drills of this kind should be continued until correct habits are formed, but should cease before the pupils become tired of them.

CHAPTER VII

SUCCESSION OF IDEAS

The next step is but a very short one in advance of the second, and yet one of exceeding importance. It deals with the succession of ideas. Every long sentence is made up of small phrases more or less intimately connected. The inflection denotes this connection. If several phrases point forward to a thought further on, the end of each of these will be marked by a rising inflection; if any one of the phrases be of sufficient importance to demand particular emphasis, its end will be marked by the falling inflection.

As was said in Chapter II, the reading of a long sentence presents great difficulties for the child. He loses himself in the maze of words, and his mental condition is clearly shown in his melody, which drifts about here and there, like a rudderless ship. It is the purpose of this step to train him in the development of his powers of continuous thinking; to enable him to keep in mind the main idea, no matter how numerous the details. This step and that dealing with subordinate ideas have much the same object in view.

The following excerpt from the *Introduction to The Song of Hiawatha* is a good illustration of a sentence in which the sense is suspended through many lines:

Ye, who sometimes, in your rambles
Through the green lanes of the country,
Where the tangled barberry-bushes
Hang their tufts of crimson berries
Over stone walls gray with mosses,
Pause by some neglected graveyard,
For a while to muse, and ponder
On a half-effaced inscription,
Written with little skill of song-craft,
Homely phrases, but each letter
Full of hope and yet of heart-break,
Full of all the tender pathos
Of the Here and the Hereafter;—
Stay and read this rude inscription,
Read this Song of Hiawatha!

It is in sentences like the following that the pupil is likely to fail. Speaking of rain, the poet says:

How it clatters along the roofs,

Like the tramp of hoofs!
How it gushes and struggles out
From the throat of the overflowing spout!

There may be some justification for the falling inflection on "roofs"; there can be no doubt that the same inflection would be incorrect on "out." And yet, the very structure of the verse would be likely to cause the careless reader to read it with that very inflection. This is a typical case, and, if this point has been made clear, one that should be very helpful to the teacher. The following passage, from the same poem, affords another exercise in succession of ideas:

In the country, on every side,
Where far and wide,
Like a leopard's tawny and spotted hide,
Stretches the plain,
To the dry grass and the drier grain
How welcome is the rain!

Let us observe that the plain does not stretch to the dry grass. There will be a falling inflection on "plain," and a rising on "grain."

The pause has nothing to do with succession of ideas. It would make little difference how long the pause after "plain" if it were read with a rising inflection. This principle must never be lost sight of.

Pupils who should know better frequently make mistakes of the kind we have been discussing, in reading the following passage:

In the furrowed land
The toilsome and patient oxen stand;
Lifting the yoke-encumbered head,
With their dilated nostrils spread,
They silently inhale
The clover-scented gale,
And the vapors that arise
From the well-watered and smoking soil.
For this rest in the furrow after toil
Their large and lustrous eyes
Seem to thank the Lord,
More than man's spoken word.
* * * * *
Near at hand,
From under the sheltering trees,
The farmer sees
His pastures, and his fields of grain.
As they bend their tops
To the numberless beating drops
Of the incessant rain.

The following extracts from *Gulliver's Travels* are within the comprehension of fairly young children, and will afford good practice:

1. The empire of Blefuscu is an island situated to the northeast of Lilliput, from which it is parted only by a channel eight hundred yards wide.

2. I had not yet seen it, and, upon this notice of a intended invasion, I avoided appearing on that side of the coast, for fear of being discovered by some of the enemy's ships, who had received no intelligence of me; all intercourse between the two empires having been strictly forbidden during the war, upon pain of death, and an embargo laid by our emperor upon all vessels whatsoever.

3. I walked toward the northeast coast, over against Blefuscu, where, lying down behind a hillock, I took out my small perspective glass and viewed the enemy's fleet at anchor, consisting of about fifty men-of-war and a great number of transports. I then came back to my house, and gave orders (for which I had a warrant) for a great quantity of the strongest cable and bars of iron. The cable was about as thick as pack-thread, and the bars of the length and size of a knitting-needle.

4. I trebled the cable to make it stronger, and for the same reason I twisted three of the iron bars together, bending the extremities into a hook. Having thus fixed fifty hooks to as many cables, I went back to the northeast coast, and putting off my coat, shoes and stockings, walked into the sea in my leathern jerkin, about half an hour before high water. I waded with what haste I could, and swam in the middle about thirty yards, till I felt ground.

5. When I had got out of danger, I stopped awhile to pick out the arrows that stuck in my hands and face, and rubbed on some of the same ointment that was given me at my first arrival, as I have formerly mentioned. I then took off my spectacles, and, waiting about an hour, till the tide was a little fallen, I waded through the middle with my cargo, and arrived safe at the royal port of Lilliput.

6. The emperor and his whole court stood on the shore, expecting the issue of this great adventure. They saw the ships move forward in a large half-moon, but could not discern me, who was up to my breast in water. When I advanced to the middle of the channel, they were yet more in pain, because I was under water to my neck. The emperor concluded me to be drowned, and that the enemy's fleet was approaching in a hostile manner.

7. But he was soon eased of his fears; for, the channel growing shallower every step I made, I came in a short time within hearing, and, holding up the end of the cable by which the fleet was fastened, I cried in a loud voice, "Long live the most puissant King of Lilliput!" This great prince received me at my landing

> with all possible encomiums, and created me a *nardac* upon the spot, which is the highest title of honor among them.

It need hardly be noted that there are many examples of momentary completeness in the preceding passages; as, for instance:

"Lilliput," in paragraph one.

"Ships," in paragraph two.

"Anchor," in paragraph three.

"Arrival," in paragraph five.

"Me," "pain," in paragraph six.

"Spot," in paragraph seven.

It will be seen that the purpose of this step is to draw the pupil's attention to two possibilities in every sentence: Does the phrase point forward, or is it momentarily complete? Great care must be observed not to confuse him with statements regarding inflections.

Momentary completeness has been so fully discussed in a preceding chapter that it need not be dwelt upon further.

The following lesson-talk may be helpful for the teacher:

> Read to yourself this little sentence: "Robert has a slate." Is that a complete picture? You see that it is. Now read this sentence: "Robert has a slate and a pencil." Here you note that Robert has two things, so the sentence is not complete when we come to the word "slate." Although we have a clear picture, yet we have not the whole picture. How do we know this? In the first sentence there was a period after "slate," but in the second sentence there was none, and because there wasn't, we kept on reading and found there was another group of words giving us the picture of something else Robert had. Now this teaches us that if we want to read just as we speak, we must be careful to get not only one picture or two, but all the pictures in the sentence.
>
> Let me show you how we often make mistakes in our reading because we don't pay attention to what I have just shown you. Suppose we have this sentence: "I saw a cat, and a mouse, and a rat." Now, some pupils are careless and they read, "I saw a cat," just as if that were the whole sentence. Then they look a little further and see the next group, "and a mouse," and they read that. Then they see the rest of the sentence, "and a rat," and they read that. But we know that is not the way to read. We must first read the whole sentence silently until we get the picture in each group, and then we shall be sure to read the sentence just as one of us would speak it if he really saw the cat, the rat, and the mouse, at the same time.

Here is a very good example for you to study. Read it through slowly and carefully, and do not try to read it aloud until you see clearly the picture in each group. If you do as I ask, you will get a complete picture of the way in which the young soldier prepares to go out to battle:

But when the gray dawn stole into his tent,
He rose, and clad himself, and girt his sword,
And took his horseman's cloak, and left his tent.

Can you not see the young warrior rising from his couch, dressing himself, girding on his sword, and so forth? If you can, then I am sure you will be able to make others see it as a complete picture, without breaking it up into many little pieces, just as we used to do in the first book. You see, he did not rise and stop; and then dress himself and stop; and gird his sword and stop; but one action followed the other, just as each car in a long, moving train, follows another. Each car is like a group of words, and the whole train is like the complete sentence.

CHAPTER VIII

THE CENTRAL IDEA

A little reflection must make it manifest that every sentence, or even phrase, has a central idea. When this idea is brought out in vocal expression it is by means of some form of emphasis, such as inflection or force or time, and so forth. The exact form of the manifestation need not concern us here.

Now that the pupils have been trained to look for the thought, the average sentence will take care of itself as far as the leading idea is concerned; but it must be admitted that in the sentence of more than average difficulty we find much obscure and more faulty reading, due, no doubt, to ignorance of the central idea. It is perhaps not wise in all cases to teach this step, as a step, to pupils under eleven years; but when it is taught, great care must be exercised to keep the class from forming the habit of pounding out every important word. Be this as it may, the attention of teachers should be directed to the great importance of such studies as are included in the present chapter. Furthermore, there can be no doubt that the step may be undertaken in the higher grades and in high schools to great advantage.

Perhaps there is no more severe test of the student's apprehension of the meaning than his emphasis—using that term in its broadest sense. Determining the central idea is essentially a logical process; the student weighs and determines the value of every word, and by a process of elimination finally fixes upon the exact thought to be conveyed.

Rules for emphasis so commonly given are, comparatively, of little value. If the student has the thought, his emphasis may be trusted to take care of itself; where he has not, the rules are confusing and misleading. Mr. Alfred Ayres says facetiously, but truly, "There is only one rule for emphasis—Gumption."

It is understood that emphasis has a much wider meaning than that of merely making a word stand out distinctly by means of force; it includes any manner of making a thought prominent. What we are here studying is simply that form of emphasis which is manifested by inflection or force, or both. The central idea in colloquial utterance is generally made significant through force; but by far the most suggestive method, when occasion requires, is through inflection. Of course, these two are very often combined in various proportions.

In the following illustrations, two classes of examples will be noticed. In the first, the central ideas are indicated by means of italics and capitals. It is not claimed that some other interpretation might not be possible; but that suggested is at least justifiable. The teacher will study these examples carefully with the object of determining the reason for the marking. In the second list of illustrations, the teacher himself will determine the central idea, and manifest it through his rendition.

By following this plan, the teacher's own reading will show much improvement, and he will probably learn better how to work out the problem with his classes.

It is to be regretted that we have no recognized symbols for showing shades and degrees of emphasis. The teacher will, no doubt, be able to determine for himself whether the element of force or that of inflection predominates.

> [10]There on the dais sat another king
> Wearing HIS HOBES, *his* CROWN, his SIGNET-RING.
>
> —*King Robert of Sicily.* LONGFELLOW.

Note that "his" and "robes" are of about equal importance, the former perhaps weighing a little heavier than the latter. In the next phrase the inflection on "his" is much narrower than on the first "his," while the "crown" becomes more important. Finally, the last "his" has no emphasis, while the climax of thought and emotion is reached on "signet-ring."

> And do you NOW put on your *best attire*!
> And do you NOW cull out a HOLIDAY?
> And do you now STREW FLOWERS in HIS way
> That comes in triumph over Pompey's blood?—*Julius Caesar,* Act i., Sc. 1.

Note the climax: "best attire" is weaker than "holiday," and it than the strewing of flowers. Conversely, the emphasis on "now" diminishes at each repetition. The context should be carefully digested.

> I rather tell thee what is to *be fear'd*
> Than what I *fear.*—*Julius Caesar,* Act i., Sc. 2.

An actor (?) was once heard to read the above passage, putting his emphasis on "thee" and the second "I." How illuminating!

> If 'twere *done* when 'tis *done,* then 'twere well
> It were done quickly.—*Macbeth,* Act i., Sc. 7.

The above is a fine illustration of the claim that the study of the "Central Idea" is essentially a logical process. Any other emphasis is puerile, and yet every other emphasis is heard except this. Let us look a little closer. The passage beginning with this line resolves itself into this: I am hampered with doubts and fears; I can find no rest by day or night until I kill the king or resolve to abandon the attempt. But if I can be assured that there shall be no after consequences here, I'll risk the life to come. Hence, the following paraphrase is the equivalent of the first line: If it [the murder] were out of people's minds, if it were blotted out of recollection, consigned to oblivion, when it is committed [when I do the murder], then the sooner

---

[10] The sources of most of the following excerpts are given in order that the student may refer to the context when necessary. It is urged, however, that, since the extracts are taken from literature quite available, the teacher refer to the context as often as possible.

it is done the better for my peace of mind. In a word, if it is all *over* when it is *committed,* "then 'twere well it were done quickly." Many purposely avoid repeating the emphasis on "done" because they believe the two "done's" are identical in meaning. Nothing could be farther from the truth, as shown above. The truth is, this line is one of those grim plays upon words in which Shakespeare is so prolific. It need hardly be added that when properly read the sense will be made clear by keeping in mind the paraphrase just given. The result will be that the first "done" will be read with a very decided falling inflection, and the second with a rising circumflex inflection (the mind looking forward at the end to the conclusion of the sentence). Perhaps to the sensitive student of literature there is another argument. Shakespeare's vocabulary would indeed have been very limited had he found it necessary to use three "done's" in the opening line of a most important soliloquy. To one who is alive to æsthetic effects, the very fact that Shakespeare does use them suggests a more careful analysis, and one soon discovers the cause. The play on the words makes the salient idea more striking.

And flood upon flood hurries on never ending;
and it never *will* rest nor from travail be free.

—*The Diver.* SCHILLER-LYTTON.

MACBETH. I dare do all that may become a man;
Who dares do more is none.

LADY MACBETH. What *beast* was't then
That made you *break* this enterprise to me?
When you *durst do* it, *then* you were a *man,*
And, to be *more* than what you were, you would
Be so much *more* the man. Nor *time* nor *place*
Did *then* adhere, and yet you would *make both,*
They have made *themselves,* and that their fitness *now*
Does *un*make *you.* —*Macbeth,* Act i., Sc. 7.

... it becomes
The thronèd MONARCH *better* than his CROWN.

—*The Merchant of Venice,* Act iv., Sc. 1.

Why is "better" not the most significant word?

Lives of great men all remind us
We can make *our* lives sublime. —*Psalm of Life.* LONGFELLOW.

Why not emphasize "we"?

... perchance to dream; ay, there's the rub!
For in that sleep of death *what* dreams may come. —*Hamlet,* Act iii., Sc. 1.

"What" is equivalent to what *horrible* or *awful.*

CASSIUS. I may do that I shall be sorry for.

Brutus. You *have* done that you *should* be sorry for.

—*Julius Caesar,* Act iv., Sc. 3.

It is the bright day that brings forth the adder,
And *that* craves wary walking. —*Julius Caesar,* Act ii., Sc. 1.

And since the quarrel
Will bear no color for the thing he *is,*
Fashion it thus; that what he *is,* AUGMENTED,
Would run to these and these extremities. —*Ibid.*

This reading brings out most clearly the *rationale* of Brutus's attitude. The soliloquy should be studied in its entirety.

Give me that man
That is not passion's slave, and I will wear him
In my *heart's core,* ay, in my HEART of heart,
As I do thee. —*Hamlet,* Act iii., Sc. 2.

This example is used in Fulton and Trueblood's *Practical Elocution.* The authors state:

> It has been a question with the actors which word of the phrase *heart of heart* should receive the chief emphasis, some claiming the reading should be "*heart* of heart," others "heart *of* heart," still others "heart of *heart.*" The first seems to us the preferable reading, for if the lines read, "I will wear him in my heart's core, ay, in the *center* of it," the case would be clear. Here "center" stands in the place of the first "heart."

She looked down to blush and she looked up to sigh,
With a *smile* on her *lip* and a *tear* in her *eye.*—*Lochinvar.* Scott.

There are those who argue that "lip" and "eye" should not be emphasized. This is a serious error. The phrases "on her lip" and "in her eye" are elaborative, and hence the emphasis is distributed over the entire phrase. If this is wrong, we must blame the writer for tautology. But literature has many similar examples. Here is another:

> Bring forth the best robe, and put it on him: and put a *ring* on his *hand,* and *shoes* on his *feet.*—*Luke* xv. 22.

There is a rule telling us to emphasize words in antithesis. In many cases we do so; but these cases would emphasize themselves, so to speak. There are, however, many cases of rhetorical antithesis where it interferes with the sense to emphasize both members of the antithesis, and here the rule steps in to lead astray the pupil. To illustrate: "I am going to town to-morrow, but *you* need not go until the day *after.*"

Mr. A. Melville Bell has put this very clearly. In his *Essays and Postscripts on Elocution,* he says:

> The emphasis of contrast falls necessarily on the second of a contrasted pair of words, but not necessarily on the first. The first word is emphatic or otherwise, according as it is new, or implied in preceding thoughts; but it is not emphatic in virtue of subsequent contrast. A purposed anticipation may give emphasis to the first word, but such anticipatory emphasis should not be made habitual.

> If the bright blood that fills my veins, transmitted free from godlike ancestry, were like the slimy ooze which stagnates in your arteries, I had remained at home.

Is it not clear that the anticipatory emphasis on "my" is not only unnecessary, but would, if given, weaken the force of the succeeding phrase?

> I have nothing more to say, but the honorable *gentleman* will no doubt speak for hours.

> What could I do *less*; what could *he* do *more*?

MESSALA. It is but change, Titinius; for Octavius
Is overthrown by noble Brutus' power,
As Cassius' legions are by Antony.

TITINIUS. These tidings will well comfort Cassius.

MESSALA. Is not that he that lies upon the ground?

TITINIUS. He lies not like the living. Oh my heart!

MESSALA. Is not that he?

TITINIUS. No, this was he, Messala,
But Cassius is no more,—O setting sun!
As in thy red rays thou dost sink to-night,
So in his red blood Cassius' day is set;
The sun of Rome is set! Our day is gone;
Clouds, dews, and dangers come; our deeds are done!
Mistrust of my success hath done this deed.

—*Julius Caesar*, Act v., Sc. 3.

It is evident that the speakers have been conversing about the two parts of the battle, and Titinius has told his friend that Cassius has been overthrown. To this Messala replies, comfortingly, Affairs are balanced, then, etc. The entire extract needs and will amply repay most critical study. It would be hard to find one containing more difficulties.

BASSANIO. This is no answer, thou unfeeling man,
To excuse the current of thy cruelty.

SHYLOCK. I am not bound to please thee with my answer.

BASSANIO. Do all men kill the things they do not love?

SHYLOCK. Hates any man the thing he would not kill?

BASSANIO. Every offense is not a hate at first.

SHYLOCK. What! wouldst thou have a serpent sting thee twice?

—*Merchant of Venice,* Act iv., Sc. 1.

DUNCAN. Go, pronounce his present[11] death,
And with his former title greet Macbeth.

ROSS. I'll see it done.

DUNCAN. What he hath lost, noble Macbeth hath won.

—*Macbeth,* Act i., Sc. 2.

Thou shalt get kings, though thou be none. —*Macbeth,* Act i., Sc. 3.

MACBETH. The thane of Cawdor lives: why do you dress me
In borrow'd robes?

ANGUS. Who was the thane, lives yet. —*Ibid.*

LIGARIUS. What's to do?

BRUTUS. A piece of work that will make sick men whole.

LIGARIUS. But are not some whole that we must make sick?

—*Julius Caesar,* Act ii., Sc. 1.

When beggars die, there are no comets seen;
The heavens themselves blaze forth the death of princes.

—*Julius Caesar,* Act ii., Sc. 2.

BRUTUS. He hath the falling sickness.

CASSIUS. No, Caesar hath it not; but you and I,
And honest Casca, we have the falling sickness.

—*Julius Caesar,* Act i., Sc. 2.

Romans now
Have thews and limbs like to their ancestors,
But, woe the while! our fathers' minds are dead,
And we are govern'd with our mothers' spirits.

—*Julius Caesar,* Act i., Sc. 3.

That you do love me, I am nothing jealous;
What you would work me to, I have some aim;
How I have thought of this, and of these times,
I shall recount hereafter; for this present,

[11] I. e., instant.

I would not, so with love I might entreat you,
Be any further mov'd. What you have said,
I will consider; what you have to say,
I will with patience hear, and find a time
Both meet to hear, and answer such high things.

—*Julius Caesar*, Act i., Sc. 2.

Cowards die many times before their deaths;
The valiant never taste of death but once.

—*Julius Caesar*, Act ii., Sc 2.

FLAVIUS. Thou art a cobbler, art thou?

CITIZEN. Truly, sir, all that I live by is with the awl.

—*Julius Caesar*, Act i., Sc. 1.

SIR PETER. Very well, ma'am, very well! So a husband is to have no influence—no authority!

LADY TEAZLE. Authority? No, to be sure! If you wanted authority over me, you should have adopted me, and not married me; I am sure you were old enough!—*The School for Scandal.* SHERIDAN.

We live in deeds, not years; in thought, not breath;
In feelings, not in figures on a dial;
We should count time by heart-throbs. He most lives,
Who thinks most, feels the noblest, acts the best. —*Festus.* BAILEY.

I must be cruel, only to be kind;
Thus bad begins, and worse remains behind.

Our new heraldry is—hands, not hearts.

He jests at scars that never felt a wound.

Friendship was in their looks, but in their hearts there was hatred.

Oh! the blood more stirs
To rouse a lion than to start a hare.

You will find it less easy to uproot faults than choke them by gaining virtues.

A maiden's wrath has two eyes—one blind, the other keener than a falcon's.

The storm that rends the oak uproots the flower.

But break, my heart, for I must hold my tongue.

Suggestions for a class lesson follow:

Let us look at the following sentence: "I heard William say it." Can you read that sentence now? I should say you could not, and my reason is, that you are not quite sure of its meaning. Let us see what that meaning is.

One person might mean that *he* had heard William say it, but that *you* had not. How would you read the sentence then? Another person might mean, "I am *sure* William said it, for I was there to hear him." How would you express that? Again, a third person might mean that he was sure *George* or *John* had not said it, but *William*. How would you read that?

We learn from this another reason why we must use great care in preparing our reading lesson. You see, if we do not, we shall not stop to consider just what the sentence means, and then in reading we shall not express the author's meaning. Let us try a few more examples. In each make up your mind just what you want to say, and then say it as if you meant it.

Example 1.—"I like geography better than I do history." Now, if you have been talking to a friend about the studies you like best, and he has just said, "I like geography as well as I do history," how would you read the above example? Of course, you see that the main idea in your mind would be to tell him that you liked geography not only as well as, but better than, history. Well then, now you may read the example.

Example 2.—"I should rather be a lawyer than a doctor." Suppose in this case a friend has said, "My father wants me to be a doctor." How would you then read the sentence?

Example 3.—"Queen Victoria has reigned longer than any other monarch who ever sat upon the English throne." Suppose you are telling this to your classmates, and that you have not been talking about Queen Victoria before, but you want only to give them a piece of information.

Let us remember, then, that every sentence has a principal, or, as we sometimes say, a central idea. We need be extremely careful to get that central idea, and if we have been, we notice that certain words will stand out very prominently in our reading. This is true because reading is just like speaking. If some one asks you where you are going, and you are going to school, what do you think of? You don't think of each word of your answer; you think only one idea—school. So you say, "I am going to school," and you make the word "school" very prominent, or important. "School" is the central idea.

Until our next step I want you to study every sentence of every reading lesson, bearing in mind this very important fact regarding the central idea. Every sentence has such a central idea, and until you have found it you cannot read the sentence.

Very few directions are necessary except to warn the teacher against speaking about the various *kinds* of emphasis. No matter what the kind, the thought will find its natural channel if the conditions be right. It is true, that sometimes a word is made prominent by inflection (rising, falling, circumflex), sometimes by slower time, sometimes by force alone. But let us remember, these various forms are the results of various forms of thinking. If those are right, correct reading will follow.

It is further worth noting that the best authorities use "emphasis" as signifying any means of making the thought stand out. Hence, the teacher is urged not to use the term "emphasis" at all. If a pupil err, tell him he has not given you the central, or leading, idea.

CHAPTER IX

SUBORDINATION

The analysis for determining the central idea must have led the student to discern subordinate ideas. As a rule, the expression of these will not be difficult, but there are certain phases of subordination that require special study. We have noted that in our desire to impress the leading thought upon another we have used significant inflection, or force or time. It must follow then that the relatively unimportant words will be read in a manner less striking. In the following speech of Portia, observe how naturally we slight the relatively unimportant ideas:

> If to do were as easy as to know what were good to do, chapels had been churches, and poor men's cottages princes' palaces. It is a good divine that follows his own instructions: I can easier teach twenty what were good to be done, than to be one of the twenty to follow mine own teaching.

There will be degrees of subordination, of course: the above marking is meant only to draw attention to the purely instinctive process as a result of which the vocal modulations manifest the relative degrees of thought value.

It is something of an art to touch lightly upon the unimportant and yet not to slur it. We are not advocating that the teacher should at any length dwell upon this, though it is well for him to recognize this feature of expression. There are two reasons for this: first, in the earlier stages of reading there is a tendency to overemphasize; second, in the later stages, the unimportant words are hurried, with the result that the reading becomes indistinct.

As there are slighted words in every phrase, so there are slighted phrases and clauses in many sentences. We are all acquainted with the time-honored advice concerning the manner in which one should read words in parentheses: "Lower the voice and read faster." It is not to be denied that the average parenthetical thought is expressed in that way, but there are many examples in which the injunction will not apply. Whether the key will be raised or lowered, and whether the time will be accelerated or retarded, will depend entirely upon the mental attitude of the reader. To illustrate: "The battle of Waterloo,—the most important battle of the nineteenth century,—ended the career of Napoleon." If one has been speaking of the great importance of this battle, and takes for granted that his audience recognizes this importance, he will probably lower the key in the subordinate sentence, and read it faster; but otherwise he would read it more slowly (as a result of the importance of the thought), even if he did not raise the key. This leads us to the conclusion that a phrase or clause may be grammatically subordinate and yet of the greatest importance. The degree of importance determines how it shall be read, and not arbitrary rules. The main result to be obtained in this step is the training of the student's mind in apprehending thought-modulation; to enable him to weigh the thought in order that he may perceive more clearly the relative values of the various phrases. This perception leads in expression to that most desirable phase of utterance—variety.

A few simple illustrations are added as examples of what may be used for class drill. The more difficult illustrations may be used for advanced classes, and for practice by the teacher himself:

> And children, coming home from school,
> Look in at the open door;
>
> And, with his hard, rough hand, he wipes
> A tear out of his eyes.

> However, as the sun baked these two very dry and hard, I lifted them very gently, and set them down again in two great wicker baskets, which I had made on purpose for them, that they might not break; and, as between the pot and the basket there was a little room to spare, I stuffed it full of the rice and barley straw; and these two pots, being to stand always dry, I thought would hold my dry corn, and perhaps the meal, when the corn was bruised.
>
> Though I succeeded so poorly in my design for large pots, yet I made several smaller things with better success, such as little round pots, flat dishes, pitchers, and pipkins, and anything my hand turned to; and the heat of the sun baked them very hard.

> Art is long, and Time is fleeting,
> And our hearts, though stout and brave,
> Still, like muffled drums, are beating
> Funeral marches to the grave.

> Then it was that Jo, living in the darkened room, with that suffering little sister always before her eyes, and that pathetic voice sounding in her ears, learned to see the beauty and sweetness of Beth's nature, to feel how deep and tender a place she filled in all hearts, and to acknowledge the worth of Beth's unselfish ambition to live for others, and make home happy by the exercise of those simple virtues which all may possess, and which all should love and value more than talent, wealth, or beauty.[12]

> It was past two o'clock when Jo, who stood at the window

[12] A good example to illustrate succession of ideas.

thinking how dreary the world looked in its winding-sheet of snow, heard a movement by the bed, and, turning quickly, saw Meg kneeling before their mother's easy-chair, with her face hidden.

In what school did the worthies of our land—the Washingtons, Henrys, Franklins, Rutledges—learn those principles of civil liberty?

Next to the worship of the Father of us all—the deepest and grandest of human emotions—is the love of the land that gave us birth.

I am not—I need scarcely say it—the panegyrist of England.

I have returned,—not, as the right honorable member has said, to raise a storm,—I have returned to discharge an honorable debt of gratitude to my country.

May that God (I do not take his name in vain), may that God forbid it.

One day—shall I forget it ever?—*ye* were present—I had fought long and well.

I was about to slay him, when a few hurried words—rather a welcome to death than a plea for life—told me he was a Thracian.

One raw morning in spring—it will be eighty years the 19th of this month—Hancock and Adams were both at Lexington.

And are we to speak and act like men who have sustained no wrong? We! Six millions of—what shall I say?—citizens?

Among the exploits of marvelous and almost legendary valor performed by that great English chieftain—who has been laid aside uncoroneted, and almost unhonored because he would promote and distinguish the men of work in preference to the men of idleness—among his achievements not the least wondrous was the subjugation of the robber tribes of the Cutchee Hills in the north of Scinde.

But if there is one man here—I am speaking not of shapes and forms, but of feelings—if there is one here that feels as men were wont to feel, he will draw the sword.

And you—you, who are eight millions strong—you, who

boast at every meeting that this island is the finest which the sun looks down upon—you, who have no threatening sea to stem, no avalanche to dread—you, who say that you could shield along your coast a thousand sail, and be the princes of a mighty commerce—you, who by the magic of an honest hand, beneath each summer sky, might cull a plenteous harvest from your soil, and with the sickle strike away the scythe of death—you, who have no vulgar history to read—you, who can trace, from field to field, the evidences of civilization older than the Conquest—the relics of a religion far more ancient than the Gospel—you, who have thus been blessed, thus been gifted, thus been prompted to what is wise and generous and great—you will make no effort—you will perish by the thousand, and the finest island that the sun looks down upon, amid the jeers and hooting of the world, will blacken into a plague spot, a wilderness, a sepulcher.

In his early manhood, at the bidding of conscience, against the advice of his dearest friends, in opposition to stern paternal commands, against every dictate of worldly wisdom and human prudence, in spite of all the dazzling temptations of ambition so alluring to the heart of a young man, he turned away from the broad fair highway to wealth, position, and distinction, that the hands of a king opened before him, and, casting his lot with the sect weakest and most unpopular in England, through paths that were tangled with trouble, and lined with pitiless thorns of persecution, he walked into honor and fame, and the reverence of the world, such as royalty could not promise and could not give him.

No one venerates the Peerage more than I do; but, my Lords, I must say that the Peerage solicited *me*,—not I the Peerage. Nay, more,—I can say, and *will* say, that, as a Peer of Parliament, as Speaker of this right honorable House, as keeper of the great seal, as guardian of his Majesty's conscience, as Lord High Chancellor of England,—nay, even in that character alone in which the noble Duke would think it an affront to be considered, but which character none can deny me, as a MAN,—I am at this moment as respectable—I beg leave to add—I am as much respected,—as the proudest Peer I now look down upon.

Fresh as the flower, whose modest worth
He sang, his genius "glinted" forth,
Rose like a star that touching earth,
For so it seems,
Doth glorify its humble birth
With matchless beams.

The piercing eye, the thoughtful brow,
The struggling heart, where be they now?
Full soon the aspirant of the plow,
The prompt, the brave,
Slept, with the obscurest, in the low
And silent grave.

True friends though diversely inclined;
But heart with heart and mind with mind,
Where the main fibers are entwined,
Through Nature's skill,
May even by contraries be joined
More closely still.

Sighing I turned away; but ere
Night fell, I heard, or seemed to hear,
Music that sorrow comes not near,
A ritual hymn,
Chanted in love that casts out fear
By Seraphim.

Too frail to keep the lofty vow
That must have followed when his brow
Was wreathed—"The Vision" tells us how—
With holly spray,
He faltered, drifted to and fro,
And passed away.

The five preceding stanzas are from Wordsworth's poem, *At the Grave of Burns.*

In the illustrations that follow, the student will note three distinct degrees of importance of thought; in other words, there is the main idea, its modifier, and the modifier of the modifier. The vocal expression of these illustrations will be affected just to the extent that the student appreciates the value of the different phrases.

At Atri in Abruzzo, a small town
Of ancient Roman date, but scant renown,
One of those little places that have run
Half up the hill, beneath a blazing sun,
And then sat down to rest, as if to say,
"I climb no farther upward, come what may,"
The Re Giovanni, now unknown to fame,
So many monarchs since have borne the name,
Had a great bell hung in the market-place.

It is my purpose, therefore, believing that there are certain points of superiority in modern artists, and especially in one or two of their number, which have not yet been fully understood,

> except by those who are scarcely in a position admitting the declaration of their conviction, to institute a close comparison between the great works of ancient and modern landscape art.

Many students who find no difficulty in silently reading such extracts as the above, will often fail in their vocal expression because of the fact that the latter is more deliberate; and consequently they may lose the trend of the main thought in rendering the explanatory and parenthetical portions. To overcome this difficulty, they are advised to read the sentence, with the omission of all but the most essential idea; then let them add one idea after another to the main idea, until the sentence is read correctly in its entirety. In the last example quoted, the main idea is, "It is my purpose ... to institute a close comparison between the great works of ancient and modern landscape art." Read this three or four times, until the idea is clearly apprehended. Now read the sentence, omitting "and especially in one or two of their number," until this larger thought is grasped; after which let the sentence be read as a whole.

Following the usual plan, a class lesson is added:

> "When I was in Paris (which is in France), I saw a great many pretty things."
>
> Read this sentence carefully and you will find something we have not had before: a group of words in parenthesis.
>
> You notice, we should have very good sense without this group. Read it: "When I was in Paris I saw a great many pretty things."
>
> So you see, the words "which is in France" are not so important as the rest of the sentence. You might say they were thrown in after you had thought of the other idea.
>
> Now, I want you to read the sentence aloud, leaving out the group, "which is in France." After you have done this five or six times, then read the whole sentence, keeping in mind that the words in parenthesis are not very important, but just thrown in to let people know that you mean Paris in France, and not some other Paris.
>
> The groups that are thrown in are not always put in parenthesis. But that does not make any difference in the reading. Here are a few examples. I want you to practice on them just as you did on the first example in this lesson.
>
> 1. "The king of England, who was a very brave man, won several victories over the French."
>
> 2. "The largest school in our city, which is Chicago, has more than five hundred children in it."
>
> 3. "During the Christmas vacation, which lasts ten days, I went to see my grandmother."

> 4. "Frank did all his mother asked him to do; but William, because he was careless and disobedient, gave his mother and teacher a great deal of trouble."
>
> This last example makes very clear what we have been studying in this lesson. You see plainly that the words, "because he was careless and disobedient," are put in simply to explain why William gave a great deal of trouble.
>
> You must be very careful about this kind of sentence, because there are a great many of them on every page, and you will be sure to miss them if you are careless.

The teacher should ask the pupils to bring in other examples, and have them read in the class. He should also select examples from the reading book.

CHAPTER X

VALUES

This feature of expression is one of the most vital. It has to do with the value of each phrase of the sentence and each phase of the whole selection. With every change of thought and emotion comes another form of expression, and these different forms we may call Values. We apply the term Transition to the act of passing from one shade of thought or feeling to another. All transitions are not necessarily emotional, and yet those most significant are certainly of this character. Let us first consider a few examples not strongly marked with emotion:

> *"Three quarters round your partners swing!"*
> *"Across the set!"* The rafters ring,
> The girls and boys have taken wing,
> And have brought their roses out!
> 'Tis *"Forward six!"* with rustic grace,
> Ah, rarer far than—*"Swing to place!"*
> Than golden clouds of old point lace,
> They bring the dance about.

In the foregoing we have a picture of the country dance. We hear the figures called out by the old fiddler, and see the ever-varying changes of *The Money Musk*. Study the lines so as to be able to bring out the calls clearly, noting the two distinct calls at the opening, and the abrupt break in the sixth line.

The next extract presents a wife confiding to a friend the story of her courtship. Her husband is a true knight, and would perhaps resent it to have even his bravery form the subject of conversation. The story has reached its conclusion when the speaker says:

> Our elder boy has got the clear
> Great brow; tho' when his brother's black
> Full eyes show scorn, it—

and she is probably about to add some such statement as, "It behooves one to look out," when suddenly the husband appears on the scene. With a woman's ready wit, she breaks off the sentence abruptly, saying:

> Gismond here?
> And have you brought my tercel back?
> I was just telling Adela
> How many birds it struck since May.

We might put into words what passes through her mind. She is about to add something further concerning the eyes of her boy, when she hears the sound of feet along the walk. Expecting her husband, the concluding words of her sentence pass from her mind as she turns to see the visitor. It is Gismond. He must not know that she has been speaking of him. The tercel in his hand gives her the opportunity of opening the conversation, which she is quick to do, adroitly pretending that it was of that very tercel she and her friend had been conversing before his arrival.

One more illustration of this kind will suffice. A tender, loving woman is talking to her husband. He is a learned poet, and perhaps just a trifle of a pedant. He is most minute and exact in all he does, ever losing sight of the spirit in the letter. The wife is the true poet, caring nothing for the archæology and philology and the geography, but quick to perceive the inner meaning of the poetic. He has told her a story in the past, and she is going now to tell it back to him with a new moral.

Here is the first stanza:

What a pretty tale you told me
Once upon a time
—Said you found me somewhere (scold me!)
Was it prose or was it rhyme,
Greek or Latin?

When the woman comes to "somewhere," she finds she has forgotten the source of the original story. That means so much to him! It is so important! With a quizzical look, she pretends to rack her brains for the missing information, knowing all the time she will not find it, and knowing equally well that it makes no difference in the story. Then, with a coy expression and a look of mock humility on her face, she lets fall her eyes, meekly acknowledging her awful guilt, and stands prepared to accept her just punishment, saying, Scold me! I deserve it. I have sinned; my punishment is just.

Many students find it no easy task to make these transitions naturally. Some do not make them at all, but run the two phases of thought or emotion together. Others anticipate the coming idea, and hurry the last two or three words before the break. The proper training is to *write or think out the incomplete sentence,* then let it more or less quickly vanish from the mind as the new conception grows clearer, without betraying the fact that one is conscious of a coming interruption. For instance, in the second example, one must read up to and through "it" without the slightest suggestion of the coming of Gismond, and even think the conclusion of the sentence. Then hear or suddenly see Gismond just as the word "it" falls from the lips, and dismissing from the mind the former idea, conclude with the joyous, wifely welcome and question.

It might be proper to remark here that the same principle applies to the reading of dialogue. Except in rare cases the reader should not in any way anticipate the speech of one character while rendering the words of another.

For those who do not intend to become readers, but who would be preachers or lawyers, the practice here recommended will prove of great value. Too many speakers, in their excitement on the one hand and in their spiritlessness on the other, glide along line after line in one monotonous drift. A study of these exercises will teach the necessity of transitions, and train in the control of the mental action in this regard,—a control antecedent to that most important requisite, variety. After almost every paragraph or stanza there is more or less of change in the thought, and the apprehension of this change will be sufficient to modulate the vocal expression.

Even where there is no abrupt change in the flow of ideas, there is often a gradual transition from one emotion to another, and these transitions may occur several times within one paragraph. Take the following excerpt from Webster's reply to Hayne. It is one paragraph; but it is divided into four smaller paragraphs, each of which is a marked "phase" of the thinking. Practice in the analysis of selections to determine these phases is the best and only rational training in transitions. But its value does not stop here; for the student not only makes transitions, but is led, through careful analysis, to discern shades of meaning and emotion he might otherwise overlook:

> Sir, the gentleman inquires why he was made the object of a reply. Why was he singled out? If an attack has been made on the East he, he assures us, did not begin it; it was made by the gentleman from Missouri.
>
> Sir, I answered the gentleman's speech because I happened to hear it, and because I chose to answer that speech which, if unanswered, I thought most likely to produce injurious impressions.
>
> I did not stop to inquire who was the original drawer of the bill. I found a responsible endorser before me, and it was my purpose to hold him liable, and to bring him to his just responsibility without delay.
>
> But, sir, this interrogatory of the honorable member was only introductory to another. He proceeds to ask whether I had turned upon him in this debate from the consciousness that I should find an overmatch if I ventured on a contest with his friend from Missouri.

Transitions in emotion do not differ in principle from those we have been considering. The student must pursue the same method with these as with the others, expressing the first emotion until he comes to the break, making then an elliptical paraphrase, and then presenting the new emotion. An excellent model is the following speech of King Lear.

The aged monarch has, in a fit of rage, cast adrift his youngest child, and his eldest has turned him from her home. He turns in despair to his remaining daughter, assured that he will here receive a filial welcome. To his surprise, she refuses to meet him; says she is sick and travel-weary; and his amazed feeling finds vent in an uncontrolled explosion of passion:

> LEAR. Vengeance! plague! death! confusion!—
> Fiery? what quality? Why, Gloucester, Gloucester,

I'd speak with the Duke of Cornwall and his wife.

GLOUCESTER. Well, my good lord, I have inform'd them so.

LEAR. Inform'd them! Dost thou understand me, man?

GLOUCESTER. Ay, my good lord.

LEAR. The King would speak with Cornwall; the dear father
Would with his daughter speak; commands her service:
Are they inform'd of this?—My breath and blood!
Fiery? the fiery Duke? Tell the hot Duke that—
No, but not yet: may be he is not well:—

—*King Lear*, Act ii., Sc. 4.

and he then proceeds to find excuses for her action, and that of her husband, the Duke of Cornwall. There is hardly a more pathetic incident in a most pathetic play than this, in which the old man, past his eightieth year, after holding undisputed sway through his long reign, is at last compelled to temporize. He is about to send a message to the Duke, the character of which is easily judged from his previous language. If that message is sent, Lear will be alone in the world. But suddenly his fearful position flashes upon him. The threat dies upon his lips, gradually blending into apology and conciliation.

EXAMPLES OF EMOTIONAL TRANSITIONS.

If you have tears, prepare to shed them now.
You all do know this mantle: I remember
The first time ever Caesar put it on;
'Twas on a summer's evening, in his tent,
That day he overcame the Nervii:
Look, in this place ran Cassius' dagger through.

—*Julius Caesar*, Act iii., Sc 2.

He spoke; but Rustum gazed, and gazed, and stood
Speechless; and then he utter'd one sharp cry:
"O boy—thy father!"—and his voice choked there.
And then a dark cloud pass'd before his eyes,
And his head swam, and he sank down to earth.

—*Sohrab and Rustum.* M. ARNOLD.

"Ferood, and ye, Persians and Tartars, hear!
Let there be truce between the hosts to-day.
But choose a champion from the Persian lords
To fight our champion Sohrab, man to man."
As in the country, on a morn in June,
When the dew glistens on the pearlèd ears,
A shiver runs through the deep corn for joy—
So, when they heard what Peran-Wisa said,
A thrill through all the Tartar squadrons ran

Of pride and hope for Sohrab, whom they loved.
But as a troop of peddlers from Cabool,
Cross underneath the Indian Caucasus,
The vast sky-neighboring mountain of milk snow;
Crossing so high, that, as they mount, they pass
Long flocks of traveling birds dead on the snow,
Choked by the air, and scarce can they themselves
Slake their parch'd throats with sugar'd mulberries—
In single file they move and stop their breath,
For fear they should dislodge the o'erhanging snows—
So the pale Persians held their breath with fear.

—*Sohrab and Rustum.* M. ARNOLD.

Note how, after the words, "whom they loved," the atmosphere changes from that of joy to that of dread and scorn—scorn at the cowardice of the Persians, and the dread that the speaker would sympathetically feel as he recounted the deed.

This too thou know'st, that while I still bear on
The conquering Tartar ensigns through the world,
And beat the Persians back on every field,
I seek one man, one man, and one alone—
Rustum, my father; who I hoped should greet,
Should one day greet, upon some well-fought field,
His not unworthy, not inglorious son.
So I long hoped, but him I never find.
Come then, hear now, and grant me what I ask.
Let the two armies rest to-day; but I
Will challenge forth the bravest Persian lords
To meet me man to man; if I prevail,
Rustum will surely hear it; if I fall—
Old man, the dead need no one, claim no kin.
Dim is the rumor of a common fight,
Where host meets host, and many names are sunk;
But of a single combat fame speaks clear.

—*Sohrab and Rustum.* M. ARNOLD.

STUDIES IN "PHASES."

This extract from Tennyson's *Charge of the Heavy Brigade* contains five distinct phases, or strata, ending respectively with the words, "fight," "close," "then," "thousands," and "Brigade."

The trumpet, the gallop, the charge, and the might of the fight!
Thousands of horsemen had gather'd there on the height,
With a wing push'd out to the left and a wing to the right,
And who shall escape if they close? but he dash'd up alone
Thro' the great gray slope of men,

Sway'd his saber, and held his own
Like an Englishman, there and then;
All in a moment follow'd with force
Three that were next in their fiery course,
Wedged themselves in between horse and horse,
Fought for their lives in the narrow gap they had made—
Four amid thousands! and up the hill, up the hill,
Gallopt the gallant three hundred, the Heavy Brigade.

As when a boar
Or lion mid the hounds and huntsmen stands,
Fearfully strong, and fierce of eye, and they
In square array assault him, and their hands
Fling many a javelin;—yet his noble heart
Fears not, nor does he fly, although at last
His courage cause his death; and oft he turns,
And tries their ranks; and where he makes a rush
The rank gives way;—so Hector moved and turned
Among the crowd, and bade his followers cross
The trench. —*The Iliad.*

Hector, thou almost ever chidest me
In council, even when I judge aright.
I know it ill becomes the citizen
To speak against the way that pleases thee,
In war or council,—he should rather seek
To strengthen thy authority; yet now
I will declare what seems to me the best:
Let us not combat with the Greeks, to take
Their fleet; for this, I think, will be the end,—
If now the omen we have seen be meant
For us of Troy who seek to cross the trench;—
This eagle, flying high upon the left,
Between the hosts, that in his talons bore
A monstrous serpent, bleeding, yet alive,
Hath dropped it mid our host before he came
To his dear nest, nor brought it to his brood;—
So we, although by force we break the gates
And rampart, and although the Greeks fall back,
Shall not as happily retrace our way;
For many a Trojan shall we leave behind,
Slain by the weapons of the Greeks, who stand
And fight to save their fleet. Thus will the seer,
Skilled in the lore of prodigies, explain
The portent, and the people will obey. —*The Iliad.*

And thus King Priam supplicating spake:—
"Think of thy father, an old man like me,
Godlike Achilles! On the dreary verge
Of closing life he stands, and even now
Haply is fiercely pressed by those who dwell
Around him, and has none to shield his age
From war and its disasters. Yet his heart
Rejoices when he hears that thou dost live,
And every day he hopes that his dear son
Will come again from Troy. My lot is hard,
For I was father of the bravest sons
In all wide Troy, and none are left me now.
Fifty were with me when the men of Greece
Arrived upon our coast; nineteen of these
Owned the same mother, and the rest were born
Within my palaces. Remorseless Mars
Already had laid lifeless most of these,
And Hector, whom I cherished most, whose arm
Defended both our city and ourselves,
Him didst thou lately slay while combating
For his dear country. For his sake I come
To the Greek fleet, and to redeem his corse
I bring uncounted ransom. O revere
The gods, Achilles, and be merciful,
Calling to mind thy father! happier he
Than I; for I have borne what no man else
That dwells on earth could bear,—have laid my lips
Upon the hand of him who slew my son."
He spake: Achilles sorrowfully thought
Of his own father. By the hand he took
The suppliant, and with gentle force removed
The old man from him. Both in memory
Of those they loved were weeping. The old king,
With many tears, and rolling in the dust
Before Achilles, mourned his gallant son.
Achilles sorrowed for his father's sake,
And then bewailed Patroclus, and the sound
Of lamentation filled the tent. At last
Achilles, when he felt his heart relieved
By tears, and that strong grief had spent its force,
Sprang from his seat; then lifting by the hand
The aged man, and pitying his white head
And his white chin, he spake these wingèd words: —*The Iliad.*

It is especially in the reading of description that the study of values will prove most beneficial. There are very few readers who can make description interesting, and their failure is in most cases due to the monotony arising from their inability to perceive and make palpable the different values. The reply of Achilles to Priam becomes most interesting reading when values are carefully observed.

Great have thy sufferings been, unhappy king!
How couldst thou venture to approach alone
The Grecian fleet, and show thyself to him
Who slew so many of thy valiant sons?
An iron heart is thine. But seat thyself,
And let us, though afflicted grievously,
Allow our woes to sleep awhile, for grief
Indulged can bring no good. The gods ordain
The lot of man to suffer, while themselves
Are free from care. Beside Jove's threshold stand
Two casks of gifts for man. One cask contains
The evil, one the good, and he to whom
The Thunderer gives them mingled sometimes falls
Into misfortune, and is sometimes crowned
With blessings. But the man to whom he gives
The evil only stands a mark exposed
To wrong, and, chased by grim calamity,
Wanders the teeming earth, alike unloved
By gods and man. So did the gods bestow
Munificent gifts on Peleus from his birth,
For eminent was he among mankind
For wealth and plenty; o'er the Myrmidons
He ruled, and, though a mortal, he was given
A goddess for a wife. Yet did the gods
Add evil to the good, for not to him
Was born a family of kingly sons
Within his house, successors to reign.
One short-lived son is his, nor am I there
To cherish him in his old age; but here
Do I remain, far from my native land,
In Troy, and causing grief to thee and thine.
Of thee, too, aged king, they speak, as one
Whose wealth was large in former days, when all
That Lesbos, seat of Macar, owns was thine.
And all in Phrygia and the shores that bound
The Hellespont; men said thou didst excel
All others in thy riches and thy sons.
But since the gods have brought this strife on thee
War and perpetual slaughter of brave men
Are round thy city. Yet be firm of heart,
Nor grieve forever. Sorrow for thy son
Will profit nought; it cannot bring the dead
To life again, and while thou dost afflict
Thyself for him fresh woes may fall on thee.

—*The Iliad.*

The subject may be presented to the class somewhat in the manner of the following lesson:

> Suppose you were very busy studying your reading lesson, and you were just about to read aloud a sentence like this:
>
> There's a good time coming, boys,
> A good time coming!
>
> But when you came to the second "good," let us suppose somebody knocks at the door and you say, "Come in." What has happened in your reading? You have broken off one thought suddenly and another has come in its place. Let us see how such a sentence would look:
>
> There's a good time coming, boys,
> A good—Come in.
>
> Now, what is the difference between this sentence and those we studied in our last lesson? It is this: In the former lesson the new thought that was thrown in was really a part of the principal thought; but in this the new thought has no connection with the principal idea. In the previous lesson the group that was thrown in was a kind of explanation; in this lesson, the first picture is driven entirely out of mind by the second.
>
> Breaks in the thought are of many kinds, and it is very necessary that you should be on the look-out for them. Here is an example of a kind you will find quite often:
>
> "Halt!" The dust-brown ranks stood fast.
> "Fire!" out blazed the rifle-blast.
>
> The words "halt" and "fire" are commands given by the general; the sentence that follows each of these words tells us what happened after the commands were given.
>
> Another kind of break is found in those selections in which there are two or more persons speaking. As in this: "Frank said, 'Will you go to school with me?' and his brother said, 'No, I don't like it.' 'Not like school?' replied Frank, who was very much surprised, 'I would rather go there than anywhere I know.'" You can see plainly that there is a break when the reader changes from one person to another.
>
> The last kind of break we shall speak about in this lesson is that which occurs between the stanzas of a poem or between the paragraphs of a prose selection. I need not give any examples here, for you will find them on every page of your reader. All I need do is tell you that the new paragraph or the new stanza generally begins with a new thought. So you must be sure to get that new thought, and hold it well in mind, before you try to express it.

> In closing this lesson I want to show you that you may learn how to read such examples as we have had, if you will but be careful. You must be sure to get each new picture before you utter a word. Take the first example. You have read the first line, "There's a good time coming, boys," and you are just about to repeat it. Now think what you are going to say, and just as you come to the word "good," imagine you hear a knocking, and say, "Come in." If you will only think what the words mean and see the picture, there will be no trouble about reading the example well.

A few examples for class use are appended. The teacher may easily invent suitable contexts:

> My servant-boy, with a reserve gun, was ten or twelve yards off—a long way at such a moment.
>
> It would make the reader pity me to learn that, after having labored hard, I could not make above two large earthen, ugly things (I can not call them jars) in about two months' labor.
>
> The tear will start, and let it flow;
> Thou "poor Inhabitant below,"
> At this dread moment,—even so—
> Might we together
> Have sate and talked where gowans blow,
> Or on wild heather.

In the above, Wordsworth laments that the death of Burns should have deprived them of the joy of communion. Note the force of the semicolon after "flow," and the pathos of "even so." The following lines are from the same poem:

> Too frail to keep the lofty vow
> That must have followed when his brow
> Was wreathed—"The Vision" tells us how—
> With holly spray,
> He faltered, drifted to and fro,
> And passed away.
>
> Now, when the Hare came to the top of the field, the Hedgehog cried out, "Hallo! here I am. Where have you been all this while?" But the Hare was out of his wits, and cried out, "Once more—turn about, and away!" "By all means," answered the Hedgehog; "for my part, as often as you please."
>
> Young Harry was a lusty drover—
> And who so stout of limb as he?
> His cheeks were red as ruddy clover;
> His voice was like the voice of three.
> Old Goody Blake was old and poor;
> Ill-fed she was, and thinly clad;
> And any man who passed her door

Might see how poor a hut she had.

There is a change of feeling in almost every stanza of the following poem. If the pupils can grasp its meaning it will be an excellent exercise in training them to perceive the relative values. It may be well to delay the study of this selection until after the principle of the next two chapters has been thoroughly grasped and put into practice:

On Linden, when the sun was low,
All bloodless lay th' untrodden snow,
And dark as winter was the flow
Of Iser, rolling rapidly.

But Linden saw another sight,
When the drum beat at dead of night,
Commanding fires of death to light
The darkness of her scenery.

By torch and trumpet fast arrayed,
Each horseman drew his battle-blade,
And furious every charger neighed,
To join the dreadful revelry.

Then shook the hills, with thunder riven;
Then rushed the steed, to battle driven;
And, louder than the bolts of heaven,
Far flashed the red artillery.

But redder yet that light shall glow
On Linden's hills of stainèd snow,
And bloodier yet the torrent flow
Of Iser, rolling rapidly.

'Tis morn, but scarce yon lurid sun
Can pierce the war-clouds, rolling dun,
Where furious Frank and fiery Hun
Shout in their sulph'rous canopy.

The combat deepens. On, ye brave,
Who rush to glory or the grave!
Wave, Munich! all thy banners wave,
And charge with all thy chivalry!

Few, few shall part where many meet!
The snow shall be their winding-sheet,
And every turf beneath their feet
Shall be a soldier's sepulcher.

—*Hohenlinden.* CAMPBELL.

CHAPTER XI

EMOTION

Teaching children to read with feeling is one of the most difficult tasks falling to the lot of the teacher, and yet it is one that has, if successfully accomplished, far-reaching results. For, apart from the legitimate development of emotion, it enlarges their sympathy and lays the foundation for a genuine love of literature.

We must confess that emotional expression is rarely found in our public schools. It would avail little to discuss the causes of this condition in detail. In this chapter we shall try to discover a remedy. Emotion in reading comes largely through the imagination. Unless the mind conceives the thought, how can the nerves thrill and tingle? It is for this that we need teachers who are themselves lovers of the beautiful, sublime, tender, in order that they may impart their appreciation and feeling to their classes. Emotion is catching, and so is the absence of it! Time, time, time, is here the great need. It takes time to think; time for the picture to come forth in its fulness out of subconsciousness. Is not imagination the basis of literary interpretation, of historical study, yes, even of mathematics and science? The time spent on the development of imagination and emotion in the reading lesson will show its results in every other study.

If, then, the teacher would get the right emotion, he must see to it that the child has the proper and adequate stimulus. Appeal to his everyday experience and make that serve as an introduction to the new experience of the poem.

Let us suppose we are speaking to the children:

> If your class were to have a contest with another class, let us say in spelling, and your class were to come out victorious, you would, no doubt, feel very joyful over the result. Now, let us suppose that after the victory one of the members of the class should get up on his seat and wave his hand above his head, crying: "Three cheers for our class!" Would there be any difference between the way in which he spoke those words and the way in which he would read the same words if they came in a sentence like this: "If we win I shall give three cheers for our class"?
>
> Of course, you will see at once that there would be a great deal of difference. In the first place, he would be very joyful, and perhaps excited, and this joy and excitement would get into his voice, and he would call out, "Three cheers for our class," with a great deal of feeling, or emotion; and everybody would see at

once just how exultant he was. Now, what is it that causes that feeling, or emotion? I do not think that there will be much difficulty in answering this question. He was very much excited before the spelling contest came off, and now that it has been decided in your favor there is a feeling of great joy that comes over the whole body, and it is almost impossible to keep back the expression of that joy. In other words, he has been strongly moved.

I want to impress now upon you that as you go on with your study of reading, you will find that there is a great deal of emotion in many of the passages you will be called upon to read, and the only way to discover what the emotion is, must be by getting a very clear picture. But remember that the picture itself is not very likely to move you unless you enter into the spirit of the picture just as you entered into the spirit of the spelling contest. Do you see my meaning? One might say the words, "Three cheers for our class," and not express very much emotion. One might even have a very clear picture of the whole spelling match, and yet not be very much moved. But if you will close your eyes and let the picture get hold of you, I think there will be no trouble about the emotion. Let me see whether I can make clear to you what I mean by letting the picture get hold of you.

Suppose we take this line from a well-known speech, "Wolsey on His Fall:"—"Farewell, a long farewell to all my greatness!" Who speaks those words? is the first question. The answer is: An old man who has been for many years one of the leading men in the court of Henry VIII. He has used every effort to gain great power, and has forgotten his God, and now at last the king has cast him off. Just after Wolsey has been informed of his loss of power, he utters the words quoted above. Just think how much these words mean to this poor man. Think how much he must suffer, and then try to feel as much as you can what it would mean to you if everything you had hoped for and struggled for were to be taken away from you. Of course, I know that you have not been so ambitious as Wolsey, but yet I think you will have no trouble in imagining just how you would feel if everything you cared for were to be taken away from you. Well, this is all that you need feel in order to read with emotion the lines of Wolsey. Just think this over for a few minutes, and then see how much regret you can feel as you utter these words. Be sure that you get the meaning of the words; be sure you get hold of the picture; try to imagine just how you would feel if you were very deeply disappointed, and then utter the words of Wolsey.

This, then, is what I mean by telling you to let the picture get hold of you. When you were exultant over the result of the spelling contest, joy possessed you. When Wolsey learned of his

> fall, sorrow and remorse possessed him. So with all emotions. You must think over the whole story; you must think over all the events connected with it until you really feel somewhat as the speaker felt whose words you are reading. Then there will be no trouble about the expression.

The teacher will observe that the two illustrations are chosen from two distinct fields: one near to the child's experience, the other far removed from it. It is further observed that both are direct discourse rather than description.

It seems the best plan to begin the definite study of emotional expression by using extracts in which the pupil uses direct rather than indirect discourse. The reason for this is that it is far more difficult to read, with expression, a passage of description in which the pupil would be expected to put emotion, than a piece of direct quotation. For instance, is it not easier for a child to enter into the spirit of the first of the following stanzas than into that of the second, granting even that it is difficult to conceive the anguish of the father?

The father came on deck. He gasped,
"O God! thy will be done!"
Then suddenly a rifle grasped,
And aimed it at his son:
"Jump—far-out, boy, into the wave!
Jump, or I fire!" he said;
"That only chance your life can save!
Jump! jump! boy!" He obeyed.

He sank—he rose—he lived—he moved,
And for the ship struck out:
On board we hailed the lad beloved,
With many a manly shout.
His father drew, in silent joy,
Those wet arms round his neck,
And folded to his heart his boy—
Then fainted on the deck.

In the second place, the reason for choosing selections in which the emotion is akin to those of the child's own experience must be clear. How many pupils ten or eleven years old can be expected to enter into the spirit of Whittier's *The Barefoot Boy*?

Blessings on thee, little man—
Barefoot boy, with cheek of tan!
With thy turned-up pantaloons,
And thy merry whistled tunes;
With thy red lip, redder still,
Kissed by strawberries on the hill;
With the sunshine on thy face,
Through thy torn brim's jaunty grace;
From my heart I give thee joy!

I was once a barefoot boy!

It is only to discourage him, to ask him to feel like an adult who looks back upon the joys of boyhood. One hears this selection read in an affected voice and manner, where it is clear that the child is simply trying to imitate his teacher. But such experiences simply go to prove the contention that children should not be called upon to represent emotions far removed from their own experience.

But how shall we get our pupils to express emotions beyond their experience? The answer is: the teacher should strive to find those experiences in the child's life that are similar to those of the selection to be read. We have shown how this might be done in the line from Wolsey's speech. The child has experienced regret; let us make use of this experience to get him to feel something of Wolsey's feeling. Again (and this applies largely to advanced classes), it is by no means necessary that the pupil should ever have come into contact with the picture that stirs the writer, in order to represent the latter's feelings. It is the joy that the lover of nature feels that finds expression in these lines:

How the robin feeds her young,
How the oriole's nest is hung;
Where the whitest lilies blow,
Where the freshest berries grow,
Where the ground-nut trails its vine;
Where the wood-grape's clusters shine;
Of the black wasp's cunning way,
Mason of his walls of clay.

—*The Barefoot Boy.* WHITTIER.

But how can we get the true expression from one who knows nothing of the joy we take in contemplating the pictures of this stanza? By reminding him that our joy is not far different from his when rejoicing in a beautiful book, a lucky hit at baseball, or a pretty Christmas gift. Let us remember that it is not enough that he shall get the pictures: he must get the joy. And if he cannot get the joy from the pictures of the poet, he must get it from the memory of his own past joy, no matter under what circumstances. It is simply a question of transferring his own past emotion to the present moment.

Summarized, our points are:

First, choose emotions near to the child's experience.

Second, transfer his past experiences and emotions to the particular poem or stanza to be read.

Third, use direct discourse, in drill work, as far as possible.

Perhaps it would not be advisable to use selections in our reading lessons that call for an extremely difficult exercise of imagination on the part of the child, but since these selections are found in our reading books it is well to know how to do the best possible under the circumstances.

The most important point of all is that children must be brought into contact with nature. We cannot expect them to delight in a description of a sunset, or a robin's nest, or a bunch of pansies, when they have never delighted in sunsets, or robins' nests or pansies. When their early training is wise they will not need to transfer their emotions from another realm to read with true expression.

We are now to enter the more complex realm of expression, in which the emotion is more intense, and instead of being a single emotion is a blending of many. Take, for example, the trial scene from *The Merchant of Venice*. There are many speeches of Shylock that might illustrate our point, and we shall take the first that presents itself. The Duke of Venice has been urging Shylock to abandon his suit, whereupon the latter replies:

> I have possessed your grace of what I purpose;
> And by our holy Sabbath have I sworn,
> To have the due and forfeit of my bond.

What emotions does Shylock portray? There is the emotion of hatred of Antonio and the feeling of obstinacy; and there is, further, the sense of wrong that has been heaped upon his race in general, and himself in particular. It would be useless to discuss how far each of these elements is an emotion. It is sufficient for our purpose to have shown that these three mental conditions are present virtually at one time in the brain of the speaker. Now, if any one of these elements (to say nothing of others that might be mentioned) is omitted, the characterization will lack truthfulness.

There is another element in complexity of expression that needs a moment's attention. The emotion itself may be a simple one, but the character we aim to represent may be so far removed from our own that one must assume or take on many attributes. For instance, if one were portraying old Adam in *As You Like It*, he would be compelled to manifest the weakness of old age in body and voice. Now, when the old man says, "Dear master, I can go no further; O, I die for food," it is not sufficient for the reader to portray simply the pathos of the line, but his expression becomes more complex in so far as it must manifest both the pathos and the weakness.

In preparing to present the emotions in the following extracts it is well for the student to study carefully the nature of the thought, the emotion, and the character separately, and conceive each of the simpler emotional elements by itself. If he is representing, let us say, pathos and dignity, let him hold dignity before his mind until the whole being responds; then let him conceive pathos by itself; and, finally, let him conceive pathos *and* dignity, and endeavor to present them. This process will not be necessary in all cases; for there are those who can conceive these more complex conditions with one effort, as it were. But unless the student has this ability, the preceding process should be followed. And even when a student has the necessary ability to conceive the complete expression at once, he is very likely to lose some of what might be called the ingredients of a composite emotion. For instance, in representing the strong language of one who might be said never to lose his anger, the student who is particularly choleric by nature is very likely to forget the dignity of the character. He may be reminded of his error by recalling dignity to his mind, and at once the natural temperament of the speaker will be modified by the new stimulus.

It might also be well to consider here another reason for the practice of these illustrations. Many students are temperamentally restricted and shy, and others have become so through training and environment. Before these can hope to become effective readers there must be a certain amount of genuine abandon. Hence, even if a student may never have any use for the ability to impersonate, the practice here recommended will prove to be one of the best, surest, and quickest methods of bringing him out of himself. The abandon thus gained will stand him in good stead in any effort he may be called upon to make as a public speaker.

Let it be remembered that niceties of form are not to be expected for a long time. If the student's abandon is developed, that is all that should be expected.

In the following speech the student must never forget that Othello is a warrior, one accustomed to command, and of large heart. His dignity, therefore, must be manifest throughout the address:

Most potent, grave, and reverend signiors,
My very noble and approv'd good masters,—
That I have ta'en away this old man's daughter,
It is most true; true, I have married her;
The very head and front of my offending
Hath this extent, no more. Rude am I in my speech,
And little bless'd with the soft phrase of peace;
For, since these arms of mine had seven years' pith,
Till now some nine moons wasted, they have used
Their dearest action in the tented field;
And little of this great world can I speak,
More than pertains to feats of broil and battle,
And therefore little shall I grace my cause
In speaking for myself. Yet, by your gracious patience,
I will a round unvarnished tale deliver
Of my whole course of love; what drugs, what charms,
What conjuration, and what mighty magic,
(For such proceeding I am charg'd withal,)
I won his daughter with.
Her father lov'd me; oft invited me;
Still question'd me the story of my life,
From year to year; the battles, sieges, fortunes,
That I have passed.
I ran it through, even from my boyish days,
To the very moment that he bade me tell it:
Wherein I spake of most disastrous chances,
Of moving accidents by flood and field,
Of hair-breadth 'scapes i' the imminent deadly breach;
Of being taken by the insolent foe,
And sold to slavery; of my redemption thence,

And portance in my travel's history.— —*Othello*, Act i., Sc. 3.

Another excellent extract for practice is the following speech of Cassius from the first act of *Julius Caesar*. Note the dignity, the sarcasm, the ridicule, the contempt, and the sense of triumph:

I cannot tell what you and other men
Think of this life; but, for my single self,
I had as lief not be, as live to be
In awe of such a thing as I myself.
I was born as free as Caesar; so were you:
We both have fed as well, and we can both
Endure the winter's cold as well as he:
For once upon a raw and gusty day,
The troubled Tiber chafing with her shores,
Caesar said to me, "Darest thou, Cassius, now
Leap in with me into this angry flood,
And swim to yonder point?" Upon the word,
Accoutred as I was, I plungèd in,
And bade him follow; so indeed he did.
The torrent roared, and we did buffet it
With lusty sinews, throwing it aside
And stemming it with hearts of controversy;
But ere we could arrive the point proposed,
Caesar cried, "Help me, Cassius, or I sink!"
I, as Æneas, our great ancestor,
Did from the flames of Troy upon his shoulder
The old Anchises bear, so from the waves of Tiber
Did I the tirèd Caesar. And this man
Is now become a god, and Cassius is
A wretched creature, and must bend his body,
If Caesar carelessly but nod on him. —*Julius Caesar*, Act i., Sc. 2.

These speeches of Cassio in *Othello* show remorse, self-contempt, with anger and regret:

CASSIO. Reputation, reputation, reputation! Oh! I have lost my reputation. I have lost the immortal part of myself, and what remains is bestial. My reputation, Iago, my reputation!

IAGO. As I am an honest man, I thought you had received some bodily wound; there is more sense in that than in reputation. Reputation is an idle and most false imposition; oft got without merit, and lost without deserving: you have lost no reputation at all, unless you repute yourself such a loser. What, man! there are ways to recover the general again: you are but now cast in his mood, a punishment more in policy than in malice; even so as one would beat his offenseless dog, to affright an imperious lion. Sue to him again, and he's yours.

CASSIO. I will rather sue to be despised, than to deceive so good a commander with so slight, so drunken, and so indiscreet an officer. Drunk? and speak parrot? and squabble? swagger? swear, and discourse fustian with one's own shadow? O thou invisible spirit of wine! if thou hast no name to be known by, let us call thee devil.

IAGO. What was he that you followed with your sword? What had he done to you?

CASSIO. I know not.

IAGO. Is't possible?

CASSIO. I remember a mass of things, but nothing distinctly; a quarrel, but nothing wherefore. O God, that men should put an enemy in their mouths, to steal away their brains! that we should, with joy, pleasance, revel, and applause, transform ourselves into beasts!

IAGO. Why, but you are now well enough: how came you thus recovered?

CASSIO. It has pleased the devil drunkenness, to give place to the devil wrath: one unperfectness shows me another, to make me frankly despise myself.

IAGO. Come, you are too severe a moraler. As the time, the place, and the condition of this country stands, I could heartily wish this had not befallen; but, since it is as it is, mend it for your own good.

CASSIO. I will ask him for my place again: he shall tell me, I am a drunkard. Had I as many mouths as Hydra, such an answer would stop them all. To be now a sensible man, by-and-by a fool, and presently a beast! O, strange! Every inordinate cup is unblessed, and the ingredient is a devil.—*Othello*, Act ii., Sc. 3.

In conclusion, begin with simple emotions. Do not ask the younger pupils to represent intense pathos, great solemnity, and the like. Reserve these for the upper grades of the high school. Again, avoid the baser emotions, such as anger, hate, jealousy. Time does not permit us to enlarge on this, but the whole trend of the best psychology is in favor of this admonition. Select extracts in which the characters manifest simple, noble, inspiring, and uplifting feeling. Patriotism, self-sacrifice, love of nature, these are the themes with which the imagination of the pupils should come into contact.

The teacher is heartily advised to gather a dozen or more extracts and speeches (from this book and elsewhere) under three or four significant heads, such as patriotism, love of nature, etc., and to keep the class at each phase until definite results are attained. There is no hesitation in deprecating the method that compels teachers to teach any lesson simply because it follows, numerically, the preceding lesson. The proper method is hinted at elsewhere. A few words are now added to justify that method. In many readers there may be two patriotic selections; one at the beginning, one at the end. Probably a year will intervene between these two. Is it not good pedagogy to take up these lessons in succession? To keep the pupils in a patriotic mood for five consecutive days must be certainly productive of better results than can be obtained by the other method of Lesson I, Lesson II, Lesson III. So also with other emotions. When a certain emotion is present in only one or two paragraphs of a selection, only those paragraphs need, of course, to be prepared.

CHAPTER XII
ATMOSPHERE

This element of expression, perhaps more than any other, manifests the artistic nature of the reader; artistic, inasmuch as the atmosphere, or vocal color, shows the sensitiveness of the reader to sense stimuli; shows that he is moved by the contemplation of the beautiful, the sublime, the tender, the pathetic. This element is called by different names, but perhaps none is more significant than Atmosphere. This effect is not easy to describe, and yet it is as real as rhythm or inflection or any other of the elements discussed in this book. Atmosphere is that sympathetic quality of voice that manifests the spirit of literature. Who can fail to notice the tender motherly sympathy that pervades every word of the lyric *Sweet and Low*? Now compare this with the knights' chorus from *The Coming of Arthur*. This is permeated throughout with the spirit of the Round Table. The spirit of motherly love in the former, and of knightly courage and the clang of arms in the latter, completely envelop these poems, and permeate every letter. Therefore, in the rendering the reader must exercise the greatest care not to dissipate this atmosphere. The least misstep, one false note, and the atmosphere is dissipated.

In longer selections there may be variety of atmosphere in the different stanzas or paragraphs, provided always that the variety enhances the poem as a whole. Mere variety in reading is not art, but chaos, says Professor Corson.

The following lines from Matthew Arnold's *Sohrab and Rustum*[13] illustrate the principle of variety in unity. The poem purports to be an extract from the epic of Rustum, the Persian Achilles, and is especially marked by a dignity truly Homeric. This atmosphere of dignity envelops every line. Hence pathos and joy, patriotism and defiance, scorn and contempt, and all the other emotions, are always dignified. The Tartar champion, Sohrab, challenges the bravest Persian champion to meet him in single combat; and the Tartar leader, Peran-Wisa, announces the challenge. The Tartars love their hero, and the thrill that pervades their army is significant of that love. But the Persian champion, Achilles-like, sulks in his tent; and the knowledge of this fact, when the announcement of the challenge is heard by the Persians, fills them with awe and dismay. Read the following lines, bringing out the significant atmosphere of the two parts of the contrast, but being careful to bear in mind the general atmosphere of dignity:

And the old Tartar came upon the sand

[13] It would occupy too much space to insert the complete poems mentioned in this chapter. These are all, however, easily available, and it is hoped that the teacher will read them.

Betwixt the silent hosts, and spake, and said:—
"Ferood, and ye, Persians and Tartars hear!
Let there be truce between the hosts to-day.
But choose a champion from the Persian lords
To fight our champion Sohrab, man to man."
As, in the country, on a morn in June,
When the dew glistens on the pearled ears,
A shiver runs through the deep corn for joy—
So, when they heard what Peran-Wisa said,
A thrill through all the Tartar squadrons ran
Of pride and hope for Sohrab, whom they loved.
But as a troop of peddlers from Cabool,
Cross underneath the Indian Caucasus,
The vast sky-neighboring mountain of milk snow;
Crossing so high, that, as they mount, they pass
Long flocks of traveling birds dead on the snow,
Choked by the air, and scarce can they themselves
Slake their parch'd throats with sugar'd mulberries—
In single file they move and stop their breath,
For fear they should dislodge the o'erhanging snows—
So the pale Persians held their breath with fear.

The reader must also bear in mind that from the very beginning of each picture the atmosphere of joy and fear respectively must be in the mind, and must never be lost sight of under any circumstances.

Sometimes the atmosphere is modified by the fact that the speaker is quoting the words of another person, and then it is often a matter of the most subtle analysis to determine the extent to which the quoted words will modify the atmosphere of the reader, whether speaking in his own person or in the person of another.

There are two kinds of literature that must be considered in this connection. First, that class in which the reader tells the story in his own person. Second, when the reading is a personation throughout. An example of the first class is *The Idylls of the King*; and of the second, the "Instigation" speech of Cassius in *Julius Caesar*. The principle governing atmosphere applies equally and in the same way to both kinds of selections. The knowledge of this fact will often be valuable to the reader.

We get a good example in the "Instigation" speech, where Cassius tells Brutus that Caesar, when he had a fever, cried, "'Give me some drink, Titinius,' as a sick girl." The whole matter of atmosphere, as far as quoted words are concerned, will be made clear by a study of this simple passage. Cassius is so exercised over the success of Caesar and his own consequent humiliation, that his scorn and rage are well-nigh boundless. As the torrent of his emotion rushes forth, is it not entirely inconsistent with our knowledge of human nature to suppose that that torrent would be so impeded or arrested when Cassius came to the above words, that he would stop to reproduce the actual manner and tones of Caesar? What Cassius probably does is to suggest something of the effeminate manner of Caesar enveloped in Cassius' own atmosphere of bitterest loathing and contempt. One will be helped in work of this kind by asking himself the question, What is the atmosphere of the speaker? Then, having determined this, he must next make up his mind, through his knowledge of human nature, to what extent this atmosphere is modified by the quoted words that are introduced into the body of the story. He may be assisted in determining this by putting a second question to himself, Is what the quoted words convey, or the manner in which they are conveyed, of the greater importance? This is well illustrated in *King Robert of Sicily*. It makes no difference in this particular poem how the sexton uttered the words, "Who is there?" and, consequently, it would be a mistake to give them any very significant atmosphere. As a matter of fact, the words are really equivalent to indirect discourse; the expression would convey exactly the same meaning to the listener if read, Asking who was within. The following from *King Lear* is full of suggestiveness in this connection. We recall that Kent has sent a gentleman to Cordelia to tell her of the condition of her father. Later in the drama, Kent meets the gentleman, and from him gets the story of the manner in which Cordelia received the sad news of her father's suffering. How truly ridiculous it would be for the gentleman to imitate the manner of Cordelia! The psychological explanation of what happens is probably this: As he relates the story to Kent, the tearful face and voice of Cordelia come into his mind, and, since there is always in human nature a tendency to become that which one describes, something of the manner of Cordelia will be suggested in the voice of the speaker; but let us bear in mind that the imitation is not intentional and detailed, but instinctive and suggestive only. It is not meant that the reader is not conscious of what he is doing, but that the gentleman (to use a concrete illustration) is not consciously imitating Cordelia. The artistic reader in reproducing this scene is conscious of what he is doing, but consciously sympathetic, not imitative:

> KENT. Did your letters pierce the queen to any demonstration of grief?
>
> GENTLEMAN. Ay, sir; she took them, read them in my presence;
> And now and then an ample tear trilled down
> Her delicate cheek: it seemed, she was a queen
> Over her passion, who, most rebel like,
> Sought to be king o'er her.
>
> KENT. O, then it moved her.
>
> GENTLEMAN. Not to a rage: patience and sorrow strove
> Who should express her goodliest. You have seen
> Sunshine and rain at once; her smiles and tears
> Were like a better May: those happy smilets
> That played on her ripe lip, seemed not to know
> What guests were in her eyes, which parted thence
> As pearls from diamonds dropped.—In brief,
> Sorrow would be a rarity most beloved,
> If all could so become it.
>
> KENT. Made she no verbal question?
>
> GENTLEMAN. 'Faith, once, or twice, she heav'd the name of "father,"

Pantingly forth, as if it pressed her heart;
Cried, "Sisters! sisters! Shame of ladies! sisters!
Kent! father! sisters! What? i' the storm? i' the night?
Let pity not be believèd!"—There she shook
The holy water from her heavenly eyes,
And clamor moistened: then away she started
To deal with grief alone. —*King Lear*, Act iv., Sc. 3.

This leads to another feature of the study of atmosphere. In the following lines from the *Elegy in a Country Churchyard*, we certainly speak slowly; but let it be remembered that this is done, not in imitation of the slow movement of the objects described, but in sympathy with them. The solemnity and dignity of the occasion so affect us that our movement becomes slow, and this movement and the right vocal quality give us the proper atmosphere.

The curfew tolls the knell of parting day,
The lowing herd winds slowly o'er the lea,
The plowman homeward plods his weary way,
And leaves the world to darkness and to me.

Now fades the glimmering landscape on the sight,
And all the air a solemn stillness holds,
Save where the beetle wheels his droning flight,
And drowsy tinklings lull the distant folds:

Save that from yonder ivy-mantled tower,
The moping owl does to the moon complain
Of such as, wandering near her secret bower,
Molest her ancient solitary reign.

Beneath those rugged elms, that yew-tree's shade,
Where heaves the turf in many a moldering heap,
Each in his narrow cell forever laid,
The rude forefathers of the hamlet sleep.

Let us remember, too, that an event which once filled us with joy may be recalled with pain and sorrow, and that it is our present condition that determines the atmosphere. Browning's *Patriot* will illustrate this.

The untrained reader is altogether too prone to imitation; but let him bear in mind that imitation, if ever art, is its lowest form. The province of the reader is to manifest, through his interpretation, the innermost spirit of the poem. Very often by imitating, by literally reproducing the voice, manner, and movements, we obscure the underlying spirit of the line, paragraph or poem. There are certain readers, for instance, who sing, *Non ti scordar di me*, in *Aux Italiens*. For the sake of argument, we might admit, that at the end of the poem there might be some slightest justification for this procedure; but in the beginning, it is absolutely indefensible. The speaker is in a deep reverie; he dwells in the past. His mind goes back to a visit to the opera-house in Paris, years before. The opera is *Il Trovatore*; and the heroine comes before us seeking her lover, who has been snatched from her arms through the jealousy of another. She arrives before the monastery as the monks chant the *Miserere*. Her prayer ascends heavenward; and when she ceases, there rises clear and passionately the voice of her lover from within his cell, singing, *Non ti scordar di me* (Forget me not). As the audience in the opera-house hear these words, their minds go back to the past. The king goes back to his early triumphs; the queen's mind reverts to her life in Spain; the wife of the Marquis of Carabas lets her thoughts glide back to her first husband; and to the speaker's mind there comes the vision of his early love. *Non ti scordar di me,* then, is the source of the poem. The tie that binds us to the past is the poet's theme, "Old things are best." Now let us look at the stanza at the end of which occurs the line we are discussing:

> The moon on the tower slept soft as snow,
> And who was not thrilled in the strangest way,
> As we heard him sing while the gas burned low,
> "*Non ti scordar di me*."

In the first place, when one sings these lines, he is just a little likely to be deemed presumptuous when it is recalled that the previous stanza has said:

> And Mario can soothe with a tenor note,
> The souls in purgatory.

It is hardly likely that the reader is a Mario; but this is a small criticism, comparatively speaking. The atmosphere of the poem is one of reverie; and what possesses the speaker is not the literal way the words were sung, but the memory of the thrill that passed through him and through the audience as these words rang out in a pause of the solemn *Miserere* of the monks. Let it be borne in mind that the argument is not against the singing as singing, but against the method that would completely destroy the atmosphere of the poem for the sake of a vocal affectation. What should be expressed is the rapture of the speaker as he recalls those passionate words and tones, in his present moment of contemplation. There are certain reprints of this poem that leave out the stanzas describing the effect of the song on the king, the queen, and the marchioness. Does this not prove that those who print such versions have missed the very essence of the story?

There is one more element that we are to discuss in this connection, and that is the atmosphere of sympathy that envelops the reading of description. This atmosphere shows the effect upon us of that which the author describes.

The tendency of most readers is toward imitation,—to groan and moan, and laugh and cry, whenever these words appear in the selection interpreted. In such passages as the following from Aldrich's *Face Against the Pane,* we have heard more than one reader imitate the screeching and the moaning, and the groaning and the breaking:

> She hears the sea bird screech,
> And the breakers on the beach
> Making moan, making moan.

And again, in the same poem, we have heard imitations of the tolling bells in:

> How it tolls for the souls
> Of the sailors on the sea;

In these passages and all similar ones, as, for instance, those already quoted from the *Elegy in a Country Churchyard*, our aim should be to manifest through the atmosphere the effect of the description upon ourselves.

Perhaps it will assist us to get a clearer conception of this important feature if we discuss a few typical examples, even repeating some of the selections already used in the discussion.

Example 1 (from *Sohrab and Rustum*). The atmosphere of the first simile is that of joy; not in imitation of the joy of the Tartars, but because we are moved to joy by our sympathy with Sohrab.

Example 2 (*ibid.*). We do not express the fear of the Persians or of the peddlers, but our contempt for the former—perhaps slightly tinged, through sympathy, with their fear.

Example 3 (from *King Robert of Sicily*). The atmosphere is that of simple narrative, which is in no wise changed by the words of the sexton.

Example 4. Eugene Field's *Little Boy Blue* presents a father standing before the dust-covered toys of his dead child. The father speaks throughout, and yet there are those who actually imitate the voice and manner of the child in the opening lines of the second stanza:

> "Now don't you go till I come," he said,
> "And don't you make any noise;"
> So toddling off to his trundle-bed
> He dreamt of the pretty toys.

It is the father we want, not the child.

Example 5 (from the *Elegy in a Country Churchyard*). We read the passage slowly, not because we desire to imitate the slow movement of the objects described, but because we are impressed by their solemnity.

It may be thought that the principle here discussed has no value except for advanced pupils or for those who desire to make a specialty of reading. This is a grave error and one that has had much to do with the spiritless reading of our schools. At least one-half of the selections in our readers, above the second, present opportunities for the expression of what we have termed sympathy. In the chapter on Values we observed that there were ever-varying phases of thought and feeling, each one of which would be read with a different atmosphere. Let us look at another complete poem solely with a view to applying the principles of phases and of atmosphere:

> Gusty and raw was the morning;
> A fog hung over the seas,
> And its gray skirts, rolling inland,
> Were torn by the mountain-trees.
> No sound was heard but the dashing
> Of waves on the sandy bar,
> When Pablo of San Diego
> Rode down to the Paso del Mar. 8

The pescador, out in his shallop,
Gathering his harvest so wide,
Sees the dim bulk of the headland
Loom over the waste of the tide;
He sees, like a white thread, the pathway
Wind round on the terrible wall,
Where the faint, moving speck of the rider
Seems hovering close to its fall!

Stout Pablo of San Diego
Rode down from the hills behind;
With the bells on his gray mule tinkling,
He sang through the fog and wind.
Under his thick, misted eyebrows
Twinkled his eye like a star,
And fiercer he sang as the sea-winds
Drove cold on the Paso del Mar.

Now Bernal, the herdsman of Corral,
Had traveled the shore since dawn.
Leaving the ranches behind him:
Good reason had he to be gone!
The blood was still red on his dagger,
The fury was hot in his brain,
And the chill, driving scud of the breakers
Beat thick on his forehead in vain.

With his blanket wrapped gloomily round him
He mounted the dizzying road,
And the chasms and steeps of the headland
Were slippery and wet as he trode.
Wild swept the wind of the ocean,
Rolling the fog from afar,
When near him a mule-bell came tinkling,
Midway on the Paso del Mar.

"Back!" shouted Bernal full fiercely,
And "Back!" shouted Pablo in wrath,
As his mule halted, startled and shrinking,
On the perilous line of the path.
The roar of devouring surges
Came up from the breakers' hoarse war;
And "Back, or you perish!" cried Bernal;
"I turn not on Paso del Mar!"

The gray mule stood firm as the headland;
He clutched at the jingling rein,
When Pablo rose up in his saddle
And smote till he dropped it again.

A wild oath of passion swore Bernal,
And brandished his dagger still red;
While fiercely stout Pablo leaned forward,
And fought o'er his trusty mule's head.

They fought till the black wall below them
Shone red through the misty blast.
Stout Pablo then struck, leaning farther,
The broad breast of Bernal at last;
And, frenzied with pain, the swart herdsman
Closed round him with terrible clasp,
And jerked him, despite of his struggles,
Down from the mule in his grasp.

They grappled with desperate madness
On the slippery edge of the wall;
They swayed on the brink, and together
Reeled out to the rush of the fall!
A cry of the wildest death-anguish
Rang faint through the mist afar,
And the riderless mule went homeward
From the fight of the Paso del Mar!

—*The Fight of Paso del Mar.* BAYARD TAYLOR.

l. 1-4.—Simple description, the last line slightly colored with emotion.

l. 5, 6.—Note how the voice becomes suppressed in sympathy with the picture.

l. 7, 8.—Simple description.

l. 9-12.—Simple description.

l. 13-16.—The important part this pathway is to play in the poem and the danger of the rider will bring the suggestion of fear into the voice of the reader. It is the effect of the picture upon us that we must manifest; this is half the art of reading.

l. 17-24.—The joy of Pablo will find an echo in our reading, as will his joyous defiance in l. 23, 24.

l. 25-27.—Simple description to "behind him," when the coming event casts its shadow before; the color of the next line is clearly anticipated on these two words.

l. 28.—The atmosphere is difficult to characterize in a word, but not to manifest.

l. 29-32.—Note the marked change. The atmosphere is largely that of sympathy—fury and dogged, gloomy determination. Perhaps there might be something of our horror and loathing in l. 29.

l. 33-36.—Simple description.

l. 37, 38.—Sympathy.

l. 39, 40.—Brighter.

l. 41, 42.—The atmosphere is that of the speakers.

l. 43, 44.—Our fear of a fatal misstep.

l. 45, 46.—The effect upon us, not imitation of the roar.

l. 47, 48.—Anger and determination.

l. 49.—See l. 45, 46.

l. 50-56.—Virtually the same atmosphere, throughout, of terror, strife, determination, hate.

l. 57, 58.—Oh! the pity of it.

l. 59-64.—See l. 50-56.

l. 65-68.—Terror and fear increase until the climax on "fall."

l. 69, 70.—Terror and pity.

l. 71.—Observe the transition. Restrained pathos to the end.

The most important fact to be borne in mind in endeavoring to develop the pupil's sympathy with what he describes is this: imitation of sounds, and of gestures, and of movement, is a very low order of art. We can not imitate thunder, but we can show in our voices the awe that it inspires. When we unconsciously hurry our reading under the impulse the imagination receives from contemplating, let us say, the rapid movement of a cavalry charge, we do so not in imitation of, but in sympathy with, the picture. This is not primarily a question of art, but of nature. It is only ignorant teaching that says to a pupil, "Is that the way the thunder roars?" or "Read more rapidly; don't you see that you are describing the flight of the horses?" Furthermore, if we read slowly a passage describing a funeral procession, there is no conscious imitation of slowness, but a sympathy with the solemnity, stateliness and dignity of the occasion.

A very little observation will show us whether the imitation is conscious or sympathetic. In the former case, the voice will be expressing *merely* speed or slowness. In the latter, there will be speed or slowness, too, but accompanied by an indefinable and yet recognizable *quality* of voice, which is the expression of our sympathy. This is an infallible criterion.

Lastly, it must be urged that we give more time to this work. The imagination cannot be developed in a week or a month; and unless there is imagination, there can be no sympathy. It is difficult to restrain one's self and not dwell longer on the value of the training of the imagination. We have no hesitation in saying that that feature of education is the most neglected. Such training as is here suggested will, in many cases, do much to bring about a more favorable condition of affairs. But it takes time, and plenty of it. The teacher should read to the class quite often such passages as are likely to stimulate the imagination. Make the class follow attentively and get them to give back the picture, as far as possible, in minutest detail. Do this again and again and improvement must follow. Just in proportion as the imagination is stimulated may we hope for a better class of reading. *We have no time to teach any subject poorly!*

This phase of the subject may be presented to pupils in some such manner as this:

> Let me tell you a story:
>
> The other day, a little child came to its mother, saying, "Oh, mother! I just saw a beautiful toy in the window: I wish you would buy it for me." *The sweet voice was full of pleading.* The mother was very poor, and had hardly earned enough to pay for fuel. *How could she spare even the few pennies for the toy?* But she said to herself, "This is Christmas time;" and the tears came into her eyes. The little one saw the tears, and said: "What are you crying for, mother?" *And then the mother hugged her child to her breast and kissed her again and again, saying over and over,* "Because I love you! Because I love you!"
>
> When Christmas morning dawned the little toy was on the mantel and the child was happy. But when the time for breakfast came, the child asked her mother why she did not eat; and the mother answered, "I am not hungry, darling; don't mind me," and she smiled tenderly upon the sweet face, upturned to kiss her.
>
> After you have read this simple tale two or three times, I think you will begin to feel some sympathy with the loving mother who would do without her food to give joy to her little child. When you read the sentences I have put in italics, if you have really tried to see the pictures, I am sure you will feel some sympathy that will make your reading so different from the reading of, let us say, the first sentence in this lesson. Take the line, "The sweet voice was full of pleading." Can't you imagine some sweet child-voice pleading for the toy? Well, then, listen to that voice, and after you have, then read, "The sweet voice was full of pleading." You will find that your voice will be so full of sympathy that it will say not only the words, but also will express love, and tenderness, and sympathy. You will think, perhaps, some such thought as, "She was such a lovely child and she wanted the toy so much. It made me feel sorry to hear her ask for it." There is another sentence in italics that I want you to think about. When you read, "And the tears came into her eyes," can you not feel something of the sadness of that mother, as she thinks how much she would like to buy the toy, and yet there is nothing to buy it with? When you express your feeling, your voice will say, "And the mother's heart was sad when she thought that her darling could have no little gift at Christmas, when it seemed everyone should be made happy. How disappointed the sweet one would be when she found out how many toys her playmates had while she had not one!" All these thoughts will run through your mind if you will only think about this scene long enough, and then your voice will express that sympathy with the picture you are describing without which

> you can never be a good reader. Let us then close this lesson by reminding you that the best way to develop our feelings as we read is through sympathy.
>
> There are several other phrases and sentences in this story that I want you to study sympathetically for to-morrow's lesson. Then, after you have grasped the idea of this lesson, be sure, in every selection you read hereafter, that you do not fail to pay particular attention to sympathy.

Let us, in closing this long but most vital discussion, direct attention in a few words to the psychology of the atmosphere of description. When we are giving the description for its own sake, desiring simply to impress the picture upon the audience, we should probably use the normal quality. To illustrate:

A fellow in a market-town,
Most musical, cried "Razors!" up and down,
And offered twelve for eighteen pence;
Which certainly seemed wondrous cheap,
And for the money quite a heap,
As every man would buy, with cash and sense.

When, however, we are somewhat moved through the contemplation of what we see, when it takes possession of us, we should be likely to manifest our feeling in a suggestive imitation of the object described. See the third stanza of *The Fight of Paso del Mar*. The third stage is reached when the picture moves us to such an extent that imitation and suggestion disappear, and we show merely our own feelings. See lines 69 and 70 of the same poem. In reading these we do not utter the cry, nor do we show the death anguish, but our own feelings of pity and perhaps terror. There is a fourth stage, in which the conditions of the second and third are blended. Again we may use the same poem as an illustration. In lines 53 and 54, one could conceive a reader partaking through sympathy of the passion of Bernal, and yet manifesting his own feeling of fear and horror at the same time.

It is believed that this classification is psychologically sound, and that it will repay close study. It need hardly be added that the attention of the pupil is not to be drawn to the details. Selections for practice follow:

As thro' the land at eve we went,
And pluck'd the ripen'd ears,
We fell out, my wife and I,
O we fell out I know not why,
And kiss'd again with tears.
And blessings on the falling out
That all the more endears,
When we fall out with those we love
And kiss again with tears.
For when we came where lies the child
We lost in other years,
There above the little grave,

O there above the little grave,
We kiss'd again with tears. —*The Princess.* TENNYSON.

The essence of these exquisite lines is in their tender simplicity.

Sweet and low, sweet and low,
Wind of the western sea,
Low, low, breathe and blow,
Wind of the western sea!
Over the rolling waters go,
Come from the dying moon, and blow
Blow him again to me;
While my little one, while my pretty one, sleeps.

Sleep and rest, sleep and rest,
Father will come to thee soon;
Rest, rest, on mother's breast,
Father will come to thee soon;
Father will come to his babe in the nest,
Silver sails all out of the west
Under the silver moon:
Sleep, my little one, sleep, my pretty one, sleep. —*Ibid.*

Blow trumpet, for the world is white with May;
Blow trumpet, the long night hath roll'd away!
Blow thro' the living world—"Let the King reign."

Shall Rome or Heathen rule in Arthur's realm?
Flash brand and lance, fall battleaxe upon helm,
Fall battleaxe, and flash brand! Let the King reign.

Strike for the King, and live! his knights have heard
That God hath told the King a secret word.
Fall battleaxe, and flash brand! Let the King reign.

Blow trumpet! he will lift us from the dust.
Blow trumpet! live the strength and die the lust!
Clang battleaxe, and clash brand! Let the King reign.

Strike for the king and die! and if thou diest,
The King is King, and ever wills the highest.
Clang battleaxe, and clash brand! Let the King reign.

Blow, for our Son is mighty in his May!
Blow, for our Son is mightier day by day!
Clang battleaxe, and clash brand! Let the King reign.

The King will follow Christ, and we the King
In whom high God hath breathed a secret thing.
Fall battleaxe, and flash brand! Let the King reign.

—"Knights' Chorus" from *The Coming of Arthur*. TENNYSON.

It would hardly be appropriate to imitate the blow of the trumpet; and, striking as the effect would be, it would not be the highest art to have an accompaniment of clanging arms.

> But Rustum eyed askance the kneeling youth,
> And turn'd away, and spake to his own soul:—
> "Ah me, I muse what this young fox may mean!
> False, wily, boastful, are these Tartar boys.
> For if I now confess this thing he asks,
> And hide it not, but say: 'Rustum is here!'
> He will not yield indeed, nor quit our foes,
> But he will find some pretext not to fight,
> And praise my fame, and proffer courteous gifts,
> A belt or sword perhaps, and go his way.
> And on a feast tide, in Afrasiab's hall,
> In Samarcand, he will arise and cry:
> 'I challenged once, when the two armies camp'd
> Beside the Oxus, all the Persian lords
> To cope with me in single fight; but they
> Shrank, only Rustum dared; then he and I
> Changed gifts, and went on equal terms away.'
> So will he speak, perhaps, while men applaud;
> Then were the chiefs of Iran shamed through me."

—*Sohrab and Rustum.* M. Arnold.

Note that when Rustum utters the supposed words of Sohrab he would still speak in the musing mood. It is still the voice and manner of Rustum, with the faint suggestion of the other's supposed boastfulness.

> He spoke, and Sohrab kindled at his taunts,
> And he too drew his sword; at once they rush'd
> Together, as two eagles on one prey
> Come rushing down together from the clouds,
> One from the east, one from the west; their shields
> Dash'd with a clang together, and a din
> Rose, such as that the sinewy woodcutters
> Make often in the forest's heart at morn,
> Of hewing axes, crashing trees—such blows
> Rustum and Sohrab on each other hail'd.
> And you would say that sun and stars took part
> In that unnatural conflict; for a cloud
> Grew suddenly in heaven, and dark'd the sun
> Over the fighters' heads; and a wind rose
> Under their feet, and moaning swept the plain,
> And in a sandy whirlwind wrapp'd the pair.
> In gloom they twain were wrapp'd, and they alone;
> For both the on-looking hosts on either hand
> Stood in broad daylight, and the sky was pure,

And the sun sparkled on the Oxus stream.
But in the gloom they fought, with bloodshot eyes
And laboring breath: first Rustum struck the shield
Which Sohrab held stiff out; the steel-spiked spear
Rent the tough plates, but fail'd to reach the skin,
And Rustum pluck'd it back with angry groan.
Then Sohrab with his sword smote Rustum's helm,
Nor clove its steel quite through; but all the crest
He shore away, and that proud horsehair plume,
Never till now defiled, sank to the dust;
And Rustum bow'd his head; but then the gloom
Grew blacker, thunder rumbled in the air,
And lightnings rent the cloud; and Ruksh, the horse,
Who stood at hand, utter'd a dreadful cry;—
No horse's cry was that, most like the roar
Of some pain'd desert lion, who all day
Hath trail'd the hunter's javelin in his side,
And comes at night to die upon the sand.
The two hosts heard that cry, and quaked for fear,
And Oxus curdled as it cross'd his stream.

—*Sohrab and Rustum.* M. ARNOLD.

The above is an interesting illustration. We are not to be eagles and the wind and the sand, but to manifest the awe which overwhelms us as we describe the terrible struggle of this father and son, each ignorant of the identity of the other.

As when some hunter in the spring hath found
A breeding eagle sitting on her nest,
Upon the craggy isle of a hill lake,
And pierced her with an arrow as she rose,
And follow'd her to find her where she fell
Far off;—anon her mate comes winging back
From hunting, and a great way off descries
His huddling young left sole; at that, he checks
His pinion, and with short uneasy sweeps
Circles above his eyry, with loud screams
Chiding his mate back to her nest; but she
Lies dying, with the arrow in her side,
In some far stony gorge out of his ken,
A heap of fluttering feathers—never more
Shall the lake glass her, flying over it;
Never the black and dripping precipices
Echo her stormy scream as she sails by—
As that poor bird flies home, nor knows his loss,
So Rustum knew not his own loss, but stood
Over his dying son, and knew him not.

—*Sohrab and Rustum.* M. ARNOLD.

Rustum has mortally wounded his son in the combat, and now the poet introduces the exquisite simile given above. It is a fine study in the reading of description.

CHAPTER XIII

CONTRASTS

It is because contrasts are a distinct feature of literature that it is well to make the study of them and their vocal presentation a feature of the reading course. It is understood, of course, that the teacher must use his discretion as to the time when the definite study of contrasts should be undertaken; but when clearly presented and discriminatingly illustrated, even young children can be led to perceive the artistic value of contrast, to enjoy it as art, and to manifest their appreciation of it in their reading. It should not be difficult to show young children that Cinderella's character is made to appear more lovable because it is set over against those of her sisters. Children enjoy such effects as well as adults, when pleasantly and suggestively presented to them.

In literature there are found illustrations of contrast upon every page. There are contrasts of ideas, contrasts of emotions, contrasts of scenes, contrasts of characters, and many others. Under the head of "The Central Idea" will be found numerous examples of the first class. We shall here consider a few illustrations of the other classes, while in later pages will be found illustrations for more extended study.

Contrast of emotion is admirably illustrated in the following scene from *The Merchant of Venice*, Act iii., Sc. 1:

> Shylock. How now, Tubal! what news from Genoa? hast thou found my daughter?
>
> Tubal. I often came where I did hear of her, but cannot find her.
>
> Shylock. Why there, there, there, there! a diamond gone, cost me two thousand ducats in Frankfort! The curse never fell upon our nation till now; I never felt it till now:—two thousand ducats in that; and other precious, precious jewels. I would my daughter were dead at my foot, and the jewels in her ear! would she were hearsed at my foot, and the ducats in her coffin! No news of them? Why so;—and I know not what's spent in the search: why, thou loss upon loss! the thief gone with so much, and so much to find the thief; and no satisfaction, no revenge: nor no ill luck stirring but what lights on my shoulders; no sighs but of my breathing; no tears but of my shedding.

TUBAL. Yes, other men have ill luck too. Antonio, as I heard in Genoa,—

SHYLOCK. What, what, what? ill luck, ill luck?

TUBAL. Hath an argosy cast away, coming from Tripolis.

SHYLOCK. I thank God, I thank God! Is it true, is it true?

TUBAL. I spoke with some of the sailors that escaped the wreck.

SHYLOCK. I thank thee, good Tubal. Good news, good news! ha, ha!—Where? in Genoa?

TUBAL. Your daughter spent in Genoa, as I heard, one night fourscore ducats.

SHYLOCK. Thou stick'st a dagger in me; I shall never see my gold again. Fourscore ducats at a sitting! fourscore ducats!

TUBAL. There came divers of Antonio's creditors in my company to Venice, that swear he cannot choose but break.

SHYLOCK. I am very glad of it: I'll plague him; I'll torture him: I am glad of it.

TUBAL. One of them showed me a ring that he had of your daughter for a monkey.

SHYLOCK. Out upon her! Thou torturest me, Tubal: it was my turquoise; I had it of Leah when I was a bachelor. I would not have given it for a wilderness of monkeys.

TUBAL. But Antonio is certainly undone.

SHYLOCK. Nay, that's true, that's very true. Go, Tubal, fee me an officer; bespeak him a fortnight before. I will have the heart of him, if he forfeit; for, were he out of Venice, I can make what merchandise I will. Go, go, Tubal, and meet me at our synagogue; go, good Tubal; at our synagogue, Tubal.

We cannot fail to remark how the contrast between Shylock's emotions (when bemoaning the loss of his ducats at one moment, and cursing the daughter who has robbed him and eloped with a Christian at another) serves to bring out his peculiar character.

Contrast of character is brought out in every great play. Horatio and Hamlet, Cordelia and her sisters, Macbeth and his wife, suggest themselves as examples. The third act of *King Lear*, where the jester's jibes are interpolated between the fearful outbursts of the king, is a striking example of character, as well as of emotional contrast.

It may be well to remark that the two parts of a contrast do not always occur in succession. Do not the last three or four speeches of Shylock depend, for their effect, upon the keeping in mind by the audience of his emotions and bearing during the former scenes? Let the audience forget these, and they have lost a most significant æsthetic detail. Similarly, when King Robert utters the speech beginning, "Thou knowest best," the whole effect is lost unless we bear in mind that never for three years has his answer to the angel's question been other than, "I am, I am the king."

The following examples will afford good practice:

> Sheltered by the verdant shores, an hundred triremes were riding proudly at their anchors, their brazen beaks glittering in the sun, their streamers dancing in the morning breeze, while many a shattered plank and timber gave evidence of desperate conflicts with the fleets of Rome.—*Regulus to the Carthaginians.* Kellogg.

> The multitude swayed to and fro like a forest beneath a tempest, and the rage and hate of that tumultuous throng vented itself in groans, and curses, and yells of vengeance. But calm, cold and immovable as the marble walls around him stood the Roman.—*Ibid.*

> If there be three in all your company dare face me on the bloody sands, let them come on. And yet I was not always thus, a hired butcher, a savage chief of still more savage men! My ancestors came from old Sparta, and settled among the vine-clad rocks and citron groves of Syrasella. My early life ran quiet as the brooks by which I sported; and when at noon I gathered the sheep beneath the shade, and played upon the shepherd's flute, there was a friend to join me in the pastime.... One evening, my grandsire, an old man, was telling of Marathon and Leuctra, and how, in ancient times, a little band of Spartans, in a defile of the mountains, had withstood a whole army. I did not then know what war was; but my cheeks burned, and I clasped the knees of that venerable man, until my mother, parting the hair from off my forehead, kissed my throbbing temples and bade me go to rest, and think no more of those old tales and savage wars. That very night the Romans landed on our coast. I saw the breast that had nourished me trampled by the hoof of the war-horse, and the bleeding body of my father flung amidst the blazing rafters of our dwelling!—*Spartacus.* Kellogg.

> O Rome, Rome, thou hast been a tender nurse to me! Ay, thou hast given to that poor, gentle, timid shepherd lad, who never knew a harsher tone than a flute note, muscles of iron and a heart of flint; taught him to gaze into the glaring eyeballs of the fierce Numidian lion, even as a boy upon a laughing girl.—*Ibid.*

> The shouts of revelry had died away.-*Ibid.*

> The roar of the lion had ceased.—*Ibid.*

You all do know this mantle: I remember
The first time ever Caesar put it on;
'Twas on a summer's evening in his tent,
That day he overcame the Nervii.
Look! in this place ran Cassius' dagger through.

—*Julius Caesar*, Act iii., Sc. 2.

The selection entitled the "Choric Song," a part of Tennyson's *The Lotos-Eaters*, is a fine study in contrast. The speakers are the followers of Ulysses, who are debating whether they shall remain in this new found land of the Lotos or return to their homes. The first, third, fifth, and seventh stanzas are in striking contrast to the others. The feelings of the sailors as they alternately contemplate their life as it is and has been, in contrast with what it might be should they remain here, are strikingly depicted.

The subject of contrasts may be presented to the class in some such manner as the following:

> Have you not noticed how much brighter the sunlight seems to be after a thunder-shower? how keenly we enjoy a victory after defeat seems certain? Why is this? Because the clouds by their blackness make us appreciate the sunlight; and the fear of losing the contest makes us doubly glad when we win. If we had sunshine all the time, how monotonous it would be, and how little we should notice it! And you must see that if the other side in a contest were very weak, we should not derive much pleasure from the outcome. All nature is full of these contrasts: joy and sorrow, light and darkness, success and failure, are always around us. So literature, which deals with nature, contains these contrasts, too.
>
> In literature, the contrast is used to impress upon us some idea or picture more completely than could be done by merely describing it. This is done by placing before us the idea and its opposite: it is like placing a dark screen behind a white marble statue. This being so, we can easily see how necessary it is for us to recognize these contrasts in order that we may present them with our voices to the listeners.
>
> Let us take a few simple examples. Our grandparents tell us that it took them sixty days to cross the ocean from England to America; and now, we know, it takes but six. The best way to show how great an advance this century has made in boat-building would be by contrasting the past and the present. We might say: "It took my grandparents sixty days, in a sailing vessel, to cross the ocean, but now we go by steam in six."
>
> Again: "Last week I was sleighing and skating in Minneapolis; but to-day I am plucking violets and japonicas in the gardens of Savannah."

In both examples you observe that the concluding idea of the sentence is made more striking because of the contrast it makes with the first part. Be sure to bear this in mind. A contrast is made up of two ideas, and you must have both of them in mind or your reading will be a failure. Do you not see that this is true? If you were to say "I am plucking violets in Savannah to-day," there would be very little emotion shown in your voice: you would be making just an ordinary statement. But if you were thinking of the great change you had made; how strange it was that you should be in the midst of winter one week and in the midst of spring the next, then the contrast would be such a pleasant one that your voice would be full of joy, and your joy would be largely the result of the contrast. If you had violets all the year round, perhaps you would hardly notice them.

Here are two more examples of contrast, more difficult to express, but more beautiful than the others.

Imagine a noble warrior whose whole life is devoted to good deeds. Imagine him as he speaks the following words descriptive of the old time tournament. Then imagine how grateful he would feel for the relief after the fierce struggle, a relief so beautifully described by the author:

My good blade carves the casques of men,
My tough lance thrusteth sure,
My strength is as the strength of ten,
Because my heart is pure.
The shattering trumpet shrilleth high,
The hard brands shiver on the steel,
The splintered spear-shafts crack and fly,
The horse and rider reel.
They reel, they roll, in clanging lists,
And when the tide of combat stands,
Perfume and flowers fall in showers,
That lightly rain from ladies' hands.

—*Sir Galahad.* TENNYSON.

In this next example, we have the picture of a king who is punished for his pride by being deprived of all his power, wealth, and friends. See how powerful the contrast he makes as he, who should be master, rides in mock state amid the splendor of his courtiers. The word "he" in the first line does not refer to the king, but to another.

Then he departed with them o'er the sea,
Into the lovely land of Italy,
Whose loveliness was more resplendent made
By the mere passing of that cavalcade,

With plumes, and cloaks, and housings, and the stir
Of jeweled bridle and of golden spur.
And lo! among the menials, in mock state,
Upon a piebald steed, with shambling gait,
His cloak of foxtails flapping in the wind,
The solemn ape demurely perched behind,
King Robert rode, making huge merriment
In all the country towns through which they went.

—*King Robert of Sicily.* LONGFELLOW.

Let us remember that contrasts are of two kinds: logical and emotional. The former are largely antitheses, such as "I said John, not Charles," and will need but casual attention. The pupils will perceive them without difficulty. The other class need much care. Perhaps the most important fact that the teacher must bear in mind concerning these, is that their successful rendition depends upon the pupils' keeping both parts of the contrasts in mind, *the first serving as a background, or relief, for the second.* Just as contrasts in literature afford variety and relief, so the reading aloud of contrasts gives great variety in vocal expression.

CHAPTER XIV

CLIMAXES

In Genung's *Practical Rhetoric* we find the following definition of Climax: "This figure, which depends upon the law that a thought must have *progress*, is the ordering of thought and expression so that there shall be uniform and evident increase in significance, or interest, or intensity."

An excellent illustration of increase in Significance is found in the following speech from Regulus:

> The artisan had forsaken his shop, the judge his tribunal, the priest the sanctuary, and even the stern stoic had come forth from his retirement.

Here the author desires to show that the return of Regulus had thrown all Carthage into a state of intense excitement. The artisan, who could ill afford to lose his day's labor, had left his shop to join the throng that was taking its way to the great square of the city. The judge, whose duty it was to administer justice, could not refrain from joining the crowd. The priest, whose sacred office was to tend the altars of the gods, he too, for once, was neglecting his duty. And even the stern stoic, whose philosophy taught him to remain unmoved under any and all conditions of life, even he, perforce, must mix with the multitude thronging the Carthaginian streets. Each succeeding clause presents to us a more unusual disturbance of the normal condition of Carthaginian affairs; and the climax is reached when even the man whose whole philosophy teaches him never to be moved, is impelled to do violence to his life-long convictions.

In the following lines from Lord Chatham's speech we have an illustration of the climax of Intensity:

> If I were an American, as I am an Englishman, while a foreign troop was landed in my country, I never would lay down my arms! Never! Never! Never!

The verbal expression does not progress; and yet the emotion increasing in force, as the mind dwells upon the thought, finds vent in increasing intensity of vocal expression. It may be well to note that by increasing the intensity is not necessarily meant greater loudness or higher pitch; but greater intensity of feeling, which may result in greater loudness or higher pitch, or, on the other hand, in deeper, more controlled, or more dignified expression.

We have thus far been considering simple and palpable forms of climaxes. Let us turn now to the examination of the more difficult and complex. The following speech is uttered by Marullus, one of the tribunes, in the first scene of the first act of *Julius Caesar*. We recall the fact that Marullus appears to be greatly surprised that the citizens of Rome should dress themselves in holiday garb and make holiday to celebrate the return of the victorious Caesar. He inquires of them what is their purpose in thus celebrating; and, after considerable bantering, one of the crowd remarks that they make holiday to see Caesar, and to rejoice in his triumph, whereupon Marullus speaks:

> Wherefore rejoice? What conquest brings he home?
> What tributaries follow him to Rome,
> To grace in captive bonds his chariot wheels?
> You blocks, you stones, you worse than senseless things!
> O you hard hearts, you cruel men of Rome,
> Knew you not Pompey? Many a time and oft
> Have you climb'd up to walls and battlements,
> To towers and windows, yea, to chimney-tops,
> Your infants in your arms, and there have sat
> The livelong day, with patient expectation,
> To see great Pompey pass the streets of Rome:
> And when you saw his chariot but appear,
> Have you not made an universal shout,
> That Tiber trembled underneath her banks,
> To hear the replication of your sounds
> Made in her concave shores?
> And do you now put on your best attire?
> And do you now cull out a holiday?
> And do you now strew flowers in his way,
> That comes in triumph over Pompey's blood?
> Be gone!
> Run to your houses, fall upon your knees,
> Pray to the gods to intermit the plague
> That needs must light on this ingratitude.

The first three ideas are arranged in order of climax. It may be termed a climax of Significance. But we must not lose sight of the fact that, throughout the speech, as the emotion of Marullus increases, we shall have a climax in Intensity. In line 4, we have another climax, reaching its height on the word "worse." Then, with "many a time and oft," begins another climax, which, with occasional diminutions, continues to "shores." In the next four lines we have a climax which is intensified by contrast. The word "now" is full of reproof and condemnation; and by the time the speaker utters the words "over Pompey's blood" he is so overcome with the enormity of the crime that, with the utmost fervor, he urges the mob to run to their houses and pray to the gods to refrain from visiting upon their heads the rightful punishment of their ingratitude.

This cursory analysis of the speech has shown us that while there is a steady increase in intensity from the first word to the last, there are, besides, many smaller climaxes in Significance. We find these in lines 1 to 3, line 4, lines 6 to 16, lines 17 to 20, lines 22 to 24. It may be said in passing, that the climax in lines 17 to 20 forms a very interesting study. "Best attire," "holiday," "strew flowers in his way," are plainly arranged in order of climax, while the three "now's" are evidently an anti-climax. The first "now" is most significant, while the last is of very little importance. On the other hand, the fact of strewing flowers in Caesar's way is clearly a very much more striking mark of their ingratitude than that of merely putting on their best attire.

Just as in the long paragraph that we have analyzed we find a climax, so in a drama or in a poem we find this steady progression. That scene which is the climax of the action is gradually led up to by successive steps, each one more significant and intense than the preceding. The artist is careful not to destroy his effect by anti-climax, for to do so would be to lessen the interest of the audience, and consequently defeat the very purpose of the drama or story. The play of *The Merchant of Venice* illustrates this. Each scene manifestly increases the intensity which finally culminates in the trial scene, after which the play, being a comedy, descends to a restful close at the end of the fifth act.

In recitation the ordinary climax of Significance presents no great difficulty for the reader. As soon as he appreciates the fact of the growth in significance, he will manifest that increase in greater loudness or intensity, or increase of passion. It may be well to repeat that the increase need not be in loudness, nor is it necessary that the pitch of the voice be raised; but there will unquestionably be some form of climax in the expression. The difficulty begins when the climax is made up of smaller climaxes, as in the example from *Julius Caesar*, or when a climax is, so to speak, one of considerable length. In the latter case, the utmost care must be used to husband one's resources, that when the moment of intensest feeling is reached, there shall be sufficient power to produce the required result. One of the most striking defects in oratory, recitation, and acting, is the inability to present climaxes artistically. Either from a failure to perceive their literary value, or from lack of control, or other limitations of technique, the effect is often spoiled, with most disastrous results. The student, then, is advised to determine carefully that point of a passage or story where the strongest effect is to be made, and then to be careful to subordinate all else to this.

GRADATION

This feature of literary art may appropriately be considered in connection with Climax. The law of gradation demands that the progress from the smaller to the greater be gradual and regular. In the musical and elocutionary arts this is by no means an easy task, and great care must be taken to reserve the strongest effects for the culmination of the climax. This is not difficult when the climax is short, but in the longer examples one requires all the art at his command.

To assist in rendering a climax artistically, let the reader bear in mind the end from the beginning. Then the temptation to overdo the less important details will be reduced.

ANTONY. O, pardon me, thou bleeding piece of earth,
That I am meek and gentle with these butchers!
Thou art the ruins of the noblest man
That ever livèd in the tide of times.
Woe to the hand that shed this costly blood!
Over thy wounds now do I prophesy,—
Which, like dumb mouths, do ope their ruby lips
To beg the voice and utterance of my tongue,—
A curse shall light upon the limbs of men;
Domestic fury and fierce civil strife,
Shall cumber all the parts of Italy;
Blood and destruction shall be so in use,
And dreadful objects so familiar,
That mothers shall but smile when they behold
Their infants quartered with the hands of war,
All pity choked with custom of fell deeds;
And Caesar's spirit, ranging for revenge,
With Até by his side, come hot from hell,
Shall in these confines with a monarch's voice
Cry "Havoc!" and let slip the dogs of war;
That this foul deed shall smell above the earth
With carrion men groaning for burial. —*Julius Caesar*, Act iii., Sc. 1.

CASSIUS. I know that virtue to be in you, Brutus,
As well as I do know your outward favor.
Well, honor is the subject of my story.—
I cannot tell what you and other men
Think of this life; but for my single self,
I had as lief not be, as live to be
In awe of such a thing as I myself.
I was born free as Caesar; so were you:
We both have fed as well, and we can both
Endure the winter's cold as well as he:
For once, upon a raw and gusty day,
The troubled Tiber chafing with her shores,
Caesar said to me, "Darest thou, Cassius, now
Leap in with me into this angry flood,
And swim to yonder point?"—Upon the word,
Accoutred as I was, I plungèd in,
And bade him follow: so, indeed, he did.
The torrent roared, and we did buffet it
With lusty sinews, throwing it aside
And stemming it with hearts of controversy;
But ere we could arrive the point proposed,
Caesar cried, "Help me, Cassius, or I sink."
I, as Æneas, our great ancestor,

Did from the flames of Troy upon his shoulder
The old Anchises bear, so from the waves of Tiber
Did I the tirèd Caesar. And this man
Is now become a god; and Cassius is
A wretched creature, and must bend his body
If Caesar carelessly but nod on him.
He had a fever when he was in Spain,
And when the fit was on him, I did mark
How he did shake: 'tis true, this god did shake:
His coward lips did from their color fly;
And that same eye, whose bend doth awe the world,
Did lose his luster. I did hear him groan;
Ay, and that tongue of his, that bade the Romans
Mark him, and write his speeches in their books,
Alas it cried, "Give me some drink, Titinius,"
As a sick girl. Ye gods, it doth amaze me,
A man of such a feeble temper should
So get the start of the majestic world,
And bear the palm alone. [*Shout. Flourish.*

Brutus. Another general shout!
I do believe that these applauses are
For some new honors that are heaped on Caesar.

Cassius. Why, man, he doth bestride the narrow world,
Like a Colossus; and we petty men
Walk under his huge legs, and peep about
To find ourselves dishonorable graves.
Men at some time are masters of their fates:
The fault, dear Brutus, is not in our stars,
But in ourselves, that we are underlings.
Brutus, and Caesar: what should be in that Caesar?
Why should that name be sounded more than yours?
Write them together, yours is as fair a name;
Sound them, it doth become the mouth as well;
Weigh them, it is as heavy;—conjure with 'em,
Brutus will start a spirit as soon as Caesar.
Now, in the names of all the gods at once,
Upon what meat doth this our Caesar feed,
That he is grown so great? Age, thou art shamed!
Rome, thou hast lost the breed of noble bloods!
When went there by an age, since the great flood,
But it was famed with more than with one man?
When could they say, till now, that talked of Rome,
That her wide walls encompassed but one man?
Now is it Rome indeed, and room enough,
When there is in it but one only man.

O, you and I have heard our fathers say,
There was a Brutus once that would have brooked
The eternal devil to keep his state in Rome
As easily as a king. —*Julius Caesar*, Act i., Sc. 2.

In the preceding illustration it must be remembered that the description of the rescue of Caesar from the Tiber is only the beginning of Cassius' plan; and that his object is to cite the illustrations of Caesar's weakness, and finally to lead up to that subtle flattery with which the "Instigation" speech closes.

It is an outrage to bind a Roman citizen; to scourge him is an atrocious crime; to put him to death is almost parricide; but to crucify him—what shall I call it?

I know it, I concede it, I confess it, I proclaim it.

When a wind from the lands they had ruin'd awoke from sleep,
And the water began to heave and the weather to moan.

If there be one among you who can say that ever, in public fight or private brawl, my actions did belie my tongue, let him stand forth and say it. If there be three in all your company dare face me on the bloody sands, let them come on.

O comrades, warriors, Thracians,—if we must fight, let us fight for *ourselves*! If we must slaughter, let us slaughter our *oppressors*! If we must die, let it be under the clear sky, by the bright water, in noble, honorable battle!

Next morning, waking with the day's first beam,
He said within himself, "It was a dream!"
But the straw rustled as he turned his head,
There were the cap and bells beside his bed;
Around him rose the bare, discolored walls,
Close by, the steeds were champing in their stalls,
And in the corner, a revolting shape,
Shivering and chattering, sat the wretched ape.
It was no dream; the world he loved so much
Had turned to dust and ashes at his touch!

Have I not, since first my youthful arms could wield a spear, conquered your armies, fired your towns, and dragged your generals at my chariot wheels?

Remember that Greece had her Alexander, Rome her Caesar, England her Cromwell, France her Bonaparte, and that, if we would escape on the rock on which they split, we must avoid their errors.

> "But, Mr. Speaker, we have a right to tax America." Oh, inestimable right! Oh, wonderful, transcendent right! the assertion of which has cost this country thirteen provinces, six islands, one hundred thousand lives, and seventy millions of money.

This last example is a peculiar one. Under ordinary circumstances thirteen provinces would be more valuable than six islands, and surely one hundred thousand lives are more valuable than seventy millions of money. On the other hand, the figures in the last three phrases certainly rise to a climax. On the whole, I think it better to regard this as an oratorical climax, understanding Burke not to have had in mind anything more than to present the losses of England, as each occurred to him, while his emotion and indignation rise with each enumeration.

The climax is a very important feature in reading. It stimulates the imagination and feelings, and, through them, the voice. It should be remembered that no definite method of expressing a climax vocally can be laid down. In one case the pitch may rise; in another it may fall. Sometimes the force increases; at other times it diminishes. Hence, the admonition so often given must be repeated: Do not tell the pupil to raise his voice, or to speak louder. Work at his imagination. If there be a climax there, it will come out in his expression.

Frequent drills in climax will do much to give flexibility, power, and range to the voice. And that, too, in a far more rational way than through any mechanical exercises in pitch and force.

The following plan of presenting climaxes to classes has been found extremely helpful:

> Read the following sentence carefully to yourself. Notice each clause, and try to discover if there is not something here that we have not had before. I want to ask you not to read more than that sentence until you have studied over it for some time. "It is an outrage to bind a Roman citizen; to scourge him is an atrocious crime; to put him to death is almost parricide; but to crucify him—what shall I call it?"
>
> We have here another method used by writers and speakers for making an idea more striking. In this case, the speaker is condemning one who has caused the crucifixion of a Roman. The orator desires to impress upon the judges the seriousness of the offense. How does he do it? Instead of speaking at once about the crucifying of the victim, he begins by showing that a far less serious punishment was a grave offense against the Roman law. He says, "It is an outrage to bind a Roman citizen." Then he goes another step, saying: "To scourge him is an atrocious crime." Worse still: "To put him to death" (by any means) "is almost parricide." And now, having shown that less extreme methods of punishment were great crimes, the orator is ready for his final statement: "But to crucify him—what shall I call it?" In other words, the speaker seems to have exhausted his vocabulary in giving names

to lower crimes; when he comes to a name with which to describe the crime of crucifying a Roman, he finds his vocabulary does not have one strong enough. Do you not see how powerful an effect such an arrangement of clauses must have? It is much stronger than if the speaker had said merely, "I know no word to describe the crime of crucifying a Roman citizen."

Analyze the following sentence, and explain how the thought is made more striking by this kind of arrangement. "I know it, I concede it, I confess it, I proclaim it."

This method of increasing the effect is called climax. Whenever, for any reason, a speaker or writer keeps on adding thought to thought, making each succeeding idea stronger than the preceding, we have a climax. Although you may never have called it by this name you have used it many times. If you were determined to do a certain thing you might say, "I can do it, I will do it, I must do it." Well, that is a climax. Or you might say, "You can't have it for ten dollars, for fifty dollars, for a hundred dollars." That is another climax.

Note this example: "If I were an American, as I am an Englishman, while a foreign troop was landed in my country, I never would lay down my arms! never! never! never!" This, too, is a climax, each of the last three "never's" being stronger than the preceding. If you will put yourself in the position of the speaker, you will soon feel that each "never" after the first is the result of stronger, more intense feeling. If you will think of it in this way you will notice the effect in your expression.

We shall close this lesson with two illustrations. Your teacher will tell you the story from which these extracts are taken, and then you will prepare them very carefully, taking particular pains to note the climax in each.

When a wind from the lands they had ruin'd awoke from sleep,
And the water began to heave and the weather to moan,
And or ever that evening ended a great gale blew,
And a wave like a wave that is raised by an earthquake grew,
Till it smote on their hulls and their sails and their masts and
    their flags,
And the whole sea plunged and fell on the shot-shatter'd navy of
    Spain,
And the little Revenge herself went down by the island crags,
To be lost evermore in the main.—*The Revenge.* TENNYSON.

And thro' the centuries let a people's voice
In full acclaim,
A people's voice,

The proof and echo of all human fame,
A people's voice, when they rejoice
At civic revel and pomp and game,
Attest their great commander's claim
With honor, honor, honor, honor to him,
Eternal honor to his name.

—*Ode on the Death of the Duke of Wellington.* TENNYSON.

CHAPTER XV

CONCLUDING REMARKS ON METHOD

In taking leave of the pedagogy of the subject it may be profitable to review some of the principal features of the method advocated, and add a few hints on minor topics not treated elsewhere.

The method herein laid down aims to present one principle at a time; calls for specific preparation on the part of the pupils; urges that there be definite grading of the difficulties encountered by children in learning to read; advises strongly against calling their attention to the vocal technique of expression; and lastly, holds out the hope that the impression will eventually find an outlet in true expression.

As at present taught, no distinction is drawn, in reading, between the easy and the difficult, the simple and the complex. We trust that in the suggestions of this book will be found at any rate a partial solution of the difficulty.

It should be impressed upon pupils from the outset that they are studying the thoughts and feelings of others that find expression in words upon the printed page. They must discover the thoughts behind the words and then express them; that is all there is to reading.

While it is believed that the order of the steps as here outlined is a rational one, it is not claimed that this order is hard and fixed. In advanced classes, where the method has not been used in the lower grades, the teacher should endeavor to discover the particular weakness of his pupils, and use with them the step most likely to produce the desired effect. Or if it is thought advisable, he may start with the first step and cover all the ground in one grade as fast as the pupils can absorb the spirit of each step. But it must never be forgotten that carelessness in reading is a habit not easily eradicated; and, further, that because a pupil satisfactorily prepares a lesson in, let us say, grouping, he will not necessarily have formed the habit of grouping correctly. We are dealing with complicated psychical phenomena, and until the eye, the memory, the voice, in fact, all the elements of expression are thoroughly co-ordinated, we are in constant danger of error.

The time deemed necessary in public schools to complete all the steps, is about two years, beginning with the grade third or fourth below the highest. Before the pupils reach that grade, the sole effort of the teacher should be directed to making the reading vital and meaningful. If this is done the work of subsequent teachers will be relatively easy.

Avoid, and the admonition is repeated once more, talking to the pupils about inflection, pause, and the like. These are instinctive manifestations of mental states, and will appear when the conditions are right.

Let the teacher not follow slavishly the order of lessons in the regular reading book. Let him choose such selections or parts of them as offer the best opportunity for practice where the class most needs it. Let him further find extracts from outside sources for class use. These may be written on the board or mimeographed.

It has been said that we must have a technique if we would read. This may be granted; but it is equally to be granted that the principal technique is mental, and, moreover, that, in the public schools, our aim is to produce simple, natural, expressive readers, not artistic actors and orators. There is, then, no necessity for drills on inflection, time, modulation, and the like, as such. Give the pupil all the drill that is necessary on the states of mind producing these effects, but let us never separate the technique from the mental condition that will find instinctive expression in that technique.[14] Expression grows through expressing. If we will bear this in mind, and present the right thoughts and emotions to be expressed, at the right time, there should and will be no difficulty.

It is suggested that, perhaps once a week, short extracts be committed and recited before the class. There need be no gesture, just simple saying. Such a procedure will give the pupil confidence, develop his earnestness, improve his voice, and in every way affect for good the reading spirit of the class. Where a suitable selection can be found, it will be well to give a stanza to each pupil. A word may be added about the recitations that form so large a part of the closing exercises in our schools. If the recitation were an honest, legitimate presentation of the reading as taught in the school, there could be no objection to it; but in most cases it is anything but this. Special teachers are called in to "coach" the students, and the result is far from satisfactory. A few lessons can seldom make a reader, and where that plan partially succeeds, so much greater is the hypocrisy; for the reading stands for the work of the school rather than for that of an individual teacher. A true showing of the work of the school, and one that would in time be heartily appreciated by parents, would be to select the good readers (a few hints to them are all that would be necessary), and let them, book in hand, read as they would in class. If the class reading has been good, so will be the individual reading; otherwise it has no business to parade under false colors at public exercises.

To what extent shall pupils imitate? No fixed rule should be laid down, but one might say that they should never attempt to imitate inflections, pauses, rate of movement, and the like. On the contrary, there seems to be much value in stimulating the pupils' imagination by having the teacher read certain emotional passages for them. They then may catch the spirit of the selection without any

---

[14] A great deal of what seems to be unnecessary confusion exists regarding the meaning of this term. It is used very freely to mean not only mechanical facility, but also that facility plus the knowledge of where and how to use it, a meaning which leads to confusion. Technique is "a collective term for all that relates to the purely mechanical part of either vocal or instrumental performance. The technique of a performer may be perfect, and yet his playing ... fail to interpret intelligibly the ideas of the composer." These words from the *Century Dictionary* ought to settle this misunderstanding effectually.

conscious effort at imitation. There are many who train a class to read in concert from imitation. The results of such training are worse than baneful, leading only to inane, affected expression.

PART THREE
LITERARY INTERPRETATION

CHAPTER XVI

LITERARY INTERPRETATION

In the concluding part of this work it is purposed to lay before the teacher some examples of literary interpretation. The object of these is to assist him to a deeper insight into literature, and hence to become a better reader and teacher of reading.

It is not too much to say that we accept as good reading what is often the reverse simply because the subject matter does not appeal to us or is only partly appreciated. A pupil may read such a passage as the following in a commonplace way, and be complimented by one teacher for his distinct articulation and forceful utterance, whereas a teacher who appreciated the true spirit of the lines would severely condemn the reading.

The curfew tolls the knell of parting day;
The lowing herd winds slowly o'er the lea;
The plowman homeward plods his weary way,
And leaves the world to darkness and to me.

The explanation of the difference in the attitudes of the teachers is that the former has no appreciation of the spirit of the lines, while the latter keenly feels their tenderness, their beauty, and their pensive solemnity.

The best way to learn to love good literature is to study only good literature, and to study it again, again and again. What is truly great art cannot be apprehended at a glance, but requires time for its fullest appreciation. We believe, however, that it is good pedagogy, in a work of this kind, to lay before the teacher certain examples of what careful analysis may reveal. The effect of such analysis upon the reading must be evident to all.

We have already discerned that all analysis preparatory to reading aloud is virtually literary analysis. This is well illustrated in the chapters on Climax and on Contrast. It remains, therefore, to deal only with certain broader aspects of literary appreciation, in connection with which we shall endeavor to show the application of the principles discussed in Parts I and II to vocal interpretation.

STUDY IN RHYTHM

It is a truism to state that every poem should be a unity, but we often forget a most important corollary, that every line should be scanned with a view to determine that unity. It is only in so far as we understand the parts that we understand the whole. Let us illustrate this principle in the following well-known poem:

HOW THEY BROUGHT THE GOOD NEWS FROM GHENT TO AIX

ROBERT BROWNING

I sprang to the stirrup, and Joris, and he;
I galloped, Dirck galloped, we galloped all three:
"Good speed!" cried the watch, as the gate-bolts undrew;
"Speed!" echoed the wall to us galloping through;
Behind shut the postern, the lights sank to rest,
And into the midnight we galloped abreast.

Not a word to each other; we kept the great pace
Neck by neck, stride by stride, never changing our place;
I turned in my saddle and made its girths tight,
Then shortened each stirrup, and set the pique right,
Rebuckled the check-strap, chained slacker the bit,
Nor galloped less steadily Roland a whit.

'Twas moonset at starting; but while we drew near
Lokeren, the cocks crew and twilight dawned clear,
At Boom, a great yellow star came out to see;
At Duffeld, 'twas morning as plain as could be;
And from Mecheln church-steeple we heard the half chime,
So Joris broke silence with, "Yet there is time!"

At Aerschot, up leaped of a sudden the sun,
And against him the cattle stood black every one,
To stare through the mist at us galloping past,
And I saw my stout galloper Roland at last,
With resolute shoulders, each butting away
The haze, as some bluff river headland its spray.

And his long head and crest, just one sharp ear bent back
For my voice, and the other pricked out on his track;
And one eye's black intelligence,—ever that glance
O'er its white edge at me, his own master, askance!
And the thick heavy spume-flakes which aye and anon
His fierce lips shook upwards in galloping on.

By Hasselt, Dirck groaned; and cried Joris, "Stay spur!
Your Roos galloped bravely, the fault's not in her;
We'll remember at Aix,"—for one heard the quick wheeze
Of her chest, saw the stretched neck and staggering knees,
And sunk tail, and horrible heave of the flank,
As down on her haunches she shuddered and sank.

So we were left galloping, Joris and I,
Past Looz and past Tongres, no cloud in the sky;
The broad sun above laughed a pitiless laugh,
'Neath our feet broke the bright brittle stubble like chaff;
Till over by Dalhem a dome-spire sprang white,
And "Gallop," gasped Joris, "for Aix is in sight!"

"How they'll greet us!"—and all in a moment his roan
Rolled neck and croup over, lay dead as a stone;
And there was my Roland to bear the whole weight
Of the news which alone could save Aix from her fate,
With his nostrils like pits full of blood to the brim,
And with circles of red for his eye-sockets' rim.

Then I cast loose my buff coat, each holster let fall,
Shook off both my jack-boots, let go belt and all,
Stood up in the stirrup, leaned, patted his ear,
Called my Roland his pet-name, my horse without peer;
Clapped my hands, laughed and sang, any noise, bad or good,
Till at length into Aix Roland galloped and stood.

And all I remember is, friends flocking round
As I sat with his head 'twixt my knees on the ground,
And no voice but was praising this Roland of mine,
As I poured down his throat our last measure of wine,
Which (the burgesses voted by common consent)
Was no more than his due who brought good news from Ghent.

The central idea in this poem is Roland; not the rider, not the historical element. As a matter of fact, the poem has no historical basis. Browning tells us somewhere that after a tiresome and tedious sea voyage he longed for a gallop over the English downs, and that this poem is a result of that longing. The rhythm of the poem is peculiarly adapted to express the bounding joy of the poet, and is in striking contrast to the long, monotonous roll of ocean waves.

On studying the poem, we note the absence of any but cursory reference to the rider, and, on the contrary, the constant reference to the real hero, Roland. One might imagine a setting for the lines something as follows: Around a camp-fire are gathered many veterans of the wars. They are telling of the gallant deeds of their war steeds, when one of their number starts up and says:

"You talk of your horses; have you ever heard of mine? Have you heard how my Roland helped to save Aix? No? Let me tell you. You remember so-and-so's famous campaign, and how the enemy were preparing to take Aix. You know, too, that the officer in command had no hope of saving the city and was preparing to capitulate the moment the enemy began the attack. Well, one night, just after we had turned in, a messenger came in hot haste to tell us that the king himself had that day started to relieve the city and that we must carry the good news to Aix and thus encourage them to hold out until his arrival. Our commander called for three volunteers to undertake the dangerous task of bearing the news. We—Joris,

Dirck, and I—offered our services. They were accepted, and a moment after we had received our instructions,

'I sprang to the stirrup, and Joris, and he;'"

From now on observe how the poet fixes our attention on Roland.

Nor galloped less steadily Roland a whit.

And I saw my stout galloper Roland at last,
With resolute shoulders, each butting away
The haze, as some bluff river headland its spray.

And there was my Roland to bear the whole weight
Of the news which alone could save Aix from her fate,

Till at length into Aix Roland galloped and stood.

And no voice but was praising this Roland of mine.

The whole of the fifth stanza is devoted to praise of Roland; while the failure of the horses of Joris and Dirck serves but to enhance the glory of Roland's feat.

As soon as we perceive the meaning of the poem—its central thought—the entire reading becomes permeated with the joy and exultation of the rider in his steed. The poem is well adapted to develop vocal flexibility, and freedom of expression.

Tennyson's *Charge of the Light Brigade* affords another opportunity for analysis.

The atmosphere of this poem is that of a dirge. This does not mean that we snivel and whine while rendering it, but that the whole poem is enveloped in the atmosphere of dignified solemnity. It is true that this is not the popular view, which seems to be that Tennyson wrote the poem to afford the reader an opportunity of making descriptive gestures. Tennyson's heart ached for those brave fellows in their useless sacrifice; and he wrote the poem, not primarily to show how they fought, but that they fought in vain. True, there is a vein of stirring patriotism in the lines, but all that is inferior in importance to the dignified solemnity and controlled pathos of the speaker.

THE CHARGE OF THE LIGHT BRIGADE

TENNYSON

Half a league, half a league,
Half a league onward,
All in the valley of Death
Rode the six hundred.
"Forward, the Light Brigade!
Charge for the guns!" he said:
Into the valley of Death
Rode the six hundred.

"Forward, the Light Brigade!"

Was there a man dismayed?
Not tho' the soldier knew
Some one had blunder'd:
Theirs not to make reply,
Theirs not to reason why,
Theirs but to do and die:
Into the valley of Death
Rode the six hundred.

Cannon to right of them,
Cannon to left of them,
Cannon in front of them
Volley'd and thunder'd;
Storm'd at with shot and shell
Boldly they rode and well,
Into the jaws of Death,
Into the mouth of Hell
Rode the six hundred.

Flash'd all their sabres bare,
Flash'd as they turn'd in air
Sabring the gunners there,
Charging an army, while
All the world wonder'd:
Plunged in the battery-smoke
Right thro' the line they broke;
Cossack and Russian
Reel'd from the sabre-stroke
Shatter'd and sunder'd.
Then they rode back, but not—
Not the six hundred.

Cannon to right of them,
Cannon to left of them,
Cannon behind them
Volley'd and thunder'd;
Storm'd at with shot and shell,
While horse and hero fell,
They that had fought so well
Came thro' the jaws of Death,
Back from the mouth of Hell,
All that was left of them,
Left of six hundred.

When can their glory fade?
O the wild charge they made!
All the world wonder'd.
Honor the charge they made!
Honor the Light Brigade,

Noble Six Hundred!

It is impossible to overlook the constant recurrence of the phrases "valley of Death;" "jaws of Death;" "mouth of Hell," and their significance. The keynote of the poem is found in the line,

Some one had blunder'd:

Here is the central thought. The men made a gallant charge, went boldly and willingly to their doom; but it was all a mistake, a fearful, horrible mistake. We care not for the *fact* that cannons were to the right, to the left, and to the front of them. The mere position is nothing. But who can repress the shudder of despair as he contemplates that heroic band surrounded by fires from death-dealing cannon?

On pages 135 and 136 will be found three poems from Tennyson, each of which presents a different aspect. The first is marked by an exquisite simplicity. It contains but one simple idea, which is set forth in the simplest language. Consequently, the reading should be equally unassuming. The least appearance of affectation or effort will dissipate the atmosphere.

The second is a lullaby. The rocking cradle is felt in every line, while in the last line of each stanza we have the rhythmic picture of the gradual cessation of the rocking, and it seems impossible to omit the long pause before the last word in each of these lines, a pause exactly equal to the time of one of the preceding feet.

The third poem is of an entirely different nature. Here we have the strength of spirit that animated King Arthur's Knights of the Round Table. When we bear in mind that this song is sung after King Arthur's claim to the throne, which has long been in doubt, has been firmly established, and he has taken Guinevere to wife, we can better understand its passionate joy.

One of the most interesting features in connection with the study of literature is rhythm. The meaning of rhythm is not always clearly apprehended, many regarding it simply as poets' playfulness, interesting in the nursery rhyme, tickling the childish ear, but beyond that a useless and even senseless filigree. Nothing could be farther from truth. Rhythm is not a conventional appendage of poetry, but its very heart, life, spirit. It springs spontaneously from the poet's heart, and is the manifestation of his deepest feeling. Who can fail to catch the bounding spirit of life and joy in the following:

I come, I come! ye have called me long;
I come o'er the mountains with light and song;
Ye may trace my step o'er the wakening earth,
By the winds which tell of the violet's birth,
By the primrose stars in the shadowy grass,
By the green leaves opening as I pass. —*Spring*. HEMANS.

Haste thee, nymph, and bring with thee
Jest, and joyful Jollity,
Quips, and cranks, and wanton wiles,
Nods, and becks, and wreathèd smiles,

Such as hang on Hebe's cheek,
And love to live in dimple sleek;
Sport that wrinkled Care derides,
And Laughter holding both his sides.
Come and trip it as you go
On the light fantastic toe;
And in thy right hand lead with thee
The mountain-nymph, sweet Liberty:
And, if I give thee honor due,
Mirth, admit me to thy crew,
To live with her, and live with thee,
In unreprovèd pleasures free: —*L'Allegro.* MILTON.

What a dignity is imparted to the scene by the rhythm in the following extracts:

Here are old trees, tall oaks and gnarlèd pines,
That stream with gray-green mosses; here the ground
Was never trenched by spade, and flowers spring up
Unsown, and die ungathered. It is sweet
To linger here, among the flitting birds
And leaping squirrels, wandering brooks, and winds
That shake the leaves, and scatter as they pass,
A fragrance from the cedars, thickly set
With pale blue berries. In these peaceful shades—
Peaceful, unpruned, immeasurably old—
My thoughts go up the long dim path of years,
Back to the earliest days of liberty. —*Freedom.* BRYANT.

A land of streams! some, like a downward smoke,
Slow-dropping veils of thinnest lawn, did go;
And some through wavering lights and shadows broke
Rolling a slumbrous sheet of foam below.
They saw the gleaming river seaward flow
From the inner land: far off, three mountain-tops,
Three silent pinnacles of aged snow,
Stood sunset-flushed: and, dewed with showery drops,
Up-clomb the shadowy pine above the woven copse.

—*The Lotos-Eaters.* TENNYSON.

Often in the same poem the emotional changes are manifested in changes of rhythm. Observe this in the following lines:

Look! look! that livid flash!
And instantly follows the rattling thunder
As if some cloud-crag, split asunder,
Fell, splintering with a ruinous crash,
On the earth, which crouches in silence under;

And now a solid gray wall of rain
Shuts off the landscape, mile by mile;
For a breath's space I see the blue wood again,
And, ere the next heart-beat, the wind-hurled pile,
That seemed but now a league aloof,
Bursts rattling over the sun-parched roof;
Against the windows the storm comes dashing,
Through tattered foliage the hail tears crashing,
The blue lightning flashes,
The rapid hail clashes,
The white waves are tumbling,
And in one baffled roar,
Like the toothless sea mumbling
A rock-bristling shore,
The thunder is rumbling
And crashing and crumbling,—
Will silence return never more? —*A Summer Shower.* LOWELL.

Or in the concluding stanzas of Wordsworth's ode on *Intimations of Immortality*:

Then sing, ye birds, sing, sing a joyous song!
And let the young lambs bound
As to the tabor's sound!
We in thought will join your throng,
Ye that pipe and ye that play,
Ye that through your hearts to-day
Feel the gladness of the May!
What though the radiance that was once so bright
Be now forever taken from my sight,
Though nothing can bring back the hour
Of splendor in the grass, of glory in the flower,
We will grieve not, rather find
Strength in what remains behind,
In the primal sympathy
Which having been, must ever be;
In the soothing thoughts that spring
Out of human suffering;
In the faith that looks through death,
In years that bring the philosophic mind.

And O ye fountains, meadows, hills and groves,
Forebode not any severing of our loves!
Yet in my heart of hearts I feel your might;
I only have relinquished one delight,
To live beneath your more habitual sway.
I love the brooks which down their channels fret,
Even more than when I tripped lightly as they:
The innocent brightness of a new-born day

Is lovely yet;
The clouds that gather round the setting sun
Do take a sober coloring from an eye
That hath kept watch o'er man's mortality;
Another race hath been, and other palms are won.
Thanks to the human heart by which we live;
Thanks to its tenderness, its joys and fears,
To me the meanest flower that blows can give
Thoughts that do often lie too deep for tears.

In blank verse we get the best and clearest illustration of the meaning of rhythm. Here the poet has the utmost freedom, untrammeled by rhyme or any limitations as to the length of his stanza. The rhythm in the description of the overthrow of Satan is most suggestive of strength and determination:

Him the Almighty power
Hurl'd headlong flaming from th' ethereal sky,
With hideous ruin and combustion, down
To bottomless perdition; there to dwell
In adamantine chains and penal fire,
Who durst defy th' Omnipotent to arms! —*Paradise Lost*, Book I. MILTON.

How clearly the frantic passion of Lear is shown in the irregular, erratic, almost chaotic, rhythm of the following speech:

Blow, winds, and crack your cheeks! rage! blow!
You cataracts and hurricanoes, spout
Till you have drench'd our steeples, drowned the cocks!
You sulphurous and thought-executing fires,
Vaunt-couriers to oak-cleaving thunderbolts,
Singe my white head! And thou, all-shaking thunder,
Smite flat the thick rotundity o' the world!
Crack Nature's moulds, all germens spill at once,
That make ingrateful man! —*King Lear*, Act iii., Sc. 2.

Note how the varying rhythm in the following passage corresponds with the ever varying moods of the King and the poet:

To whom replied King Arthur, much in wrath:
"Ah, miserable and unkind, untrue,
Unknightly, traitor-hearted! Woe is me!
Authority forgets a dying king,
Laid widow'd of the power in his eye
That bow'd the will. I see thee what thou art
For thou, the latest-left of all my knights,
In whom should meet the offices of all,
Thou wouldst betray me for the precious hilt;
Either from lust of gold, or like a girl
Valuing the giddy pleasure of the eyes.
Yet, for a man may fail in duty twice,

And the third time may prosper, get thee hence:
But, if thou spare to fling Excalibur,
I will arise and slay thee with my hands."
Then quickly rose Sir Bedivere, and ran,
And, leaping down the ridges lightly, plunged
Among the bulrush-beds, and clutch'd the sword,
And strongly wheel'd and threw it. The great brand
Made lightnings in the splendor of the moon,
And flashing round and round, and whirl'd in an arch,
Shot like a streamer of the northern morn,
Seen where the moving isles of winter shock
By night, with noises of the northern sea.
So flash'd and fell the brand Excalibur:
But ere he dipt the surface, rose an arm
Clothed in white samite, mystic, wonderful,
And caught him by the hilt, and brandish'd him
Three times, and drew him under in the mere.
And lightly went the other to the King. —*Morte d'Arthur.* TENNYSON.

In order to give a clear conception of the meaning and purpose of rhythm, the analysis of an entire poem is given.

THE REVENGE

A BALLAD OF THE FLEET

TENNYSON

I

At Flores in the Azores Sir Richard Grenville lay,
And a pinnace, like a flutter'd bird, came flying from far away:
"Spanish ships of war at sea! we have sighted fifty-three!"
Then sware Lord Thomas Howard: "'Fore God I am no coward;
But I cannot meet them here, for my ships are out of gear,
And the half my men are sick. I must fly, but follow quick.
We are six ships of the line; can we fight with fifty-three?"

II

Then spake Sir Richard Grenville: "I know you are no coward;
You fly them for a moment to fight with them again.
But I've ninety men and more that are lying sick ashore.
I should count myself the coward if I left them, my Lord Howard,
To these Inquisition dogs and the devildoms of Spain."

III

So Lord Howard past away with five ships of war that day,
Till he melted like a cloud in the silent summer heaven;

But Sir Richard bore in hand all his sick men from the land
Very carefully and slow,
Men of Bideford in Devon,
And we laid them on the ballast down below;
For we brought them all aboard.
And they blest him in their pain, that they were not left to Spain,
To the thumbscrew and the stake, for the glory of the Lord.

IV

He had only a hundred seamen to work the ship and to fight,
And he sailed away from Flores till the Spaniard came in sight,
With his huge sea-castles heaving upon the weather bow.
"Shall we fight or shall we fly?
Good Sir Richard, tell us now,
For to fight is but to die!
There'll be little of us left by the time this sun be set."
And Sir Richard said again: "We be all good English men.
Let us bang these dogs of Seville, the children of the devil,
For I never turn'd my back upon Don or devil yet."

V

Sir Richard spoke and he laugh'd, and we roar'd a hurrah, and so
The little Revenge ran on sheer into the heart of the foe,
With her hundred fighters on deck, and her ninety sick below;
For half of their fleet to the right and half to the left were seen,
And the little Revenge ran on thro' the long sea-lane between.

VI

Thousands of their soldiers look'd down from their decks and laugh'd,
Thousands of their seamen made mock at the mad little craft
Running on and on, till delay'd
By their mountain-like San Philip that, of fifteen hundred tons,
And up-shadowing high above us with her yawning tiers of guns,
Took the breath from our sails, and we stay'd.

VII

And while now the great San Philip hung above us like a cloud
Whence the thunderbolt will fall
Long and loud,
Four galleons drew away
From the Spanish fleet that day,
And two upon the larboard and two upon the starboard lay,
And the battle-thunder broke from them all.

VIII

But anon the great San Philip, she bethought herself and went
Having that within her womb that had left her ill content;
And the rest they came aboard us, and they fought us hand to hand,
For a dozen times they came with their pikes and musqueteers,
And a dozen times we shook 'em off as a dog that shakes his ears
When he leaps from the water to the land.

IX

And the sun went down, and the stars came out far over the summer
sea,
But never a moment ceased the fight of the one and the fifty-three.
Ship after ship, the whole night long, their high-built galleons came,
Ship after ship, the whole night long, with her battle-thunder and flame;
Ship after ship, the whole night long, drew back with her dead and her
shame.
For some were sunk and many were shatter'd, and so could fight us
no more—
God of battles, was ever a battle like this in the world before?

X

For he said "Fight on! fight on!"
Tho' his vessel was all but a wreck;
And it chanced that, when half of the short summer night was gone,
With a grisly wound to be drest he had left the deck,
But a bullet struck him that was dressing it suddenly dead,
And himself he was wounded again in the side and the head,
And he said "Fight on! fight on!"

XI

And the night went down, and the sun smiled out far over the summer
sea,
And the Spanish fleet with broken sides lay round us all in a ring;
But they dared not touch us again, for they fear'd that we still could sting,
So they watch'd what the end would be.
And we had not fought them in vain,
But in perilous plight were we,
Seeing forty of our poor hundred were slain,
And half of the rest of us maim'd for life
In the crash of the cannonades and the desperate strife;
And the sick men down in the hold were most of them stark and cold,
And the pikes were all broken or bent and the powder was all of it spent;
And the masts and the rigging were lying over the side;
But Sir Richard cried in his English pride,
"We have fought such a fight for a day and a night

As may never be fought again!
We have won great glory, my men!
And a day less or more
At sea or ashore,
We die—does it matter when?
Sink me the ship, Master Gunner—sink her, split her in twain!
Fall into the hands of God, not into the hands of Spain!"

XII

And the gunner said "Ay, ay," but the seamen made reply:
"We have children, we have wives,
And the Lord hath spared our lives.
We will make the Spaniard promise, if we yield to let us go;
We shall live to fight again and to strike another blow."
And the lion there lay dying, and they yielded to the foe.

XIII

And the stately Spanish men to their flagship bore him then,
Where they laid him by the mast, old Sir Richard caught at last,
And they praised him to his face with their courtly foreign grace;
But he rose upon their decks, and he cried:
"I have fought for Queen and Faith like a valiant man and true;
I have only done my duty as a man is bound to do:
With a joyful spirit I Sir Richard Grenville die!"
And he fell upon their decks, and he died.

XIV

And they stared at the dead that had been so valiant and true,
And had holden the power and glory of Spain so cheap
That he dared her with one little ship and his English few;
Was he devil or man? He was devil for aught they knew,
But they sank his body with honor down into the deep,
And they mann'd the Revenge with a swarthier alien crew,
And away she sail'd with her loss and long'd for her own;
When a wind from the lands they had ruin'd awoke from sleep,
And the water began to heave and the weather to moan,
And or ever that evening ended a great gale blew,
And a wave like the wave that is raised by an earthquake grew,
Till it smote on their hulls and their sails and their masts and their
    flags,
And the whole sea plunged and fell on the shot-shatter'd navy of Spain,
And the little Revenge herself went down by the island crags
To be lost evermore in the main.

NOTES ON RHYTHM

Stanza I

l. 1-2.—Normal rhythm.

l. 3.—Note the emphasis imparted to the call by the trochees.

l. 4-6.—The effect of the internal rhymes *Howard—coward, here—gear, sick—quick,* is very marked. Similar effects are frequently introduced in the poem.

Stanza II

l. 10.—The two emphatic syllables, *I've* and *nine-*, coming in succession, add force to Sir Richard's statement.

Stanza III

l. 13.—Note how the author retards his movement and hence impresses us with the slow moving picture, by drawing his emphatic syllables together, as *So Lord How-; five ships;* and *that day*. This effect is one of the commonest in literature, and one of the most natural. This line will scan as a normal line; but let us bear in mind that sense accent determines the rhythm in English, not quantity.

l. 16.—A strange device, the effect of which is to cause Sir Richard's gallantry to stand out most strikingly. In spite of the fact that fifty-three Spanish galleons were coming down upon him, the brave captain was as considerate in the handling of his sick sailors as a mother of her babe. And this is emphasized by making this statement in a line by itself.

Stanza IV

l. 24.—Again note the strength imparted by the successive accents in *huge sea-castles heaving.*

l. 25-27.—The abruptness aptly fits in with the sentiment. Observe that the effect of the short line is brought out by the rhyme, *fly—die.* The further apart the rhyme, the less striking it becomes. See lines 43-45, and 57-59.

Stanza V

l. 32.—Full of strength and admirably expressive in rhythm.

l. 36.—Again we observe the retardation and its effect. Observe further, that this is the first time the concluding line of a stanza has deviated from the normal, and note how appropriate is the deviation; not merely for the sake of variety, but the spontaneous expression of feeling.

Stanza VI

l. 37-38.—How forceful is the effect of beginning each line with the accented syllable!

l. 42.—The contrast of this line with the preceding is most marked. Line 41 is long drawn out, while in 42 one can feel the shock of the abrupt stop.

Stanza VIII

l. 53-54.—The first four lines of this stanza are quite regular, but when we reach the last two, observe the correspondence between the rhythm and the sense.

Stanza IX

l. 56-60.—How admirably the rhythm lends itself to the expression of the feelings of the narrator as he recalls the terrible strain of that never-ending night! One must read the passage aloud to appreciate this effect.

Stanza X

l. 63.—Observe the strength of *Fight on! Fight on!* and also the contrast between the rhythm of this stanza and that of Stanza IX.

The stanza as a whole moves quite rapidly, owing to the preponderance of unaccented syllables. The appropriateness of this rapid movement is recognized when we bear in mind that the stanza is intended to cite but one incident of that awful night, and serves only as a link between Stanzas IX and XI.

Stanza XI

l. 70.—Compare this rhythm with that of line 56, and observe how the emotion of Stanza IX is recalled by the similarity of rhythm.

l. 83-90.—Compare with lines 25-28 and 91-95.

Stanza XIII

l. 100.—Compare with lines 42 and 103, and note similarity of mood.

Stanza XIV

l. 112-119.—It is almost impossible to analyze the effect of these lines, so admirably do sound, sense, and rhythm correspond. We can, however, clearly observe the forceful effect of *great gale blew*; the accumulation of power and size in line 115; the exultant joy of the speaker as he describes the effect of the storm in lines 116 and 117; and the gradual diminution of the passion as the poem comes back to normal movement in the concluding line.

INTERPRETATIVE NOTES

The poem as a whole is a magnificent specimen of vigorous Anglo-Saxon. There are few inversions, the style is simple and direct, and the imagery peculiarly appropriate. The speaker is a survivor, and brings us face to face with one of the proudest moments in the history of English naval warfare.

The poem deals with an event at the close of the expedition of the Spanish Armada against Great Britain, and it is interesting to know that it is almost literally true to fact and history.

Stanza I

l. 4-7.—The opening words seem a little like brag. But Sir Richard's reply, which is borne out by history, proves the contrary. The oath is not the vain oath of a braggart, but the solemn words of one who believes in God and calls upon Him to bear witness to the truth of his statement.

Stanza II

l. 8.—The delivery of the first five words will certainly manifest the pride of the narrator in such a leader.

l. 12.—Note the contempt expressed in *dogs* and *devildoms*.

Stanza III

l. 15-18.—Be sure to bring out the speaker's emotion. How the common sailor worships him who stayed to certain death to save the lives of his sick men!

l. 21.—Note the irony, contempt, and even hate.

Stanza IV

l. 25-28.—The rhythm clearly indicates the abrupt manner in which these lines should be read.

l. 29.—*We be all good English men*: this is Sir Richard's answer to their appeal.

Stanza V

l. 33.—*Heart*: right into the midst of the fleet. The Spaniards came down in double line of battle. It was evidently Sir Richard's intention to attempt to escape with his fleet craft by running the gauntlet of heavy, large, unwieldy Spanish galleons. A picture of these galleons, with their triple and quadruple decks, will greatly assist us to comprehend the disastrous outcome of one of the most elaborate naval demonstrations in the history of the world. The vessels were so unwieldy that only a few at a time could attack the Revenge, and, by constant maneuvering, Sir Richard could almost always avoid the effect of their cannonading.

Stanza VI

l. 37-38.—There is bitter sarcasm in these lines as the speaker recalls the outcome of the fight.

Stanza VIII

l. 50.—*Bethought herself*: note the sarcasm.

Stanza IX

l. 56-60.—The emotion of these five lines is very striking. Oh! the anguish, horror, and suspense of that awful night. The sun went down, but the battle went on. The stars came out, but still no rest. And so on, on, on, through that dreadful night.

l. 62-61.—Observe the sudden transition and the exultant shout at the end.

Stanza X

See note on rhythm.

Stanza XI

l. 72.—Observe the note of pride and grim determination.

l. 74.—The speaker apologizes for even an appearance of boastfulness.

l. 75-81.—Pathos.

l. 83-90.—Note the contrast between the emotion of Sir Richard in these lines and that of the speaker in uttering lines 75-81.

Stanza XII

l. 92-95.—The sailors would naturally speak rapidly. The rhythm helps us to understand their feelings.

l. 93.—And therefore we have no right to kill ourselves. A most significant line.

Stanza XIII

l. 99.—Observe the tribute the Englishman pays to his foe. See also line 108. The voice should manifest the speaker's attitude and will when we grasp the situation.

l. 101-103.—Note and bring out the blunt defiance of Sir Richard.

Stanza XIV

l. 111.—How natural seems the use of *her*! It is expressive of the sailor's love for his vessel. And further, we remark that the Revenge becomes human as she yearns for those who so long have seemed her very children.

l. 112.—Here we have one of the most significant lines in the whole poem. History tells us that a storm arose and shattered the remnant of the Armada, and sunk the battered hulk of the little Revenge. Poetry conjures up this storm as an avenging Nemesis. Out of the lands *they had ruined* comes the storm that avenges the Revenge.

l. 118.—What tenderness is there in that word *little*!

l. 118-119.—There is no regret in these lines. On the contrary, they are full of exultation. Remember, the poet was limited by history. He could not save the Revenge, but he could sink her on the spot where the glorious victory had been won. The picture of shattered greatness is not an inspiring one. If the Revenge had not sunk, she would have been dragged ignominiously at the hawser's end into some Spanish port, to become the object of every Spaniard's petty spite, and finally to fall into decay and ruin. Now she lives evermore as she was in that fight, a glorious inspiration to every son of England.

HINTS ON READINGS

YOUNG LOCHINVAR

SIR WALTER SCOTT

Oh, young Lochinvar is come out of the west,
Through all the wide Border his steed was the best:
And save his good broad-sword he weapon had none,
He rode all unarmed, and he rode all alone;
So faithful in love, and so dauntless in war,
There never was knight like the young Lochinvar!

He stayed not for brake, and he stopped not for stone,
He swam the Esk river where ford there was none—
But, ere he alighted at Netherby gate,
The bride had consented, the gallant came late:
For a laggard in love and a dastard in war,
Was to wed the fair Ellen of brave Lochinvar.

So boldly he entered the Netherby hall,
'Mong bride's-men, and kinsmen, and brothers and all:
Then spoke the bride's father, his hand on his sword—
For the poor craven bridegroom said never a word—
"O come ye in peace here, or come ye in war?
Or to dance at our bridal, young Lord Lochinvar?"

"I long wooed your daughter, my suit was denied;
Love swells like the Solway, but ebbs like its tide!
And now am I come, with this lost love of mine,
To tread but one measure, drink one cup of wine!
There be maidens in Scotland, more lovely by far,
That would gladly be bride to the young Lochinvar."

The bride kissed the goblet; the knight took it up,
He quaffed off the wine, and he threw down the cup!
She looked down to blush, and she looked up to sigh,
With a smile on her lips and a tear in her eye.
He took her soft hand ere her mother could bar—
"Now tread we a measure!" said young Lochinvar.

So stately his form, and so lovely her face,
That never a hall such a galliard did grace!
While her mother did fret and her father did fume,
And the bridegroom stood dangling his bonnet and plume,
And the bride-maidens whispered, "'Twere better by far,
To have matched our fair cousin to young Lochinvar!"

One touch to her hand, and one word to her ear,
When they reached the hall door, and the charger stood near.
So light to the croupe the fair lady he swung,
So light to the saddle before her he sprung!

"She is won! we are gone, over bank, bush, and scaur;
They'll have fleet steeds that follow!" quoth young Lochinvar.

There was mounting 'mong Graemes of the Netherby clan;
Fosters, Fenwicks, and Musgraves, they rode and they ran;
There was racing and chasing on Cannobie Lea,
But the lost bride of Netherby ne'er did they see!
So daring in love, and so dauntless in war,
Have ye e'er heard of gallant like young Lochinvar!

We observe, in the first place, that the rhythm is very pronounced. It reminds us of the rhythm of *The Ride from Ghent*, and suggests, in fact, what we soon discover to be true, that the two poems are in spirit very closely allied.

l. 2-6 are intended to win our sympathy for the hero. Observe his courage in riding unarmed and alone.

l. 10.—The accent on *gallant* is on the final syllable. Observe how the emphasis on *-lant, came,* and *late* retards the movement and suggests the contrast between Lochinvar's hope and his failure to arrive in time.

l. 11.—Note the contempt in *laggard* and *dastard*. Also in line 16, where the movement is again retarded.

l. 19-24.—How cleverly Lochinvar conceals his true intention, under the guise of indifference!

l. 20.—Love swells like ocean tides, but diminishes with equal rapidity: I can get along without your daughter.

l. 32.—*Galliard*: a lively dance.

l. 33-34.—Bring out the pictures clearly. Do not slur.

l. 37.—Accelerate the movement, but not with a manufactured speed. Catch the spirit of haste and the movement will accelerate itself.

l. 41-42.—Note the triumphant joy of Lochinvar.

l. 41.—*Scaur*: a steep bank; pronounced *scar*.

l. 43-45.—The lively movement continues throughout these lines.

l. 46.—This is a summary. The time will be slow when we recognize and endeavor to express the full import of the passage.

Longfellow's *Peace-Pipe*, from *The Song of Hiawatha*, is particularly adapted to analytic study. We shall confine our study principally to questions of sense relations, such as Momentary Completeness, Values, and the like.

THE PEACE-PIPE

LONGFELLOW

On the Mountains of the Prairie,

On the great Red Pipe-Stone Quarry,
Gitche Manito, the mighty,
He the Master of Life, descending,
On the red crags of the quarry
Stood erect, and called the nations,
Called the tribes of men together.
From his footprints flowed a river,
Leaped into the light of morning,
O'er the precipice plunging downward
Gleamed like Ishkoodah, the comet.
And the Spirit, stooping earthward,
With his finger on the meadow
Traced a winding pathway for it,
Saying to it, "Run in this way!"
From the red stone of the quarry
With his hand he broke a fragment,
Moulded it into a pipe-head,
Shaped and fashioned it with figures;
From the margin of the river
Took a long reed for a pipe-stem,
With its dark green leaves upon it!
Filled the pipe with bark of willow,
With the bark of the red willow;
Breathed upon the neighboring forest,
Made its great boughs chafe together,
Till in flame they burst and kindled;
And erect upon the mountains,
Gitche Manito, the mighty,
Smoked the calumet, the Peace-Pipe,
As a signal to the nations.
And the smoke rose slowly, slowly,
Through the tranquil air of morning,
First a single line of darkness,
Then a denser, bluer vapor,
Then a snow-white cloud unfolding,
Like the tree-tops of the forest,
Ever rising, rising, rising,
Till it touched the top of heaven,
Till it broke against the heaven,
And rolled outward all around it.
From the Vale of Tawasentha,
From the Valley of Wyoming,
From the groves of Tuscaloosa,
From the far-off Rocky Mountains,
From the Northern lakes and rivers
All the tribes beheld the signal,

Saw the distant smoke ascending,
The Pukwana of the Peace-Pipe.
And the Prophets of the nations
Said: "Behold it, the Pukwana!
By this signal from afar off,
Bending like a wand of willow,
Waving like a hand that beckons,
Gitche Manito, the mighty,
Calls the tribes of men together,
Calls the warriors to his council!"
Down the rivers, o'er the prairies,
Came the warriors of the nations,
Came the Delawares and Mohawks,
Came the Choctaws and Camanches,
Came the Shoshonies and Blackfeet,
Came the Pawnees and Omahas,
Came the Mandans and Dacotahs,
Came the Hurons and Ojibways,
All the warriors drawn together
By the signal of the Peace-Pipe,
To the Mountains of the Prairie,
To the Great Red Pipe-Stone Quarry.
And they stood there on the meadow,
With their weapons and their war-gear,
Painted like the leaves of Autumn,
Painted like the sky of morning,
Wildly glaring at each other;
In their faces stern defiance,
In their hearts the feuds of ages,
The hereditary hatred,
The ancestral thirst of vengeance.
Gitche Manito, the mighty,
The creator of the nations,
Looked upon them with compassion,
With paternal love and pity;
Looked upon their wrath and wrangling
But as quarrels among children,
But as feuds and fights of children!
Over them he stretched his right hand,
To subdue their stubborn natures,
To allay their thirst and fever,
By the shadow of his right hand;
Spake to them with voice majestic
As the sound of far-off waters,
Falling into deep abysses,
Warning, chiding, spake in this wise:—

"O my children! my poor children!
Listen to the words of wisdom,
Listen to the words of warning,
From the lips of the Great Spirit,
From the Master of Life, who made you!
"I have given you lands to hunt in,
I have given you streams to fish in,
I have given you bear and bison,
I have given you roe and reindeer,
I have given you brant and beaver,
Filled the marshes full of wild-fowl,
Filled the rivers full of fishes;
Why then are you not contented?
Why then will you hunt each other?
"I am weary of your quarrels,
Weary of your wars and bloodshed,
Weary of your prayers for vengeance,
Of your wranglings and dissensions;
All your strength is in your union,
All your danger is in discord;
Therefore be at peace henceforward,
And as brothers live together.
"I will send a Prophet to you,
A Deliverer of the nations,
Who shall guide you and shall teach you,
Who shall toil and suffer with you.
If you listen to his counsels,
You will multiply and prosper;
If his warnings pass unheeded,
You will fade away and perish!
"Bathe now in the stream before you,
Wash the war-paint from your faces,
Wash the blood-stains from your fingers,
Bury your war-clubs and your weapons,
Break the red stone from this quarry,
Mould and make it into Peace-Pipes,
Take the reeds that grow beside you,
Deck them with your brightest feathers,
Smoke the calumet together,
And as brothers live henceforward!"
Then upon the ground the warriors
Threw their cloaks and shirts of deer-skin,
Threw their weapons and their war-gear,
Leaped into the rushing river,
Washed the war-paint from their faces.
Clear above them flowed the water,

Clear and limpid from the footprints
Of the Master of Life descending;
Dark below them flowed the water,
Soiled and stained with streaks of crimson,
As if blood were mingled with it!
  From the river came the warriors,
Clean and washed from all their war-paint;
On the banks their clubs they buried,
Buried all their warlike weapons.
Gitche Manitou, the mighty,
The Great Spirit, the creator,
Smiled upon his helpless children!
  And in silence all the warriors
Broke the red stone of the quarry,
Smoothed and formed it into Peace-Pipes,
Broke the long reeds by the river,
Decked them with their brightest feathers,
And departed each one homeward,
While the Master of Life, ascending,
Through the opening of cloud-curtains,
Through the doorways of the heaven,
Vanished from before their faces,
In the smoke that rolled around him,
The Pukwana of the Peace-Pipe!

It is to be hoped that the following notes will be carefully considered. Inflections are most subtle indications of interpretation, and their meaning none too well apprehended. Time spent in such an analysis as that herein undertaken should solve all the ordinary difficulties of the class-room.

l. 1.—Incomplete, hence rising inflection[15] on *Prairie*.

l. 2.—The same inflection on *Quarry*.

l. 3-5.—(*a*) *Gitche Manito* is the central idea; hence there will be more force on those words. (*b*) Note that *descending* is separated from the next line by a comma. This is a good illustration of the function of punctuation; for if the comma were not inserted we should read, *descending On the red crags of the quarry*, and should not learn of our mistake until we came to the next line.

l. 6.—*Nations*: falling inflection. A good illustration of the principle that punctuation does not determine inflection: the sense is complete, and the falling inflection instinctively denotes that fact. The whole paragraph is pointing forward to the main statement, *called the nations*. There might be some reason in the use of a falling inflection on *erect*, but perhaps the other interpretation is to be preferred.

[15] Let it be understood once for all that the various elements in expression should be the spontaneous outcome of the mental action. As has been so often stated, to tell a pupil to use a rising inflection or to emphasize this word or that, is a violation of the fundamental principle of correct teaching.

l. 8-9.—Falling inflections on *river* and on *morning*.

l. 10.—Rising inflection on *downward*. There is likelihood of misinterpretation here. Paraphrased, lines 10 and 11 are equivalent to, And the river, plunging downward over the precipice, gleamed like Ishkoodah, the comet.

l. 11.—Falling inflection on *Ishkoodah*, because the river did not gleam like the comet Ishkoodah, but like Ishkoodah, which is the Indian name for comet.

l. 12.—*Stooping earthward*: subordinate idea.

l. 12-15.—It is surprising how careless pupils are in reading these lines. They nearly always read them to convey the idea that the Spirit stooped earthward with his finger on the meadow. Observe how the meaning is brought out by the following reading:

And the Spirit (*pause*), stooping earthẃard (*pause*),
With his finger (*pause*) on the meadoẃ (*pause*),
Traced a winding pathẁay for it̀ (*pause*),
Saying to it́ (*pause*), "Run in th̀is way!"

l. 17-19.—The melody is virtually the same in each of these lines, with a falling inflection on *fragment*, *pipe-head* and *figures*.

l. 21.—Rising inflection preferable on *pipe-stem*. The poem abounds in lines ending with falling inflections; hence, one should be on the alert for such lines as this.

l. 23.—Falling inflection on *willow*.

l. 25-26.—Rising inflection on *forest* and on *together*. We note that these two lines point forward.

l. 28-31.—Rising inflections throughout, even on *calumet*, upon which word the pupil often errs.

l. 30.—*The Peace-Pipe* is not a subordinate idea; it is an idea coördinate with *calumet*.

l. 32.—Observe the rhythmic change and its meaning.

l. 33.—Falling inflection on *morning*. Lines 32 and 33 contain the general statement, and

l. 34-39 contain the particular. When we perceive this latter fact we will use the rising inflection at the end of each line until we reach *heaven* in line 39, when, of course, we shall have the falling.

l. 37.—Subordinate.

l. 40.—Observe that *broke* is the emphatic word, not *against*. Rising inflection on *heaven*.

l. 42-46.—It is an open question whether we should use a rising or a falling inflection at the end of each of these lines. To use the falling would convey the idea that each detail was important; to use the rising, to lay the stress upon the whole. (See Momentary Completeness, page 32, *et seq.*) The former reading seems the better.

l. 51.—Falling inflection on *Behold it.*

l. 53-54.—Subordinate.

l. 56.—Falling inflection on *together.*

l. 58.—An interesting point is presented in this line. The poet intends to convey the idea that some tribes came *down the rivers* and others *o'er the prairies.* Hence the melody and force of the two phrases will be identical.

l. 59.—Falling inflection on *nations.*

l. 60-65.—The most natural interpretation seems to be to use a rising inflection on the name of the first tribe in each line, and a falling on the second.

l. 66-67.—Rising inflection on *together* and on *Peace-Pipe.*

l. 68.—Falling inflection on *Prairie.*

l. 70.—Rising inflection on *meadow.*

l. 71-74.—Falling inflection on *war-gear, Autumn, morning,* and *other.*

l. 74.—This is the strongest line of the four.

l. 75-76.—*Faces* and *hearts* are not contrasted. The melody of the two lines is virtually the same.

l. 81.—Falling inflection on *compassion.*

l. 86.—Falling inflection on *hand* is to be preferred.

l. 87-89.—These three lines should be construed as one idea. Hence rising inflection will be given on *natures* and on *fever.*

l. 90-93.—Rising inflections on *majestic, waters, warning, chiding.* Why? Falling inflection on *abysses.* Why?

l. 94.—Does he use rising inflection or falling on *children*? What would be the difference in the idea conveyed by each?

l. 95-96.—Do these lines mean "Will you not listen?" If so they are full of pleading. If the speaker is imperative the inflection will be falling.

l. 98.—Falling inflection on *Life.* Observe how meaningful are the words *who made you.*

l. 99-105.—Shall there be rising or falling inflection at the end of these lines? What would each convey respectively?

l. 112.—Observe the radical change in the speaker's attitude. He has been asserting; now he argues and pleads.

l. 116-117.—Falling inflection on *you* and on *nations.*

l. 118.—Rising inflection on *guide.*

l. 119.—*Toil* and *suffer* should be joined together, with the main pause after *suffer.* Do not emphasize *with.*

l. 121.—Rising inflection on *multiply.*

l. 122.—Note the contrast on *unheeded.*

l. 124-127.—Falling inflection on all the emphatic words. There will be a tendency to use the rising inflection on *war-paint, blood-stains, war-clubs.*

l. 128.—Rising inflection on *quarry.* Why?

l. 130.—Rising inflection on *you.*

l. 131.—Falling inflection on *feathers.*

l. 133.—Principal pause after *brothers,* with perhaps a brief pause after *live.*

l. 134.—Short pause after *then;* longer after *ground.*

l. 135.—Rising inflection on *deer-skin* seems preferable.

l. 136.—Falling inflection on *war-gear.*

l. 138.—Falling inflection on *faces.*

l. 139.—Falling inflection on *water.*

l. 140.—Falling inflection on *limpid.*

l. 142.—Rising inflection on *water.*

l. 143-144.—Falling inflection on *crimson* and on *blood.*

l. 134-144.—This is the climax of the poem. When one grasps this idea the voice becomes full of joy. Be sure to get the picture of the clear and limpid water as it flows down to where the warriors are, and note the change as it passes *below* them, tinged with the war-paint it has washed away. Note the emphasis on *clear above,* and on *dark below.*

l. 145.—Rising inflection on *warriors.*

l. 148.—Falling inflection on *weapons.*

l. 149-150.—Rising inflection on *mighty* and on *creator.*

l. 151.—Falling inflection on *smiled.*

l. 152.—Pause after *silence;* rising inflection on *warriors.*

l. 153.—Rising inflection on *quarry.*

l. 154.—Falling inflection on *Peace-Pipes.*

l. 155-156.—Rising inflection on *river, feathers.*

l. 158.—Note the pause after *ascending.* He ascended *through* and *vanished in.*

l. 158-160.—Rising inflection on *Life, ascending, curtains,* and *heaven.*

l. 161.—Falling inflection on *vanished;* rising on *faces.*

l. 162.—It seems that the rising inflection would be preferable on *him.*

In the following poem it is purposed to offer comments principally as to the movement. There is nothing that conduces more to variety in reading than frequent changes in movement. Not that these changes should be haphazard; on the contrary, as we have seen in Chapter I, there is a definite principle underlying movement. The analysis should reveal that the various ideas are of different degrees of importance, and the recognition of these differences will lead to the variety of movement.

Attention is also directed to transitions, and occasionally to the atmosphere.

Every comment should be carefully considered and challenged. The printed page is a monochrome of type. The danger is, therefore, that we read monotonously. With the years we acquire a fatal facility for pronouncing words without getting the underlying thought. The object of these analyses is to take the mind from the words to the ideas which they express, and so to improve the reading.

HORATIUS

A LAY MADE ABOUT THE YEAR OF THE CITY CCCIX

I[16]

Lars Porsena of Clusium
By the Nine Gods he swore
That the great house of Tarquin
Should suffer wrong no more.
By the Nine Gods he swore it,
And named a trysting day,
And bade his messengers ride forth,
East and west and south and north,
To summon his array.

* * * * *

XI

And now hath every city
Sent up her tale of men:
The foot are fourscore thousand,
The horse are thousands ten.
Before the gates of Sutrium
Is met the great array.
A proud man was Lars Porsena
Upon the trysting day.

XII

For all the Etruscan armies
Were ranged beneath his eye,
And many a banished Roman,
And many a stout ally;
And with a mighty following
To join the muster came

[16] The stanzas are numbered as in the original poem.

The Tusculan Mamilius,
Prince of the Latian name.

XIII

But by the yellow Tiber
Was tumult and affright:
From all the spacious champaign
To Rome men took their flight.
A mile around the city,
The throng stopped up the ways:
A fearful sight it was to see
Through two long nights and days.

XIV

For aged folks on crutches,
And women great with child,
And mothers sobbing over babes
That clung to them and smiled,
And sick men borne in litters
High on the necks of slaves,
And troops of sunburned husbandmen
With reaping-hooks and staves,

XV

And droves of mules and asses
Laden with skins of wine,
And endless flocks of goats and sheep,
And endless herds of kine,
And endless trains of wagons
That creaked beneath the weight
Of corn-sacks and of household goods,
Choked every roaring gate.

XVI

Now, from the rock Tarpeian,
Could the wan burghers spy
The line of blazing villages
Red in the midnight sky.
The Fathers of the city,
They sat all night and day;
For every hour some horseman came
With tidings of dismay.

*   *   *   *   *

XIX

They held a council, standing
Before the River-Gate:
Short time was there, ye may well guess,
For musing or debate.
Out spake the Consul roundly:
"The bridge must straight go down;
For, since Janiculum is lost,
Naught else can save the town."

XX

Just then a scout came flying,
All wild with haste and fear:
"To arms! to arms! Sir Consul:
Lars Porsena is here."
On the low hills to westward
The Consul fixed his eye,
And saw the swarthy storm of dust
Rise fast along the sky.

XXI

And nearer fast, and nearer,
Doth the red whirlwind come;
And louder still, and still more loud,
From underneath that rolling cloud,
Is heard the trumpet's war-note proud,
The trampling and the hum.
And plainly, and more plainly,
Now through the gloom appears,
Far to left, and far to right,
In broken gleams of dark-blue light,
The long array of helmets bright,
The long array of spears.

* * * * *

XXV

But when the face of Sextus
Was seen among the foes,
A yell that rent the firmament
From all the town arose.
On the housetops was no woman
But spat towards him, and hissed;
No child but screamed out curses.
And shook its little fist.

XXVI

But the Consul's brow was sad,
And the Consul's speech was low;
And darkly looked he at the wall,
And darkly at the foe.
"Their van will be upon us
Before the bridge goes down;
And if they once may win the bridge,
What hope to save the town?"

XXVII

Then out spake brave Horatius,
The Captain of the Gate:
"To every man upon this earth,
Death cometh soon or late.
And how can man die better
Than facing fearful odds
For the ashes of his fathers,
And the temples of his gods,"

* * * * *

XXIX

"Hew down the bridge, Sir Consul,
With all the speed ye may:
I, with two more to help me,
Will hold the foe in play.
In yon strait path a thousand
May well be stopped by three.
Now, who will stand on either hand,
And keep the bridge with me?"

XXX

Then out spake Spurius Lartius,—
A Ramnian proud was he,—
"Lo, I will stand at thy right hand,
And keep the bridge with thee."
And out spake strong Herminius,—
Of Titian blood was he,—
"I will abide on thy left side,
And keep the bridge with thee."

XXXI

"Horatius," quoth the Consul,
"As thou sayest, so let it be."
And straight against that great array

Forth went the dauntless Three.
For Romans in Rome's quarrel
Spared neither land nor gold,
Nor son nor wife, nor limb nor life,
In the brave days of old.

*   *   *   *   *

XXXIV

Now, while the Three were tightening
Their harness on their backs,
The Consul was the foremost man
To take in hand an axe.
And Fathers mixed with commons
Seized hatchet, bar, and crow,
And smote upon the planks above,
And loosed the props below.

XXXV

Meanwhile the Tuscan army,
Right glorious to behold,
Come flashing back the noonday light,
Rank behind rank, like surges bright
Of a broad sea of gold.
Four hundred trumpets sounded
A peal of warlike glee,
As that great host, with measured tread,
And spears advanced, and ensigns spread,
Rolled slowly towards the bridge's head,
Where stood the dauntless Three.

XXXVI

The Three stood calm and silent,
And looked upon the foes,
And a great shout of laughter
From all the vanguard rose:
And forth three chiefs came spurring
Before that deep array;
To earth they sprang, their swords they drew,
And lifted high their shields, and flew
To win the narrow way.

*   *   *   *   *

XXXVIII

Stout Lartius hurled down Aunus
Into the stream beneath;

Herminius struck at Seius,
And clove him to the teeth;
At Picus brave Horatius
Darted one fiery thrust,
And the proud Umbrian's gilded arms
Clashed in the bloody dust.

* * * * *

XL

Herminius smote down Aruns;
Lartius laid Ocnus low;
Right to the heart of Lausulus
Horatius sent a blow.
"Lie there," he cried, "fell pirate!
No more, aghast and pale,
From Ostia's walls the crowd shall mark
The track of thy destroying bark.
No more Campania's hinds shall fly
To woods and caverns when they spy
Thy thrice accursèd sail."

XLI

But now no sound of laughter
Was heard among the foes.
A wild and wrathful clamor
From all the vanguard rose.
Six spears' lengths from the entrance
Halted that deep array,
And for a space no man came forth
To win the narrow way.

XLII

But hark! the cry is Astur;
And lo! the ranks divide,
And the great Lord of Luna
Comes with his stately stride.
Upon his ample shoulders
Clangs loud the fourfold shield,
And in his hand he shakes the brand
Which none but he can wield.

XLIII

He smiled on those bold Romans,
A smile serene and high
He eyed the flinching Tuscans,

And scorn was in his eye.
Quoth he, "The she-wolf's litter
Stand savagely at bay;
But will ye dare to follow
If Astur clears the way?"

XLIV

Then, whirling up his broadsword
With both hands to the height,
He rushed against Horatius,
And smote with all his might.
With shield and blade Horatius
Right deftly turned the blow.
The blow, though turned, came yet too nigh:
It missed its helm, but gashed his thigh.
The Tuscans raised a joyful cry
To see the red blood flow.

XLV

He reeled, and on Herminius
He leaned one breathing-space,
Then, like a wild-cat mad with wounds,
Sprang right at Astur's face.
Through teeth and skull and helmet,
So fierce a thrust he sped,
The good sword stood a hand-breadth out
Behind the Tuscan's head.

XLVI

And the great Lord of Luna
Fell at that deadly stroke,
As falls on Mount Alvernus
A thunder-smitten oak.

* * * * *

XLVII

On Astur's throat Horatius
Right firmly pressed his heel,
And thrice and four times tugged amain,
Ere he wrenched out the steel.
"And see," he cried, "the welcome,
Fair guests, that waits you here!
What noble Lucumo comes next
To taste our Roman cheer?"

* * * * *

LI

Yet one man for one moment
Strode out before the crowd:
Well known was he to all the Three,
And they gave him greeting loud.
"Now welcome, welcome, Sextus!
Now welcome to thy home!
Why dost thou stay, and turn away?
Here lies the road to Rome."

LII

Thrice looked he at the city;
Thrice looked he at the dead;
And thrice came on in fury,
And thrice turned back in dread,
And, white with fear and hatred,
Scowled at the narrow way,
Where, wallowing in a pool of blood,
The bravest Tuscans lay.

LIII

But meanwhile axe and lever
Have manfully been plied;
And now the bridge hangs tottering
Above the boiling tide.
"Come back, come back, Horatius!"
Loud cried the Fathers all.
"Back, Lartius! back, Herminius!
Back, ere the ruin fall!"

LIV

Back darted Spurius Lartius:
Herminius darted back:
And, as they passed, beneath their feet
They felt the timbers crack.
But when they turned their faces,
And on the farther shore
Saw brave Horatius stand alone,
They would have crossed once more.

LV

But with a crash like thunder
Fell every loosened beam,
And, like a dam, the mighty wreck
Lay right athwart the stream:

And a long shout of triumph
Rose from the walls of Rome,
As to the highest turret-tops
Was splashed the yellow foam.

LVI

And like a horse unbroken,
When first he feels the rein,
The furious river struggled hard,
And tossed his tawny mane,
And burst the curb, and bounded,
Rejoicing to be free,
And whirling down, in fierce career,
Battlement and plank and pier,
Rushed headlong to the sea.

LVII

Alone stood brave Horatius,
But constant still in mind;
Thrice thirty thousand foes before,
And the broad flood behind.
"Down with him!" cried false Sextus,
With a smile on his pale face.
"Now yield thee," cried Lars Porsena,
"Now yield thee to our grace."

LVIII

Round turned he, as not deigning
Those craven ranks to see;
Naught spake he to Lars Porsena,
To Sextus naught spake he;
But he saw on Palatinus
The white porch of his home,
And he spake to the noble river
That rolls by the towers of Rome.

LIX

"O Tiber! father Tiber!
To whom the Romans pray,
A Roman's life, a Roman's arms,
Take thou in charge this day!"
So he spake, and, speaking, sheathed
The good sword by his side,
And with his harness on his back,
Plunged headlong in the tide.

LX

No sound of joy or sorrow
Was heard from either bank:
But friends and foes in dumb surprise,
With parted lips and straining eyes,
Stood gazing where he sank;
And when above the surges,
They saw his crest appear,
All Rome sent forth a rapturous cry,
And even the ranks of Tuscany
Could scarce forbear to cheer.

LXI

But fiercely ran the current,
Swollen high by months of rain:
And fast his blood was flowing,
And he was sore in pain,
And heavy with his armor,
And spent with changing blows;
And oft they thought him sinking,
But still again he rose.

* * * * *

LXIII

"Curse on him!" quoth false Sextus:
"Will not the villain drown?
But for this stay, ere close of day
We should have sacked the town!"
"Heaven help him!" quoth Lars Porsena,
"And bring him safe to shore;
For such a gallant feat of arms
Was never seen before."

LXIV

And now he feels the bottom;
Now on dry earth he stands;
Now round him throng the Fathers,
To press his gory hands;
And now, with shouts and clapping,
And noise of weeping loud,
He enters through the River-Gate,
Borne by the joyous crowd.

* * * * *

Stanza I

l. 1-4.—The exalted position of Lars Porsena, the oath, and the grandeur of the Tarquin house, all contribute to make the movement slow and the atmosphere dignified.

l. 5.—Note the repetition and its effect on the movement.

l. 7.—Rather fast.

l. 8.—According to the importance we attach to this line will be the rate of movement. If it means simply in all directions, the time will be moderate. If, however, we desire to emphasize that the messengers rode far to the east, and far to the west, and so forth, the time will be slow. Probably the former is the better interpretation.

Stanza XI

Colloquial style and moderate time prevail throughout the stanza except in

l. 16, where the transition is marked.

Stanza XII

The atmosphere is that of the pride of Porsena in his army.

Stanza XIII

l. 26.—Observe the transition to the atmosphere of fright and terror that pervades the entire stanza.

l. 30.—Conceive that mass of humanity and note how the length of the inflection on *mile* is extended.

l. 33.—Very slow; each day and each night seems to be endless.

Stanzas XIV and XV

Observe that the principal verb does not appear until line 49. Hence there will be a rising inflection at the end of every line of these stanzas except 49.

The movement is rather fast and the atmosphere that of despair.

l. 49.—Very slow.

Stanza XVI

l. 50-54.—Narrative style.

l. 55.—Slow.

l. 56.—Note the longer inflections on *every hour*.

Stanza XIX

l. 58.—Be careful to separate the last two words.

l. 63.—Slower time and marked transition.

Stanza XX

l. 66-67.—Fast time; not in imitation of the speed of the scout, but in sympathy with his feelings.

l. 68-69.—No effort should be made to shriek these words; it is sufficient to suggest the fact that he is calling, and his fear. The time will be fast.

l. 70.—Observe the change in time and atmosphere.

l. 73.—A good illustration of the principle underlying movement. This line is read slowly, for it announces the doom of the city.

Stanza XXI

l. 74-75.—Moderate time.

l. 76-79.—Note that the time grows gradually slower as the mind becomes more and more engrossed with the picture, and how the voice swells with increasing grandeur.

l. 80-85.—Prevailingly moderate movement.

l. 84.—Rising inflection on *bright* because the speaker no doubt has in mind the two lines, 84 and 85.

Stanza XXV

The hatred and contempt of the speaker will color the entire stanza. The movement will be on the whole moderate.

l. 88.—Slow.

Stanza XXVI

l. 94.—Slower time, and an atmosphere of sadness. Bear in mind the speaker sympathizes with the Consul.

l. 98.—Despair and sadness.

Stanza XXVII

l. 102-103.—Manifest the speaker's pride in Horatius, and note the striking contrast between the atmosphere of these lines and that of the concluding lines of the preceding stanza.

l. 104-109.—Solemn and deliberate.

Stanza XXIX

l. 110-115.—Note the change in Horatius.

l. 116-117.—As if addressing the crowd; a marked transition.

Stanza XXX

A good study in variety; nearly every line presents a change of atmosphere.

Stanza XXXI

l. 126-127.—Very deliberately the Consul speaks. Why? What are his feelings?

l. 128-129.—Observe the patriotic ring in the speaker's words.

Stanza XXXIV

The stanza is in simple narrative style, and contains but little emotion. The significant idea is that the patricians in this hour of trial worked side by side with plebeians.

Stanza XXXV

The time is moderate at the beginning, becoming gradually slower to the end.

Observe the change in atmosphere in the last line. Once more it is well to remind the reader that the speaker is a patriot.

Stanza XXXVI

The movement of the first two lines is rather slow; after that it accelerates to the end, in sympathy with the fast moving picture.

Stanza XXXVIII

The atmosphere is that of struggle and of the joy of victory.

The time will be rather fast, retarding towards the close.

Stanza XL

l. 170-173.—See note on preceding stanza.

l. 174.—Transition. Observe the hate of Horatius.

Stanza XLI

The time is prevailingly slow, and the atmosphere in marked contrast to that of the preceding stanza. There is, too, a note of contempt and irony.

Stanza XLII

l. 189.—Abrupt transition to atmosphere of what is almost fear. Time fast.

l. 190-196.—Time slow, and atmosphere in sympathy with the size and strength of Astur.

Stanza XLIII

l. 197-198.—Observe the contrast between the atmosphere of these lines and that of the succeeding two.

l. 201-202.—Astur's contempt for his own allies.

l. 203.—Boastfully.

Stanza XLIV

l. 205-208.—Fast and strong.

l. 209-210.—Fast.

l. 211-212.—Slower, and note change in feeling: Horatius is wounded.

l. 213-214.—The joy of the enemy serves but to increase the speaker's sorrow.

Stanza XLV

l. 217-222.—Note the intensity of the speaker's feeling and his savage joy at the close.

Stanza XLVI

Slow time throughout.

Stanza XLVII

l. 227.—Moderate time.

l. 231-234.—Transition to the proud and contemptuous defiance of Horatius. The time is moderate; the key is high, because Horatius is calling to the opposing army.

Stanza LI

l. 235-236.—Simple narrative.

l. 237-238.—Contemptuous.

l. 239-242.—Sarcastic throughout. Time quite slow.

Stanza LII

l. 246.—Very slow and contemptuous, especially the last four words. Falling inflection on *dread*.

Stanza LIII

l. 251.—Note the transition.

l. 251-254.—Rather fast.

l. 255.—Suggest the sustained call and the warning.

l. 256.—Subordinate.

l. 257-258.—Faster and with greater trepidation.

Stanza LIV

l. 259-262.—Fast.

l. 263.—Transition.

Stanza LV

This stanza is the climax of the poem. Horatius' work is done! The atmosphere is that of joy, triumph, and exultation.

Stanza LVI

The excitement of the speaker carries him on with headlong speed as he recalls the picture described in this stanza.

Stanza LVII

l. 284.—The excitement subsides.

l. 286-287.—No hope.

l. 289.—What is the emotion of Sextus? Note the *smile.*

l. 290.—Observe the difference between Lars Porsena and Sextus in their feelings toward Horatius.

Stanza LVIII

l. 292.—Slower time. Is there not a note of pride in the speaker's voice as he recalls the bravery of Horatius?

l. 297-299.—Tender and slow.

Stanza LIX

l. 300-303.—Slow and reverential.

l. 304-307.—Rather fast, with pause before and after *headlong.*

Stanza LX

l. 308-312.—Rather slow.

l. 313.—Note transition to the feeling of joy.

Stanza LXI

The entire stanza is permeated with the speaker's suspense and with his sympathy with the struggles of the wounded man.

Stanza LXIII

Observe again the contrast between Sextus and Lars Porsena, both enemies of Horatius.

Stanza LXIV

If we will follow the picture and describe it as we see it and as the speaker now recalls it, we will make long pauses after *bottom* and *stands.*

The time increases in rapidity through the first four lines, and then is retarded to the end.

The atmosphere of the first four lines is that of joy, and it is hardly possible to keep back the tears as we utter the last four.

In the final selection we shall call attention to all the interpretative difficulties which the teacher is likely to meet with in the class-room. There is no reason why such a piece of literature as this cannot be used to advantage even in the public school, provided we take the time for careful analysis.

JULIUS CAESAR.—Shakespeare

Act IV., Scene 3

Brutus's Tent

Enter Brutus *and* Cassius

Cas. That you have wrong'd me doth appear in this:
You have condemn'd and noted Lucius Pella
For taking bribes here of the Sardians;
Wherein my letters, praying on his side,
Because I knew the man, were slighted off.

Bru. You wrong'd yourself to write in such a case.

Cas. In such a time as this it is not meet
That every nice offence should bear his comment.

Bru. Let me tell you, Cassius, you yourself
Are much condemn'd to have an itching palm;
To sell and mart your offices for gold
To undeservers.

Cas. I an itching palm!
You know that you are Brutus that speak this,
Or, by the gods, this speech were else your last.

Bru. The name of Cassius honours this corruption,
And chastisement doth therefore hide his head.

Cas. Chastisement!

Bru. Remember March, the ides of March remember:
Did not great Julius bleed for justice sake?
What villain touch'd his body, that did stab,
And not for justice? What, shall one of us,
That struck the foremost man of all this world
But for supporting robbers, shall we now
Contaminate our fingers with base bribes,
And sell the mighty space of our large honours
For so much trash as may be grasped thus?
I had rather be a dog, and bay the moon,
Than such a Roman.

CAS. Brutus, bay not me;
I'll not endure it; you forget yourself,
To hedge me in; I am a soldier, I,
Older in practice, abler than yourself
To make conditions.

BRU. Go to; you are not, Cassius.

CAS. I am.

BRU. I say you are not.

CAS. Urge me no more, I shall forget myself;
Have mind upon your health, tempt me no farther.

BRU. Away, slight man!

CAS. Is't possible?

BRU. Hear me, for I will speak.
Must I give way and room to your rash choler?
Shall I be frighted when a madman stares?

CAS. O ye gods, ye gods! must I endure all this?

BRU. All this! ay, more: fret till your proud heart break;
Go show your slaves how choleric you are,
And make your bondmen tremble. Must I budge?
Must I observe you? must I stand and crouch
Under your testy humour? By the gods,
You shall digest the venom of your spleen,
Though it do split you; for, from this day forth,
I'll use you for my mirth, yea, for my laughter,
When you are waspish.

CAS. Is it come to this?

BRU. You say you are a better soldier;
Let it appear so; make your vaunting true,
And it shall please me well: for mine own part,
I shall be glad to learn of noble men.

CAS. You wrong me every way; you wrong me, Brutus;
I said, an elder soldier, not a better:
Did I say 'better'?

BRU. If you did, I care not.

CAS. When Caesar lived, he durst not thus have moved me.

BRU. Peace, peace! you durst not so have tempted him.

CAS. I durst not!

BRU. No.

CAS. What, durst not tempt him!

Bru. For your life you durst not.

Cas. Do not presume too much upon my love;
I may do that I shall be sorry for.

Bru. You have done that you should be sorry for.
There is no terror, Cassius, in your threats,
For I am arm'd so strong in honesty
That they pass by me as the idle wind,
Which I respect not. I did send to you
For certain sums of gold, which you denied me:
For I can raise no money by vile means:
By heaven, I had rather coin my heart,
And drop my blood for drachmas, than to wring
From the hard hands of peasants their vile trash
By any indirection: I did send
To you for gold to pay my legions,
Which you denied me: was that done like Cassius?
Should I have answer'd Caius Cassius so?
When Marcus Brutus grows so covetous,
To lock such rascal counters from his friends,
Be ready, gods, with all your thunderbolts;
Dash him to pieces!

Cas. I denied you not.

Bru. You did.

Cas. I did not: he was but a fool that brought
My answer back. Brutus hath rived my heart:
A friend should bear his friend's infirmities,
But Brutus makes mine greater than they are.

Bru. I do not, till you practise them on me.

Cas. You love me not.

Bru. I do not like your faults.

Cas. A friendly eye could never see such faults.

Bru. A flatterer's would not, though they do appear
As huge as high Olympus.

Cas. Come, Antony, and young Octavius, come,
Revenge yourselves alone on Cassius,
For Cassius is aweary of the world:
Hated by one he loves; braved by his brother;
Check'd like a bondman; all his faults observed,
Set in a note-book, learn'd, and conn'd by rote,
To cast into my teeth. O, I could weep
My spirit from mine eyes! There is my dagger,
And here my naked breast; within, a heart

Dearer than Plutus' mine, richer than gold:
If that thou be'st a Roman, take it forth;
Strike, as thou didst at Caesar; for, I know,
I, that denied thee gold, will give my heart:
When thou didst hate him worst, thou lovedst him better
Than ever thou lovedst Cassius.

BRU. Sheathe your dagger:
Be angry when you will, it shall have scope;
Do what you will, dishonour shall be humour.
O Cassius, you are yoked with a lamb
That carries anger as the flint bears fire;
Who, much enforced, shows a hasty spark,
And straight is cold again.

CAS. Hath Cassius lived
To be but mirth and laughter to his Brutus,
When grief, and blood ill-temper'd, vexeth him?

BRU. When I spoke that, I was ill-temper'd too.

CAS. Do you confess so much? Give me your hand.

BRU. And my heart too.

CAS. O Brutus!

BRU. What's the matter?

CAS. Have not you love enough to bear with me,
When that rash humour which my mother gave me
Makes me forgetful?

BRU. Yes, Cassius; and, from henceforth,
When you are over-earnest with your Brutus.
He'll think your mother chides, and leave you so.

A few words of introduction are first necessary. We should understand the play as a whole, and be conversant with the events that lead up to this particular scene; further, we should bear in mind the tense, splenetic character of Cassius, and the calm, controlled, stoical disposition of Brutus.

l. 1.—In Scene 2 we get the keynote to Cassius' manner. He is so full of his supposed wrong that he pays no heed to the surroundings, and bluntly plunges into the matter in hand. Brutus restrains him, and together they move to the former's tent. No sooner do they enter than again Cassius bursts forth.

l. 4.—Cassius is piqued that his letters should have failed to shield Lucius Pella from the punishment for his wrongdoing.

l. 5.—Subordinate and explanatory.

l. 6.—Brutus's answer is simple and direct, yet without feeling.

l. 8.—*Nice* is equivalent to unimportant, small. There is a touch of contempt in this speech.

l. 9.—Again we note the directness of Brutus's statement, and the absence of feeling. Note, too, that he in no way seeks to soften his charges.

l. 12.—Imagine the surprise and rage of Cassius. There will be a sweeping upward inflection on *I*. It is only with the utmost effort that the fiery Cassius can control himself.

l. 15-16.—Paraphrased, these lines mean, The name of Cassius is associated with this corruption, and hence the hands of justice are tied. For, to bring the corrupters to trial would be to drag in Cassius with them.

l. 17.—Do you dare to use the term *chastisement* in connection with *my* name?

l. 18.—Unmoved by the anger of Cassius, Brutus proceeds calmly and perhaps too ruthlessly to arraign his friend.

l. 21.—Observe the high moral standard of Brutus.

l. 21-26.—Rising inflections throughout.

l. 27.—Observe the contempt.

l. 28.—During the speech of Brutus, Cassius can scarcely contain himself. Never has any one dared to arraign him. Now he is even forgetting the deference he has been wont to show to one whom he recognizes as his superior.

l. 32-34.—Rapidly, as the passion of the men rises.

l. 35-36.—Now Cassius begins to threaten.

l. 37.—There is no anger in this. Brutus knows that Cassius is beside himself, and brushes him aside as one would brush an insignificant dust speck from his clothing.

l. 38.—Such treatment Cassius cannot understand. The line is exclamatory rather than interrogative. It is equivalent to, Can I believe my ears?

l. 38.—Brutus now begins to assert himself. It is a new aspect of his character, which we can comprehend only when we learn, as we do later, that Portia is dead.

l. 40.—Brutus must be greatly moved to call his dearest friend a madman.

l. 41.—The strain of listening to such words is becoming too great for Cassius to bear.

l. 42.—Brutus seems almost to enjoy the terrible lesson he is reading Cassius. It is well-nigh incredible that the thoughtful, loving husband of Portia, and the considerate master of Lucius, should speak thus to any one, let alone his best friend.

l. 50.—There seems to be no feeling but surprise in this, surprise verging on bewilderment. As Brutus grows more passionate Cassius seems to subside.

l. 51-54.—It is Brutus now who appears to lose self-control. Cassius never said he was a better soldier.

l. 55-57.—Anger and bewilderment give way to a sense of having been wronged: the last sentence is almost pathetic in its humility.

l. 57.—Anger and contempt.

l. 58.—Cassius' passion is again beginning to rise.

l. 59-62.—Note the increasing astonishment in the speeches of Cassius, and the superciliousness of Brutus.

l. 63-64.—A threat uttered not so much in anger as in fear that he may not be able to control his feelings.

l. 65.—*Have* and *should* are the emphatic words.

l. 65-82.—This speech needs no commentary. It is a plain and unmistakable arraignment, uttered in unequivocal language, and in simple, direct manner.

l. 82.—Cassius is pained that his friend should so misunderstand him. From now to line 93 Cassius seems to throw himself upon the mercy of his friend, while the latter repels his advances, each time with greater harshness.

l. 93-107.—Cassius' heart is broken. If his best friend can so wantonly misunderstand him, what can he hope from his enemies? There is nothing left to live for, and he would eagerly welcome death even at the hands of Antony. The passage is overflowing with heartbreak, and gains our sympathy for one who else would seem but a crafty, self-seeking schemer.

l. 107.—The speech of Cassius brings Brutus back to himself. Here is the real Brutus, full of tenderness and love.

To understand fully the unusual display of feeling in this scene we should read further to the stage direction, *Re-enter Lucius, with wine and taper*.

INDEX TO FIRST LINES OF SELECTIONS

LIST OF POEMS AND SELECTIONS ANALYZED

INDEX

A

C

D

E

F

G

H

I

L

M

N

O

P

R

S

T

V

W

Printed by Libri Plureos GmbH in Hamburg, Germany